PIPPA GREENWOOD

Garden Problem Solver

PIPPA GREENWOOD

Garden Problem Solver

A Dorling Kindersley Book

Dorling **DK** Kindersley
LONDON, NEW YORK, SYDNEY, DELHI, PARIS,
MUNICH and JOHANNESBURG

*With lots and lots of love to Alice and Callum, the best
pair of children in the whole, wide world.*

Senior Editor Pamela Brown
Art Editor Murdo Culver

Senior Managing Editor Anna Kruger
Senior Managing Art Editor Lee Griffiths

Illustrator Gill Tomblin

DTP Designer Louise Waller
Media Resources Romaine Werblow
Picture Research Deborah Pownall
Production Controllers Elizabeth Cherry, Sarah Coltman

First published in Great Britain in 2001 by
Dorling Kindersley Limited
9 Henrietta Street
Covent Garden, London WC2E 8PS

A CIP catalogue record for this book is
available from the British Library.

ISBN 0751 327670

Reproduced by Colourscan, Singapore
Printed and bound in Italy by Printer Trento S.r.l.

See our complete catalogue at
www.dk.com

CONTENTS

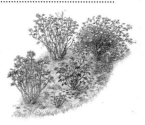

GARDEN TREES

TREES FORM AN IMPORTANT PART of the garden, giving living height and structure for twelve months of the year, year in and year out. They have the potential to become the stately elders of the garden, increasing in size and beauty as they mature. In large gardens, the range you can grow is obviously much greater than in a small space but there is usually room for one tree in all but the tiniest backyard. Maintenance is important – making sure that any tree stays healthy and in good shape yet keeping growth in check is something you always need to watch out for.

DYING SHOOTS
Parts of a tree have died but there seems no obvious reason. **6**

BROKEN BRANCH
A torn limb is a hazard and needs to be cut out. **5**

DEAD STUMP
An old tree stump is causing concern because it may invite disease. **10**

TREE FOR REMOVAL
A small conifer has become very scruffy and would be better removed. **9**

UNWANTED SUCKERS
Suckers keep on sprouting around a tree and are causing a nuisance. **1**

SURFACE TREE ROOTS
Roots emerge in the lawn and make mowing difficult. **3**

1 What is the best way to prevent suckers?

Several garden trees have an annoying habit of producing suckers from their roots, often at some distance from the trunk. These can cause a nuisance in flower beds, lawns or even in your neighbour's garden.

Suckers may sprout from roots a long way from the tree itself

REMOVE SUCKERS THAT GROW FROM TREE ROOTS

Sucker removal

Trees notorious for suckering include sumachs (*Rhus*), lilacs, poplars, robinias, ornamental cherries and crab apples. When cutting off suckers, take them right back to the root from which they appear. This may need to be done on a regular basis, and unfortunately you may stimulate the growth of further suckers.

Another option is to remove the part of the root that is producing the suckers, but take great care this does not affect the tree's stability or overall health. You can either dig out the offending root or first sever it from the main root system and treat the foliage on the suckers with a systemic weedkiller. This will kill off that part of the root and make it much easier to remove, but it is important to make sure that the root is completely severed or the weedkiller will contaminate the tree.

Competitive growth

Sometimes rootstock growth on a grafted tree can become too competitive, often on various types of cherry and crab apple. This rootstock growth may grow up, unnoticed, into the crown of the tree and, because it is more vigorous, will overtake the true leader. It is important to cut off competitive growth as soon as it is noticed, before it has any adverse effect on the tree, taking it right back to the root from which it grows.

2 Tilting tree

Venerable old trees may start to lean because of age, but in a young tree a tilt may signal a problem.

Causes and remedies

If a tree starts to lean, it may be due to a weakness in its structure or a problem with extensive shade. You can often winch or pull the tree back to the correct position. Stake it until it is again growing upright and give it plenty of water, since roots are likely to be damaged in the manoeuvre.

If an older tree starts to lean, perhaps due to strong winds, you may be able to winch it back into position, but good aftercare is even more important. It may help to reduce the size of the crown and consequently the weight the trunk has to support.

3 Tree roots in the lawn hinder the mower

Surface roots growing in the lawn are a problem with some trees, in particular ornamental cherries and poplars.

Dig out or cover up

Woody roots that protrude above the surface of a lawn can do considerable damage to a lawnmower and make the task of mowing more difficult than it should be. If the roots are injured by the mower blades they may also be stimulated into producing a forest of small suckers.

Sometimes it is possible to remove particularly troublesome roots (*see Sucker removal, above*), but there is a limit to how much you can safely do without affecting the tree's stability. The soil level around the base of the tree can be raised slightly, but only by a maximum depth of about 5cm (2in). Any greater build-up is likely to affect the tree's health. The other option is to cover the entire area with landscape fabric (which should also keep some of the sucker growth down) and put a thin layer of soil on top. You can then sow the area with grass seed or plant it up with ground-cover plants or small bulbs which will provide an attractive display in which roots and any suckers will be more readily hidden.

NEIGHBOUR'S ROOTS
If surface roots come from a tree next door, be extra cautious about taking any action that may harm the tree and discuss the problem with your neighbour first.

❹ A large tree casts a lot of shade

There are various ways in which shade can be reduced, but dealing with large trees requires the skill of a professional and it is important to check if any legal restrictions apply.

Reduce, thin or lift

To let more light past a tree you could consider having the crown reduced. This involves making the overall size of the crown smaller, almost as if it had been shrunk, so that the tree's shape and character is not significantly altered. You could also have the crown thinned (*see p.121*), so that it stays much the same size but is less dense and so lets more light through. Or the crown can be lifted; removing some of the lower branches extends the opportunities to plant beneath.

These are definitely jobs for the professional and it is important to choose a good tree surgeon, both from a safety point of view and for good quality work. In the UK, the Arboricultural Association should be able to supply a list of approved contractors, or you may be able to get similar information from your local council. It is also worth seeking the advice of friends and neighbours who have employed similar craftsmen. Be wary of employing a "cowboy", whose work is unlikely to be satisfactory.

Remove the lower branches

CROWN LIFTING

Tree Preservation Orders

Many large trees are covered by Tree Preservation Orders and it is essential to check with your local council (usually the planning department) whether such an order covers the tree in question. Carrying out work without permission can result in hefty fines for the tree surgeon and tree owner. Trees may also be affected by other restrictions – for instance if your house is in a conservation area.

Making cuts

If a tree is sizeable, hire a tree surgeon. Using chainsaws not only requires skill, it is also potentially extremely dangerous. Where a tree is reasonably small, however, and you want to avoid it becoming a cause of annoyance to you or your neighbours, you may be able to prune it yourself.

As well as improving shape, this involves taking out dead, dying, diseased and crossing branches to keep the crown relatively open. Always cut back to a vigorous-looking bud, pair of buds or sideshoot. Try to keep the amount of wood that you expose to a minimum, since it can act as an entry point for disease. Where there is a pair of opposite buds, make a straight cut immediately above them. With alternate buds, make a slightly sloping cut so that any water will be shed from the surface. It is important not to leave long stubs of wood, as these usually eventually die back to the nearest growth point and, in the meantime, can become infected. If cutting out whole branches, avoid cutting too close to the branch collar (*see Removing a small branch, opposite*).

It is important to use appropriate tools. Take safety precautions seriously and, if you hire a chainsaw, wear all the necessary protective clothing such as helmet, visor and padded safety trousers and gloves. Generally, though, if a chainsaw is needed, it is advisable to call in a professional.

THE CORRECT TOOLS FOR THE JOB

MAKE SURE that you have suitable tools for any work you need to carry out on a tree – without these you may damage one of the most important and attractive long-term features of your garden. You may also injure yourself. Good quality tools are well worth the extra initial investment; make sure that they feel comfortable to hold and lift before you buy. Keeping them rust-free and properly sharpened should ensure that they perform well for many years.

GARDEN OR PRUNING KNIFE
A sharp knife can be used to smooth away rough edges around a wound that may encourage risk of infection.

SECATEURS
Use these for cutting smaller stems, not more than 1cm (½in) in diameter, or they may damage tissue.

PRUNING SAW
The curved blade makes it easy to saw through branches and stubs without damaging nearby growth.

LOPPERS
Use loppers to cut thick stems, but for a clean cut the stem must fit comfortably between the blades.

➎ A broken branch needs to be removed

Tackle only branches that are of a size you can safely handle yourself, and try to ascertain what caused the branch to break in the first place.

Investigate the cause

If it isn't obvious, try to find out what caused the damage. It may be simply that the tree, having reached a certain age, is prone to branch shedding (cedar and beech often do this), or it could have been physically damaged, perhaps by a passing vehicle. On the other hand, some kind of disease may be responsible. Look out for obvious problems such as bracket fungi, which can weaken the structure of a branch and so make it far more likely to snap or break, even in fairly light wind. Unless the branch is very large or in a potentially dangerous position, such as over a road, pathway, house or greenhouse, you may be able to deal with it yourself. However, if you are in any way unsure, it is wisest to enlist professional help.

To paint or not to paint?

Wound paints are not now generally used since they seem to be of scant benefit and may in fact encourage the development of fungal rots. However, there is an exception – a wound paint is still advisable for trees susceptible to silver leaf (*see p.167*), a disease caused by a fungal parasite which enters fresh wounds. It is particularly common on ornamental and edible cherries and plums. Apply the paint as soon as you have created the wound.

Removing a small branch from a tree

Stems smaller than 2.5cm (1in) in diameter can often be removed using loppers but anything larger than this requires a pruning saw. Removing the majority of the branch first reduces the weight of the wood that will fall and makes it easier to achieve a clean final cut. Undercutting helps to prevent the bark from tearing. Avoid cutting too close to the branch collar, the slightly swollen ring usually found where one large branch joins another or the trunk. If this is damaged, the healing process tends to be much slower and less effective.

1 MAKE THE FIRST CUT on the underside about 30cm (12in) from the branch's joint with the trunk. The cut should penetrate a quarter of the way into the branch.

2 SAW THE BRANCH from above, 2.5cm (1in) further away from the trunk than the initial undercut until the two cuts meet. Allow the branch to fall or lift it away.

3 MAKE ANOTHER undercut 5–8cm (2–3in) from the trunk and then saw down from the top to join it. Take care not to cut into the branch collar.

4 THE FINISHED CUT should be completely smooth. If necessary, smooth away any rough edges using a sharp knife but do not enlarge the wound in the process.

➏ Part of a tree seems to be dying

If a tree is clearly suffering, try to pinpoint the factors involved.

Possible causes

There are numerous causes for a tree dying including soil contamination, soil-borne diseases, trunk or branch infections, unsuitable growing conditions or even extensive root damage due to building work. If there is no obvious cause, such as disease, you may need a tree surgeon to examine the tree *in situ*. They will advise on the most likely cause and if remedial action can be taken, or at worst, whether the tree needs to be removed. Since a large tree is likely to have an extensive root system, bear in mind that root injury, waterlogging or similar problems may have occurred in a neighbouring garden. If there is any chance that a dying tree could be easily blown down or broken in heavy winds, or endanger people, animals or property, it should be removed. Bear in mind that you are legally responsible for trees growing in your garden and so need to consider any effect on highways and neighbouring properties as well as your own.

LIGHTNING DAMAGE
A badly injured tree, such as one struck by lightning, needs attention from a tree surgeon.

❼ Is there an easy way to deal with fallen leaves?

Gathering up leaves is undoubtedly one of the more tedious jobs in the garden, but it is unavoidable if you are to enjoy the benefits trees bring.

Raking up

If leaves are not removed they soon clog lawns and may kill the grass. They can also clog the crowns of herbaceous plants and cause them to deteriorate in damp weather. It is possible to remove small quantities using a besom, but a spring-tined rake is far better and has other uses, such as scarifying the lawn. For large areas, you could buy or hire a leaf-blower, garden vacuum or leaf sweeper (*see p.60*) to speed the task. It is much

LEAVES INTO LEAF-MOULD
A spring-tined rake (far left) is a good tool for gathering leaves, and stacking them in a wire bin, an excellent way of turning them into leaf-mould.

GUTTERS AND PONDS
Check that leaves are not blocking gutters or downpipes and put a net over ponds. If ice forms, disintegrating leaves may release gases toxic to fish and other pond life.

easier to rake up freshly fallen, relatively dry leaves than those that have been trodden down or rained on.

Make leaf-mould

Use the leaves to make leaf-mould, an excellent mulching material or soil conditioner, especially for sandy and heavy soils. The leaves take about 18 months to break down, depending partly on temperature and moisture levels. Leathery leaves and those with tough, prominent veins take the longest. Chopping these first with

a sharp spade will speed things up. You can also buy special activators to help the breakdown process.

Make a heap by driving four posts into the ground to form the corners of a chicken-wire bin into which you can pile the leaves. In a small space, you can make leaf-mould in a black plastic bin liner. Fill it about two-thirds full with leaves, add a litre (2 pints) of water, some activator if you wish, and fold the top over, weighing it down with a brick. Prick a few holes in the sides to provide aeration.

❽ Glorious for two weeks in flower, but dull for the rest of the year

Some trees look lovely in blossom but contribute little to the garden scene for the majority of the year.

Add bulbs or a climber

If underplanted with bulbs, the area beneath a deciduous tree can make an otherwise dull corner look really attractive for at least part of the year (*see p.23 and p.122*). Or consider growing a climber through the tree to extend the season of interest. A good choice will introduce a decorative element at the time of year when the tree needs it most.

It is important to match eventual size of climber to size of tree, so that the climber doesn't grow faster and larger than the tree itself. The climber will need a good-sized root run of its own. This means planting it some distance from the trunk and improving the soil thoroughly with plenty of organic matter before

planting. Take care when digging the planting hole to minimize injuring nearby tree roots. Good after-care is important to help the plant get established. You may need to set up some form of support to enable the climber to reach the tree branches above. A system of canes and wires or rope should do the trick. Suitable

Length of rubber hose threaded onto rope prevents it from biting into the branch fork

TRAIN A CLIMBER INTO THE LOWER BRANCHES

climbers include clematis, *Tropaeolum speciosum* (good with conifers), *Eccremocarpus scaber* or, in a sunny position, the cup-and-saucer plant, *Cobaea scandens*. Roses such as 'Albéric Barbier', 'Paul's Himalayan Musk', 'Bobby James' and 'Rambling Rector' are ideal. If the tree is particularly large, you could try *Rosa filipes* 'Kiftsgate', but beware, it is very vigorous and heavily thorned.

Replace the tree?

You may instead decide to plant a tree that gives better value throughout the year. Apart from obvious factors such as type of flower and ultimate height and spread, consider leaf shape, changing foliage colour through the seasons, summer or autumn fruits, and the colour and texture of the bark (*see p.15*). Consider also the outline the tree will make, since this can have great impact, particularly in winter.

9 What is the best way to remove a small tree?

It is safe to tackle only small trees yourself. Anything taller than 5m (15ft) needs a skilled tree surgeon.

Removal method

Make sure there is room for the tree to fall safely. If necessary, take off some top-growth and side branches to make the job more manageable, but leave a sufficient length of trunk to give adequate leverage to remove the stump and roots. As the tree starts to fall, you can push it in the right direction, if necessary. Dig a circle around the roots and loosen them so that the stump and rootball can be levered or winched out. Severed large roots can be dug out afterwards.

1 CUT OUT A WEDGE, about 1m (3ft) from the ground, on the side of the trunk where you want the tree to fall. Make sure there is sufficient space.

2 SAW TOWARDS the wedge from the opposite side of the trunk, positioning the cut just above the base of the wedge. Let the tree fall.

3 DIG A TRENCH around the stump, severing any large roots. Loosen those still attached and dig, lever or winch out the stump.

10 Dead stumps

Although tree stumps are often regarded as an ornamental feature if covered in a scrambling clematis, in reality they are best removed. If left in the ground, they increase the risk of diseases such as honey fungus.

Removing a stump

Ideally the stump should be removed when the tree is felled. A stump that has been cut close to the ground can be very difficult to dig out. If there is a sufficient length of trunk, you may be able to hire equipment to winch it out, or you could call in a tree surgeon to do this.

Tree stumps can also be chipped or ground out using a stump chipper. These can be pedestrian-operated or tractor mounted, in which case good access is required. Stump chippers and grinders will remove only the main body of the stump and roots in close proximity; you should also try to dig out the remaining roots.

Stump chippers and grinders are no help if a stump is in an inaccessible position and you will need to rely on being able either to winch it out (if there is a suitable winching point) or dig it out.

11 A neighbour's tree blocks out light

Trees that cast shade are the cause of many a dispute. Discussing the problem may facilitate action.

Open negotiations

Always start by trying to discuss the matter in a friendly fashion with the tree's owners. People are more likely to understand the problem if you give them the chance to come into your garden and see just how much shade or other problems the tree is causing.

If amicable negotiations fail and you are left still wanting to carry out work, check the legal position carefully. This varies from country to country. In the UK it is legally permissable to cut back any growth to the fence-line or official garden boundary. If you are in any doubt as to where this is, check your property deeds. You should not attempt to cut anything that does not directly overhang your own garden. Once branches have been removed, you are legally obliged to offer them back to your neighbour.

Before proceeding, check whether the tree is covered by any kind of legislation which prevents you doing any work on it at all. If removing branches on only one side of a tree is not appropriate or feasible because it would make it too lopsided, and if you can get permission from your neighbour, it may be possible to lift, thin or reduce the crown (*see p.10 and p.121*) so that it blocks less light.

TOO CLOSE TO THE HOUSE?

WHETHER A TREE may damage a building depends on various factors, including age, structure, foundations, and soil type, and the size and variety of tree. The main risk results from the tree interfering with foundations or water or drainage pipes. Generally speaking, trees are more likely to affect buildings on heavy clays that shrink when dry rather than sandy soils. A reputable tree surgeon should be able to advise on the possible dangers and action, if any, that should be taken. Remember that if a tree is removed the amount of water being withdrawn from the soil is suddenly reduced which in itself could result in a problem. This is known as heave, the opposite of subsidence.

TREE PESTS, DISEASES AND DISORDERS

LIKE EVERY OTHER PLANT, trees are susceptible to a range of pests and diseases. A few, such as honey fungus, bracket fungi and deer, may threaten a tree's survival or make it unsafe; many, however, are unlikely to do serious injury or reduce its long-term vigour. Rusts, leaf spots and mildews or even an infestation of aphids may cause leaves to discolour and drop, but if this occurs quite late in the season, a tree is generally able to shrug off the problem. In any case, spraying is rarely feasible.

Honey fungus

This disease attacks woody plants and can spread rapidly from one to another, occasionally rendering a tree dangerous once it has killed its roots. If an aggressive species (there are many strains and species) attacks at the base of the trunk, it can kill a tree in a very short time; a tree may be able to fight off a weaker strain or it may die over a period of years. This is usually the case if the fungus attacks individual roots rather than the trunk. Infected trees should be removed, roots, stump and all.

Symptoms include honey-coloured toadstools which appear around the base or along the root system of infected trees in autumn. It is essential that these are identified correctly, as there are many similar-looking, perfectly harmless toadstools. Infected roots or trunk bases do, however, show more obvious symptoms. If the bark is lifted, a creamy white fungal sheet which smells distinctly of mushrooms will be found sandwiched between the bark and main woody part of the root or trunk. You may also find tough black strands (rhizomorphs), commonly known as bootlaces, growing through the soil and attached to affected roots. Avoid growing highly susceptible trees in the area. Good pest and disease books should give detailed lists, but certainly avoid apples, rhododendrons, privet and roses. Yew is relatively resistant.

Coral spot

Bright orange-red, raised fungal spots or pustules appear on dead wood. Though once considered a saprophyte (something which lives only on dead wood), coral spot fungus appears to have become more aggressive in recent years and may enter the plant through diseased or sometimes even perfectly healthy tissue and colonize and kill living growth. In most trees it is not too serious a problem. However, on some, such as maples (*Acer*) and magnolias, it can cause extensive dieback. Remove infected areas promptly, cutting right back into healthy growth.

Witches' brooms

Small clusters of shoots and/or leaves develop in a branch. In winter, they look rather like birds' nests, but in summer show up as dark green blobs of closely packed foliage. Although these often cause concern and sometimes result from a pest or disease problem, witches' brooms are unlikely to cause any significant damage to the tree itself. If you find them unsightly, prune them out.

Tar spot

This is seen as slightly raised black patches on the leaves of sycamores (*Acer pseudoplatanus*), which, although rather unsightly, do not cause significant harm, partly because the attack normally occurs towards the end of the season. Rake up and burn infected leaves or put them in the dustbin to limit the spread.

Deer and rabbit damage

In rural areas deer and rabbits can do extensive damage to trees, the former cropping off top-growth and sometimes attacking trunks, and the latter being quick to ringbark unprotected trunks, particularly on young trees. The only real solution is to fence off either the individual tree or the entire garden. Individual spiral rabbit guards can be fitted to newly planted trees and will largely prevent rabbit damage. Once a tree is much larger and the bark tougher, the problem should cease. (*See also pp.182–83*.)

Aphids and honeydew

When aphids (greenfly and blackfly) feed on tree sap, with its high-sugar content, their excreta is extremely sticky. Commonly known as honeydew, this drops onto everything beneath the tree and may cause a nuisance. Don't put the garden bench under a lime (*Tilia*), for instance, since it is a particularly attractive tree to aphids. Control is impossible on large trees but, if the problem is severe, you may be able to spray small trees with a suitable aphicide.

Constriction

If not checked regularly, tree ties or any other rope or line attached to a tree (for example, a washing line or child's swing) can cut into it and may even ring the bark. Use purpose-designed tree ties and check them regularly, loosening them as the trunk expands. If a tie of any sort has already become partially embedded, remove it only if this will not incur further damage to the tree.

Damaged bark

The bark of a tree may be damaged by the careless use of a lawn mower or strimmer, by passing vehicles, bonfires, or natural phenomena such as an erratic water supply or the effect of early morning sun on frosted bark, both of which can cause splitting. Try to work out what caused the problem, so that it can be avoided in the future. Do not interfere with damaged bark unless there is a large, loose flap which, if blown in the wind, could cause further damage. Covering with wound paints or "bandages" of any sort is not advisable as this seems to encourage the development of problems rather than helping to alleviate them.

HONEY FUNGUS

CORAL SPOT

WITCHES' BROOM

TAR SPOT

CONSTRICTION

Tree chooser

Trees for alkaline soils
Acer pseudoplatanus,
   including cultivars such as
   'Brilliantissimum'
Cercis siliquastrum (Judas
   tree)
Crataegus laevigata and
   cultivars
Malus (crab apple)
Morus nigra (black mulberry)
Prunus (ornamental cherry)
Salix (willow)
Sorbus aria (whitebeam), *S.
   thuringiaca, S. intermedia*

Trees for acid soils
Acer negundo and cultivars
   including 'Flamingo'
Arbutus menziesii
Betula (birch), most
Cercidiphyllum japonicum
Cercis canadensis
Gleditsia triacanthos (honey
   locust)
Ilex aquifolium (holly) and
   cultivars
Robinia pseudoacacia (false
   acacia)

Trees for clay soils
Acer (maple), most
Alnus (alder)
Betula (birch), most
Cercidiphyllum japonicum
Crataegus (hawthorn)
Eucalyptus
Ilex (holly), most
Laburnum
Liriodendron (tulip tree)
Magnolia
Malus (crap apple)
Prunus (ornamental cherry)
Salix (willow)
Sorbus, most

Good autumn colour
The following should all
develop bright autumn tints.
Acer, many including
   *A. rubrum, A. capillipes,
   A. platanoides*
Amelanchier lamarckii (snowy
   mespilus)
Betula (birch), most
Cercidiphyllum japonicum
Cercis canadensis, especially
   'Forest Pansy'

MALUS 'JOHN DOWNIE'

Liquidambar
Parrotia persica
Photinia, most
Prunus (ornamental cherry)
Sorbus, many
Stewartia

Interesting bark or stems
Textured or coloured bark
gives these trees particular
appeal in winter.
Acer, many including
   A. palmatum 'Sango-kaku',
   A. davidii 'George Forrest',
   A. griseum
Betula (birch), many
Eucalyptus
Parrotia persica
Prunus (ornamental cherry),
   many including *P. serrula*
Salix, many including
   S. alba 'Britzensis',
   S. babylonica 'Tortuosa',
   S. 'Erythroflexuosa'
Stewartia

Attractive fruits
These are all worth growing
for their eye-catching fruits.
Arbutus (strawberry tree)
Catalpa bignonioides (Indian
   bean tree)
Cercis siliquastrum (Judas tree)
Crataegus (hawthorn), many
Ilex (holly), female forms
Koelreuteria paniculata
   (golden-rain tree)
Malus, especially *M. x zumi*
   'Golden Hornet', 'John
   Downie' and *M. x robusta*
   'Red Sentinel'
Sorbus, many

BETULA NIGRA

Trees for small gardens
Some good choices for
limited spaces.
Acer, many including *A.
   callipes, A. crataegifolium,
   A. griseum, A. negundo*
   'Flamingo', *A. negundo*
   'Elegans', *A. palmatum,
   A. pseudoplatanus*
   'Brilliantissimum'
Betula pendula 'Youngii'
Catalpa bignonioides 'Aurea'
Cercis siliquastrum (Judas
   tree)
Koelruteria paniculata
   (golden-rain tree)
Magnolia stellata

Magnolia x *loebneri*
Malus (crab apple), most
Prunus (ornamental cherry),
   most
Pyrus salicifolia 'Pendula'
Robinia pseudocacia 'Frisia'
Sorbus, most

Weeping trees
The following have a graceful
weeping habit.
Betula pendula, B. pendula
   'Youngii'
Cercidiphyllum japonicum
   'Pendulum'
Fagus sylvatica 'Pendula'
   (beech)
Larix kaempferi 'Pendula'
   (larch)
Prunus x *subhirtella* 'Pendula'
Pyrus salicifolia 'Pendula'

Trees for seaside gardens
These should be able to
withstand salty winds.
Acer pseudoplatanus
Arbutus unedo
Cryptomeria japonica
Eucalyptus
Quercus ilex (holm oak)
Quercus robur (oak)
Sorbus aria (whitebeam)

LIQUIDAMBAR STYRACIFLUA 'GOLDEN TREASURE'

HEDGES & SCREENS

EVERY GARDEN HAS A BOUNDARY of some sort to define its limits. Hedges or plant screens are widely used to create boundaries, and sometimes internal divisions as well, but even if chosen and grown with care they may fail to perform in the way you had hoped. Choosing the most suitable shrubs or trees, planting them properly and then ensuring that the hedge is kept well maintained should not be too difficult a task, but there are pitfalls to be avoided.

Q *What is the best way to deal with a cypress hedge that has grown much too tall and wide and is shading both garden and house? There is no reason why it should not be cut back as much as is feasible, but how should this be done?*

A Unfortunately, once a cypress hedge, whether it is of Leyland cypress (x *Cupressocyparis leylandii*) or Lawson cypress (*Chamaecyparis lawsoniana*), has got too big there is little you can do. These trees do not respond well to severe cutting back.

You could generally reduce the height of the trees by up to 30 per cent without significantly affecting their health or vigour, but this would leave you with a row of unattractive lopped trunks surrounded by dead foliage which would look particularly unappealing from upstairs windows.

Reducing the width of the hedge will also pose problems. Deciduous hedging plants, and evergreens such as holly and yew, have dormant buds which are triggered into producing new growth when the hedge is clipped. These buds are absent in cypresses (and in many other conifers such as *Thuja plicata*). On an old or overgrown hedge, a relatively thin outer layer of green foliage conceals an inner mass of dead, brown leaves and stems. This will be revealed when the hedge is cut back, and new green growth will not be produced to hide it. You could use the remains of the heavily pruned hedge as a framework for training climbers to mask its ugly appearance, but it may be difficult to get them established near the root system of a large old hedge.

Q *What is the best way of ensuring that a newly planted conifer hedge does not get out of hand?*

A Regular trimming is essential, at the both top and sides, to keep the hedge's growth dense and green. Despite its poor reputation, even Leyland cypress can make an excellent hedge provided it is kept frequently clipped. A fast-growing tree such as this needs clipping at least twice a year, if not more. This is best done in spring and late summer or early autumn. Having determined the eventual height you want, keep the leader pruned out to approximately 15cm (6in) below this. The branches around it will then be able to mask any obvious cut.

Other conifer hedges such as *Thuja* and yew need somewhat less clipping. Once a year is usually sufficient unless you want to keep them very, very neat.

Q *What are the best plants for an evergreen hedge, avoiding conifers?*

A To help you in your choice, first decide the ultimate height needed and whether you want to keep the hedge trimmed to a neat, formal shape or whether an informal style would be more appropriate. Some shrubs are perfectly suitable for either.

Evergreen formal hedging plants include *Lonicera nitida* (and its yellow-leaved variety 'Baggesen's Gold'), privet (*Ligustrum*), many varieties of holly (*Ilex*), escallonia and, for a low hedge, lavender. The amount of clipping needed is an important consideration. Some, such as *Lonicera nitida,* may need clipping at least two or three times a year.

For informal hedges, the options include pyracantha, *Berberis × stenophylla, Garrya elliptica* (which looks particularly effective in winter) and *Cotoneaster lacteus.*

Q *What can be done about a hedge that has become very sparse at the base, and how could this have been prevented?*

A Once the hedge base has become thin there is not much you can do to improve its condition. The only solution may be to mask the problem by some careful planting nearby. A few well-sited, dense, evergreen shrubs can often be used to hide trouble spots. It may also be possible to brighten up the whole area using colourful climbers, but many of these tend to scramble upwards for light and do not have much in the way of leafy growth at the base. To some extent, regular feeding, watering and clipping from the early stages will help keep the problem to a minimum.

Q *Is it possible to create a more interesting effect by mixing a variety of cypress trees in the same hedge, or will they grow at such different rates or make such different shapes that it will look an untidy mess?*

A Provided you choose different cultivars of the same sort of cypress (that is, do not mix Lawson and Leyland cypresses) there is no reason why this should not work. There are plenty of instances where two or more cultivars of Leyland cypress have been used to dramatic effect, producing alternating stripes of gold and green.

Q *What hedging plants, apart from cypresses, can be used in a fairly formal mixed hedge?*

A If you want an evergreen tapestry hedge, try mixing green and golden forms of yew. Remember, however, that yew is not a speedy grower and you generally need to allow at least six years for a hedge to become well established. There are also numerous varieties of holly you could use, including the many variegated varieties.

For a mixed deciduous hedge, a combination of green and copper beech is hard to beat. When regularly clipped, both types attractively retain their dead, russet-coloured leaves in winter, and for the rest of the year you can enjoy the striking combination of rich green and purple-brown.

Q *What is the best way to restore an old and rather neglected hedge?*

A If extensive pruning is needed, you should try to do it in several stages so that the hedge's overall vigour is not affected and the plants are not put under too much stress. In the first year, cut the growth back hard on one side of the hedge and trim the other side in the normal way. The following year, lightly trim the growth on the side you have already renovated in the first year, but cut the other side back hard.

On the whole, extensive renovation of evergreens is best carried out in mid-spring, while a deciduous hedge is best pruned during frost-free weather in winter.

Bear in mind that not all hedges respond well to renovation, and there is an element of risk involved. Some plants such as yew, laurel, holly, hawthorn, beech, privet and hornbeam generally grow back well. Others, including lavender, cypresses and *Thuja plicata*, do not.

To make sure that plants stand a good chance of recovery and that the hedge grows away well after heavy pruning, feed and mulch it well the season before it is pruned and again after you have carried out the work.

Q *How can a perfectly acceptable but rather dull hedge be made more interesting?*

A One of the best ways is to plant some attractive flowering climbers close by and allow them to scramble through the hedge. Clematis is often used but, whatever you choose, make sure that the clipping and pruning times for hedge and climber do not differ so greatly that it will make the hedge difficult to manage.

You could also consider using annual climbers such as morning glory or sweet peas. Both can produce a lovely display in just a few months, and sweet peas will also add fragrance. Whatever you use, it will need to have an adequate supply of moisture if it is to thrive; sweet peas in, particular, will not perform well without it.

Q *What can be done to kill brambles running through a hedge without harming the hedge itself?*

A This is not an easy problem to tackle. You could try weeding the brambles out by hand (wearing really tough gloves) but do not risk injuring the roots of the hedging plants. Regular weeding will, however, stop brambles from spreading by tip-layering. A suitable weedkiller can be applied to bramble foliage or cut stumps, but take extreme care.

Q *Which are the most suitable hedging plants for creating a barrier that will deter intruders?*

A Certainly, hedges well-armed with prickles or thorns help to keep out humans and animals. Popular choices include pyracantha, holly, hawthorn, berberis, blackthorn (*Prunus spinosa*) and roses such as 'Roseraie de l'Haÿ' or a wild rose or, for a slightly lower hedge, flowering quince (*Chaenomeles*). Plant to create a hedge that is wide and dense by arranging the plants in a double, staggered row. Good soil preparation and regular watering will help get the hedge growing thickly and vigorously. Frequent clipping will also help to prevent gaps developing at the base.

Q *What is meant by planting in a double, staggered row?*

A This is the method to choose if you are trying to achieve a dense, wide hedge. Arrange the plants in two parallel rows about 45cm (18in) apart. Within each row, space the plants about 90cm (3ft) apart, but stagger them so that the plants form a zigzag pattern – in each row, every gap should have a plant directly opposite it in the other row.

Q *What is the optimum planting distance where only a single row of plants is needed?*

A This will vary with your choice of hedging, but most plants need to be spaced 30–60cm (12–24in) apart. For a particularly vigorous tree or shrub, such as Leyland cypress, increase the distance to about 75cm (30in), and for small shrubs, such as lavender, a spacing of 25–30cm (10–12in) is more usual. Once you have decided which plant to use in your hedge, check its needs and growth habits before calculating the number of plants required. It is often wise to buy a few extra, in case you need some replacements should any plants fail. Heel these in, in a spare piece of ground.

Q *What is the best types of hedging to reduce noise and pollution problems from a busy, major road nearby?*

A The problem of lead fumes is not as great as it used to be with the increasing use of unleaded petrol, so pollution is likely to occur only where traffic is heavy and slow-moving. Lead particles, being very dense, tend to land fairly close to the road. However, any hedge will help to filter the air to some extent and conifers would do the job well. They would also help to reduce noise pollution but, if you have the space, you would get even greater benefit if you planted on top of a solid mound of soil. One of the best plants to use is the willow *Salix viminalis*. If you drive in a row of stakes along the boundary line and weave planted willow stems horizontally in and out of them, the willow will gradually root into the mound of soil to create an attractive living wall. Regularly clipping the sides and top will keep the growth dense and a good shape.

Q *The top of a hedge always seems to have a few dips and peaks after it has been clipped. Is there an easy way to ensure a straight, even line?*

A If your hedge requires a flat, level top, a piece of string tied taut between two posts, one at either end of the hedge, should provide an accurate line for you to cut to. For a more complicated shape, for instance a rounded top, it is worth making a template (out of extra-stiff card or plywood) to use as a guide. Place it over the top of the hedge and move it along the hedge as you cut. Also make sure that your shears or other tools are kept really sharp.

Q *In an exposed garden, is there any way that a hedge can be made less susceptible to damage from wind and snow? Previous hedges have suffered badly.*

A From the start, try to clip a hedge so that the sides slope inwards slightly with the base a little wider than the top. This will help the hedge to shed snow and prevent a heavy accumulation lying on top that would weigh on the hedge and break it open. Shaping a hedge in this way also helps to minimize wind damage.

Q *Which are the best hedging plants for supporting and attracting native wildlife to the garden?*

A In many parts of Britain, a mixture of blackthorn (*Prunus spinosa*), hawthorn (*Crataegus monogyna*), guelder rose (*Viburnum opulus*) and dog rose (*Rosa canina*) is ideal. The fruits from these plants, combined with their dense growth once established, will provide a source of food and shelter for wildlife, in

particular birds. Field maple (*Acer campestre*) is also often recommended but it is extremely vigorous and may eventually swamp the others unless carefully managed. To some extent, choice of plant relates to area and type of soil. So, for good examples, look at what grows naturally in your part of the country.

Q *What does it mean when hedging plants are described as bare-rooted, and are they the best type of plant to use?*

A Bare-rooted hedging plants are grown in open ground and lifted for sale while dormant. They are a great deal cheaper than pot-grown shrubs (especially plants such as beech). Although the plants themselves may initially look a lot less impressive than their pot-grown counterparts – they sometimes resemble leafless, rooted sticks – they usually establish and grow away faster and better. The season for buying and planting bare-rooted hedging is much shorter (generally winter only). Container-grown plants can be purchased at almost any time of year.

Q *The foliage of conifers can look gloomy, and deciduous hedging offers insufficient privacy once the leaves fall in autumn. Which other plants make a good screen all the year round?*

A There are plenty of hedging plants which are evergreen (hold their leaves all winter) but are not coniferous. A variegated holly, for instance, would look far from gloomy. You could still consider using a conifer, but one which has golden or variegated foliage. Although beech is deciduous, when regularly clipped as a hedge it holds its brown, autumnal leaves for much of the winter (as does hornbeam, *Carpinus*, to a lesser extent). The dry foliage is finally pushed from the branches when the new leaves unfurl in spring.

Q Apart from conventional hedging, what other types of plant could be used to create a screen?

A Many bamboos make good screens. The different types provide a range of heights and densities and are good for muffling unwanted noise while producing their own soothing rustle. They can be invasive, so choose with care unless you have plenty of space.

Plenty of shrubs, for example roses and forsythia, can be grown in an informal fashion – not clipped to follow a straight, disciplined line – so that they create a screen rather than a conventional hedge. Trellis well-decked with climbers often allows a degree of visibility from one "area" of the garden to another. If you want something really eye-catching, a screen made from parallel lengths of copper tubing (the sort used for domestic water systems) arranged vertically, horizontally or diagonally can look wonderful, especially once it has started to age and become covered in verdigris.

Once established, rooted stems of willow, if kept well clipped, make a lush living barrier. More solid-looking hurdles of woven willow or hazel blend in well in a rural setting, or ready-made heather or bamboo screens suit almost any garden style.

Q Do hedges need special soil preparation before planting ?

A It is worth trying to improve the soil before almost any kind of planting, especially if it is to become a long-term feature of the garden.

Prepare the ground in much the same way as for planting individual trees or shrubs, by digging it over and killing all weeds, especially perennials such as brambles. Incorporate organic matter along the entire length of the hedge to a width of 60–90cm (2–3ft). Native hedging plants do not seem to need the same degree of soil improvement, but, as with other hedges, once planted, it is important to remove competing weeds regularly. Even the toughest hedging plants require good aftercare, particularly watering, if they are to establish well. An annual mulch and application of general fertilizer is also a good idea.

Q Does a newly planted deciduous hedge require pruning?

A The pruning needed varies from plant to plant, but as a rule most hedging shrubs which have a naturally bushy shape should have their leaders cut back by about 30 per cent immediately after planting. Any really bushy laterals should be pruned back by a similar amount. In the second winter after planting, prune the hedge again to a similar extent. Doing this should encourage good dense growth in all areas of the new hedge.

Some vigorous plants, such as hawthorn, which have a naturally upright habit, can have all growth cut back to 15–30cm (6–12in) above ground level towards the end of spring. The laterals will then need some further clipping towards the end of summer. In the second winter, you will need to prune the plants back hard again, taking off about 50 per cent of the growth that was made in the previous season. This may seem as though you are never giving the plants a chance to grow before attacking them again. However, such seemingly drastic treatment will pay off in the end by developing dense growth.

Q One end of a conifer hedge has started to die. The ground is fairly damp just there, so could this be the reason? There are no signs of honey fungus.

A An excessively wet soil could indeed cause the roots to die, particularly if the soil actually becomes waterlogged during the wetter parts of the year. If this is all that is wrong you should at least be able to prevent the situation from worsening by doing all you can to improve drainage in the area. It is, however, obviously far easier to do whatever is needed to ensure good drainage before planting the hedge.

A wet soil also often encourages development of a fungal disease known as *Phytophthora*. This microscopic fungus will kill the roots and may cause a staining, usually a blackish discolouration, beneath the bark. Many plants may be attacked, but this disease does seem especially common on conifers. Unfortunately, there is no control measure available, and you will need to remove all the infected plants and burn or dispose of them. They should not be chipped or composted, as this may not kill off the fungus. The infection may spread to other plants but hopefully will be less likely to cause problems at the drier end of the hedge.

If you decide to replace the entire hedge, it is advisable first to remove all traces of the plants and then change the soil in the area. Where this is not possible, you must at least dig out the soil in the wetter parts and, before replacing it with fresh soil, break down any hard pans beneath the surface and dig in lots of additional grit and bulky organic matter to help improve drainage. Ideally, replant with a deciduous hedge or at least one which is not coniferous. Or, better still, replace the boundary with a non-living structure such as a fence or wall.

ORNAMENTAL SHRUBS

SHRUBS ARE AN IMPORTANT ELEMENT in most gardens, bringing structure and form throughout the year. If chosen carefully, perfumed flowers, evergreen leaves or tolerance of a less-than-perfect site can all be attributes, too. If planted well in the first instance, and given adequate attention until they get established, most are easy-going plants that will probably not present any problems unless they get too big for their place in the border. Some, however, do have particular demands over site and soil and it will be apparent if they are not happy.

PRUNING DILEMMA
When should a buddleja and other flowering shrubs be pruned? **6**

NO BERRIES
Each autumn, a holly fails to produce any berries. **9**

BROWN SHOOTS IN SPRING
The new growth on a pieris is often spoilt by frost damage. **1**

CHANGE OF COLOUR
A blue hydrangea has started to produce flowers in a murky shade of pink. **5**

WINTER'S VICTIM
A lavender looks as though it may not have survived the winter. **1**

UNHEALTHY FOLIAGE
Leaves on a heather have started to turn a sickly-looking yellow. **2**

REFUSAL TO GROW
A newly planted shrub has not put on any fresh growth. **10**

WINTER VULNERABILITY

• **YOUNG SHRUBS** in their first winter, especially those only recently planted in autumn or imported from warmer climes, are particularly susceptible to frost damage. Protect for the first couple of winters until established.

• **MEDITERRANEAN NATIVES**, such as cistus, lavender, *Convolvulus cneorum*, rosemary and many grey-leaved plants, easily succumb to a combination of damp and cold. Good drainage improves their chances of survival.

• **WALL SHRUBS**, such as camellias, can easily have flowers and shoots scorched if early morning sun catches them while covered in frost. Site them where they will receive sun later in the day.

1 Dead stems and brown shoots in spring

Withered shoots in spring don't necessarily mean that a shrub has succumbed to winter weather, but if large areas of a plant have turned brown, further checks are needed.

Investigate the damage

To find out whether a plant is dead or dying, carefully remove a small piece of bark close to an affected shoot tip using a sharp knife. If the stem beneath is dry and brown rather than cream or pale green and sappy, it is dead. To check the extent of the die-back, make similar cuts at intervals towards the main body of the shrub. Where damage is extensive or the main stems are affected, you would probably do best to remove the plant; where minor, prune out affected stems. It is worth waiting until the weather starts to warm up before doing this, since the damaged stems will help to protect the remaining growth. When pruning dying or damaged stems, always cut well back into healthy growth to a vigorous, outward-facing bud.

Don't promote soft growth

Pruning late in the season encourages new soft growth that is easily damaged in winter because stems have not had time to ripen and toughen up. Similarly, feeding in late summer and autumn may promote soft growth that is easily killed by frost. Avoid feeding shrubs after early summer except with a specially formulated fertilizer containing a high level of potash (or simply use sulphate of potash itself). This helps to ripen and toughen the wood.

Protect from frost

If a shrub has only recently been planted, is not reliably hardy or is in an exposed site, you may need to supply winter protection. A cloak of horticultural fleece, old net curtains or some similar material will provide a couple of degrees' protection. It will also help to protect susceptible new

USE FLEECE TO PROTECT EARLY SPRING FLOWERS

shoots on shrubs such as pieris or vulnerable early spring flowers such as magnolia and camellia.

If something more substantial is required, create a chicken-wire "cage" around the plant and fill it with dry leaves or straw (*see p.140*). You can also use bubble-wrap polythene, but with any sort of protection, especially polythene, it is essential to allow adequate air circulation. Damp conditions inside can cause fungal die-back. Some plants, such as tree ferns and bananas, may be potentially hardy in a sheltered garden but will definitely need extra protection over the winter. In most cases the foliage can be loosely bound together, then a coat of dry material such as straw or bracken padded around the outside.

The damp factor

A combination of cold and wet can be lethal for some shrubs, particularly Mediterranean natives. Avoid planting these in heavy, poorly drained ground, or improve drainage first by digging in grit or plenty of organic matter. Planting on a slight ridge or mound also helps to improve drainage. Alternatively, consider creating a raised bed with free-draining soil for plants that are intolerant of cold, damp conditions.

2 Leaves have unexpectedly turned a sickly-looking yellow

When foliage turns yellow unexpectedly, it can indicate that a plant is suffering or it may be nothing to worry about at all.

Mineral deficiencies

Leaves may yellow if soil is deficient in nitrogen or magnesium. With nitrogen deficiency, yellowing is widespread through the leaf, whereas with magnesium, it is generally restricted to leaf edges and between the veins, especially on older leaves. Apply a supplementary fertilizer, such as a high-nitrogen feed or, for magnesium deficiency, Epsom salts. Epsom salts can be applied either to the root system or as a foliar application, which has a quicker effect (*see p.184 for dilution rates*). Deficiencies can be caused when vital nutrients are washed out of the soil by heavy rainfall or excessive watering.

Viral infections

Certain virus infections cause leaf yellowing, usually in distinct patterns such as streaking, striping, ring spots or mosaic patterns. In most cases, shrubs seem to be able to fight off the infection with little ill effect.

Discoloured evergreens

Just like other plants, evergreen shrubs make new leaves and shed old ones, which often turn yellow before they drop. Often, this is barely

SIGNS OF MAGNESIUM DEFICIENCY

SIGNS OF NITROGEN DEFICIENCY

noticeable, but sometimes lots of leaves are affected, and on shrubs such as *Elaeagnus* × *ebbingei* it can look worrying. It is, however, a completely natural occurrence.

Needs an acid soil

In an alkaline soil, the leaves of acid-loving plants turn yellow because iron and manganese become "locked up" and so are unavailable to certain plants, such as rhododendrons.

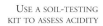

USE A SOIL-TESTING KIT TO ASSESS ACIDITY

Wrong moisture levels

Too much water and occasionally too little can result in root die-back which causes leaves to yellow and drop. Make sure that drainage is adequate, especially for shrubs in containers. In the border, improve soil before planting if necessary, especially in damp areas. If noticed in time, a plant that has received too much water should recover provided the situation improves. Regular applications of a foliar feed to the remaining green leaves should help since this stimulates root growth and will allow the plant to take in nutrients at a time when its root system is probably not functioning nearly as well as it should.

SHRUBS FOR ACID SOIL

Andromeda	Helianthemum (rock
Arbutus	rose)
Berberis	Hibiscus
Calluna (heather)	Ilex crenata (holly)
Camellia	and cultivars
Cistus	Kalmia latifolia
Corylopsis	(calico bush)
Cotoneaster	Leucothöe
Enkianthus	Magnolia, most
Erica (heath)	Pieris
Fothergilla	Rhododendron
Gaultheria	Salix caprea
mucronata	'Kilmarnock'
Genista (broom)	Tamarix
Hamamelis (witch	Vaccinium
hazel)	(blueberry)

3 Do bamboos die after flowering, and can they be contained?

Bamboos are striking architectural plants, make excellent screens and help to muffle noise. But some are invasive and if they flower, you could be left with a gap in the border.

Dying bamboos

Bamboos that have flowered do tend to die back in their entirety and, sadly, nothing can be done to prevent this. However, most species reach a ripe old age before they produce any

flowers, anything up to 50 years. If you buy a replacement plant put it in a new position or, if you are intent on putting it in the same spot as the original, remove all remains of the root system and thoroughly improve the soil before replanting.

Methods of containment

Most bamboos have a habit of spreading further than you want. However, they can be restricted to

quite an extent by creating an underground barrier when planting. For example, make a planting "box" by inserting paving slabs on their sides into the soil. Leave the base open for the roots to receive moisture and nutrients. In addition, if you regularly cut around the edges of a clump by driving a sharp spade firmly into the ground and severing all the creeping roots and stems, you should be able to keep the bamboo in check.

4 A shrub is dull except at flowering time

*Some shrubs, such as mock orange
(Philadelphus) and lilac (Syringa) are
glorious in flower but decidedly dull
for the rest of the year. There are
ways, though, of extending the
season of interest.*

CHIONODOXA FORBESII

COLCHICUM SPECIOSUM 'ALBUM'

SMALL BULBS

Colchicum
Crocus (spring and autumn)
Iris reticulata
Narcissi, especially those that
flower early in spring such as
'Hawera', 'Tête-à-Tête' and
'Peeping Tom'
Scilla

Arrange a floor show

Brighten up a shrub by underplanting
with bulbs, seasonal bedding or early
flowering herbaceous plants. It is
easier to plant under shrubs than
trees, because their root systems are
less extensive and there are fewer
problems with shade and drought.
Choose small or miniature bulbs and
low-growing plants for best effect.
Making a link between the shrub and
the underplanting can be particularly
effective. For instance, you could
coordinate a crocus flower with the
colour in a shrub's variegated leaf. It is
also possible to use autumn-flowering
bulbs such as autumn crocus and
colchicums to add interest towards
the back end of the year.

Let a climber scramble through the shrub

Training a climber through larger
shrubs can help to extend the season.
Clematis are ideal for the job, as are
more delicate climbers such as the
Chilean flame flower (*Tropaeolum
speciosum*). As a temporary measure,
use annual climbers such as morning
glory or tender perennials such as
Eccremocarpus scaber, often grown
as an annual though it may come
up year after year. Annuals have the
advantage that they do not generally
interfere with pruning the shrub.

SUITABLE CLIMBERS

Clematis (except very
vigorous types such
as *C. montana*)
Cobaea scandens
Ipomoea
(morning glory)

Lathyrus (annual sweet
pea, *L. odoratus*,
and perennial
L. grandiflorus and
L. latifolius)
Thunbergia alata

EXTEND THE SEASON OF INTEREST
*The clematis 'Cardinal Wyszynski' puts on
a show long after the rhododendron through
which it twines has finished flowering.*

5 A hydrangea has changed colour

*Hydrangeas can be affected by soil
alkalinity or acidity, and very dry
conditions may weaken flower colour.*

Colour effects

On an alkaline soil, blue-flowered
varieties of *Hydrangea macrophylla* will
look washed-out or even slightly pink.
For a good blue, soil pH needs to be
5.5 or less. If you can't supply these
conditions, consider growing the
hydrangea in a large container.
Regular applications of chopped
bracken and use of sequestered iron
or aluminium sulphate will lower pH
very slightly. When grown on an acid
soil, pink hydrangea flowers tend to
be a less exciting shade and sometimes
develop purple tints. In this case,
apply limestone at the rate of about
70g (2½oz) per square metre (yard)
annually to maintain a strong pink.

ACID SOIL PRODUCES THE BEST BLUE FLOWERS

SHRUB PESTS AND DISEASES

• RHODODENDRON BUD BLAST
Numerous tiny black bristles develop
on dry, brown buds. There is no
effective control, but pick off infected
buds by early summer to limit spread.

• VINE WEEVIL Adults often take
notches out of the edges of leaves.
There may be no significant loss of
vigour if the shrub is in open ground.
Use suitable controls against the grubs
in the soil (*see p.83*).

• HOLLY LEAF MINER Raised yellow or
brown blotches on leaves are caused by
the larva eating its way within the leaf.
Infested leaves may fall early but there
is no significant loss of vigour. Collect
up and dispose of infested leaves.

(*Other pests and diseases, see pp.178–85.*)

⑥ When is the best time to prune a shrub?

Many shrubs need no pruning at all except to cut out congested growth and dead, dying or damaged stems. But with some, pruning improves flowering; when to do it depends largely on when the shrub blooms.

Easy guide

As a very broad rule – which must be used with caution – if a shrub flowers in spring or early summer it should be pruned shortly after flowering (but generally by midsummer). Where a shrub flowers later in the summer, it is best pruned in late winter during the dormant period. When pruning, always make a clean cut, back to healthy wood, just above a sideshoot, leaf or bud. Where shrubs that form a thicket of stems have become congested, it is usually best to remove a proportion at the base, but not more than about one stem in four.

How far to go?

Some plants can be cut back fairly hard; for instance, many hypericums and varieties of cornus and willow (*Salix*) that are grown for their brightly coloured winter stems. Many plants, however, would show extreme distress or could even be killed by cutting back hard, for example ceanothus and lavender, so it is essential to check the specific needs of your plant, either on the label or in a good reference book.

Pruning evergreens

Evergreen shrubs are generally only pruned if they have become too big for their site. Do this in spring. A few, however, will put up with quite extensive pruning. These include aucuba, box, *Choisya ternata*, many types of euonymus, most hollies, cherry and Portuguese laurel, *Sarcococca humilis* and *Viburnum tinus*.

WHEN TO PRUNE WHAT

NO PRUNING NEEDED
Amelanchier, Chimonanthus, Buddleja globosa, Daphne, Hamamelis (witch hazel), *Viburnum* (deciduous types)

PRUNE AFTER FLOWERING
Chaenomeles, Deutzia, Kolkwitzia, Magnolia stellata, Philadephus, Photinia villosa, Ribes (flowering currant), *Spiraea* x *arguta, Syringa* (lilac), *Weigela*

PRUNE LATE WINTER/EARLY SPRING
Buddleja davidii, Caryopteris, Cotinus, Fuchsia (hardy types), *Hibiscus syriacus Lavatera, Perovskia, Spiraea japonica*

Pruning hydrangeas

Mophead and lacecap hydrangeas flower in late summer on shoots made the previous season. In cool climates, leave dead flowers on until spring to protect new growth. Then, also take out one or two old stems at the base.

HARD PRUNING IN LATE WINTER
A vigorous shrub such as Buddleja davidii, *which flowers in summer on the current year's growth, can be hard pruned in late winter.*

PRUNING AFTER FLOWERING
A shrub such as Spiraea x arguta, *which flowers in spring on the previous year's growth, is pruned once flowering has finished.*

PRUNING A HYDRANGEA
On mature mophead and lacecap hydrangeas, cut back old, flowered stems in mid-spring by up to 30cm (12in) to a pair of healthy buds.

⑦ Can an overgrown, misshapen shrub be cut back?

Some shrubs, but not all, can be rejuvenated by cutting back. If you are unsure about a shrub you have inherited, establish first what it is and how much pruning it will tolerate.

Proceed with caution

If extensive pruning is needed, unless you are sure that the shrub can be cut back hard without suffering, it is best to spread the work over several seasons, cutting back a proportion at a time. Large-scale pruning is generally best carried out in very early spring or while the plant is dormant. Renovate evergreens in early spring. Follow the general rules for pruning and remove dead, diseased, crossing or damaged branches first. Always cut back to a vigorous-looking growing point to reduce the risk of the shrub suffering stress and dying back. After heavy pruning, feed well. You may find that flowering and berrying are not up to scratch after extensive renovation, because you have had to prune out stems on which the flowers and fruits would have formed. But with feeding and maintenance the shrub should perform perfectly after a few years.

8 Disappointing display of flowers

It may take several years for a shrub to establish and start flowering reliably. For instance, many daphnes rarely get under way until about three years after planting. Even if the plant was flowering when purchased, it may have been induced to flower early and then settled back into its normal routine once planted in the garden. But if you have waited and still been rewarded with a feeble show, it might be a sign that something else is amiss.

Feeding fault

Excessive application of nitrogen, whether in the form of well-rotted manure or fertilizer, may encourage a shrub to produce foliage at the expense of flowers. Make up for an over-supply of nitrogen by applying a high-potash fertilizer such as a liquid tomato feed, or sulphate of potash, in early spring and autumn.

Poor pruning

If you have pruned a shrub unnecessarily or at the wrong time of year, you may well have pruned out the wood that would have borne the flowers. Check the correct pruning time and give the shrub a chance to recover before attacking it with the secateurs again.

Deadhead for more flowers

A few shrubs can sometimes be persuaded to flower for a little longer or produce a second, albeit much smaller, flush if the spent flowers are removed before they have a chance to set seed. Carefully remove flowers that are borne on very short stalks, for instance rhododendrons and camellias (twist them off between finger and thumb), but cut back other flowering stems to the next sideshoot or pair of shoots. Cut back choisya stems by about 15cm (6in).

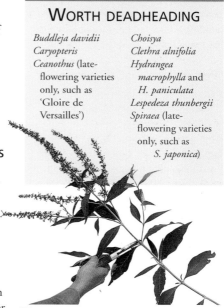

WORTH DEADHEADING

Buddleja davidii	*Choisya*
Caryopteris	*Clethra alnifolia*
Ceanothus (late-flowering varieties only, such as 'Gloire de Versailles')	*Hydrangea macrophylla* and *H. paniculata*
	Lespedeza thunbergii
	Spiraea (late-flowering varieties only, such as *S. japonica*)

TAKE OFF FADED BLOOMS
Buddleja davidii can be encouraged to produce more, if smaller, flowerheads by cutting back to the next pair of sideshoots.

9 Berries are few and far between or non-existent

With some shrubs, gender is the crucial factor if fruits fail to form. Birds might also be stealing berries, or you, the gardener, might be the culprit if your pruning was too hasty.

Sex matters

A few shrubs, such as hollies and skimmias, produce male and female flowers on separate plants, and if you have unwittingly bought a male plant only, it will never be able to bear berries. Similarly, if you have a female plant but no suitable partner within pollination distance, berries will be sparse or not form at all. Buy more than one shrub to guarantee berries. Gender varies with variety, but good catalogues or plant directories usually supply the necessary information. Cultivar names can be misleading; 'Golden Queen' is a male holly.

Occasionally, a shrub that has been laden with berries year after year suddenly stops producing them. This suggests that a pollinating partner in a nearby garden has been removed and you need to plant a replacement.

Fallen fruit

Occasionally berries form but quickly drop. This may be due to extreme lack of moisture, in which case regular watering and a good bulky organic mulch are essential and should

YELLOW FRUITS MAY BE LESS TEMPTING TO BIRDS

remedy the problem the following year. In some plants, diseases such as pyracantha scab may spoil the berries or cause them to drop prematurely.

Untimely pruning

If you have pruned away faded flowers you may, without thinking, have cut out the stems that would have borne the berries. This often happens with shrubs such as pyracantha, where cutting back the extremely thorny stems is often necessary but removes the plant's berrying potential.

Food for the birds

Although birds are a real pleasure to see in the garden, they may strip the berries from shrubs before you have had time to enjoy them. Netting or scaring devices may work, but you could also try planting a shrub with yellow berries which birds often (but not always) find less appetizing.

⑩ Why won't it grow?

Instead of growing into a fine, healthy specimen, the occasional shrub refuses either to grow at all or goes into a decline.

Poor plant, poor planting

If the plant was pot-bound when purchased, or the root ball too dry when planted, the roots may never manage to move out into the surrounding soil and take up water and minerals. Consequently, the plant will gradually run out of steam and may start to die back.

Make sure you prepare a really good-sized planting hole, with plenty of well-rotted organic matter or planting compost incorporated into the soil, and that the plant's root ball is in good condition. If dry or at all pot-bound, thoroughly moisten the root ball (*above right*). Spread the roots in the hole and check that the plant is at the same depth as it was in its container before backfilling with soil.

Keep it watered

After planting, the shrub must be watered in well and kept moist during its first summer at least, probably the second summer too. On light soils or

MOISTEN THE ROOT BALL
If pot-bound, soak the root ball in water for a few hours or overnight, then gently but firmly tease out the outer roots and trim off some of the excess.

sloping ground, making a circular ridge of soil around the area of the root ball helps to prevent run-off. Inserting a short piece of hose (*see p.94*) ensures that water is channelled directly to the roots.

Gradual decline

If a shrub appears to have taken well but then shows signs of distress or fails to grow it is often due to poor planting, perhaps combined with environmental factors such as dry soil. Investigate the state of the root ball in

autumn or very early spring. If the roots are dry and congested, carefully lift the plant, soak the root ball and replant, preferably in a new site or at least surrounded by fresh soil.

Soil and environment

If the soil is too dry, too wet, too acid or too alkaline for the plant's needs, it may survive but never thrive and leaf size and colour may be diminished. Check a shrub's requirements before buying and then give it the most suitable position possible.

⑪ Can a large shrub be transplanted?

Disturbance is never good for a plant, and the longer it has been in the same position, the more it is likely to suffer. If you need to move a shrub, the smaller it is and the better the preparations, the greater your chances of success.

Moving strategy

Generally speaking, shrubs should be moved while dormant, from late autumn to very early spring. Take as large a root ball as possible to minimize root damage. The spread of the roots usually at least matches the spread of the branches. Ideally, make the new planting hole before digging up the shrub. It must be large enough

to accommodate the roots easily plus a good planting mix of organic matter and soil. To move large shrubs, you may need two or more people, so get help if necessary.

Using a sharp spade, cut around the roots in a circle and dig out the root ball to the greatest depth possible. Move the shrub on a large tarpaulin or sheet of hessian or polythene. If there is any delay in replanting, keep the roots well covered with soil or tie the polythene or tarpaulin around them to prevent them drying out.

If time allows, shrubs are best moved in two stages, using a process known as under-cutting. Take out a circular trench, at least 20cm (8in)

deep, around the roots in autumn and fill with planting compost. The shrub will be ready to move one year later, by which time fine feeding roots should have formed in the compost. Dig out the root ball around the outermost edge of the trench so that you include the newly formed roots.

Good aftercare

A transplanted shrub needs good aftercare, because the root system may have been damaged. Regular watering and the use of a good mulch are essential. In the first year or two after transplanting, some protection in summer and winter from extremes of temperature is also advisable.

Shrub chooser

Shrubs for acid soils

These shrubs will do well in gardens where soil has a low pH (6.5 or under).
Camellia
Erica carnea, and cultivars
Eucryphia
Fothergilla
Gaultheria mucronata, and cultivars
Pieris
Rhododendron
Vaccinium
Zenobia

Year-round interest

In a small garden it is worth including shrubs which have at least one attractive feature in each of the seasons.
Convolvulus cneorum
Corylus avellana 'Contorta'
Dwarf conifers (strictly trees, but smaller than many shrubs)
Elaeagnus × *ebbingei*, and cultivars, *E. pungens*, and cultivars
Euryops acraeus
Lavandula (lavender)
Ozothamnus ledifolius
Pieris (particularly those with foliage that turns colour, such as 'Forest Flame')

Damp, shaded areas

Provided the soil does not become waterlogged, a number of shrubs will thrive in areas of fairly damp shade.
Aucuba
Buxus sempervirens (box)
Camellia
Cornus (dogwood)
Daphne laureola
Euonymus fortunei, and cultivars, *E. japonicus*, and cultivars
Fatsia japonica
Lonicera pileata
Mahonia aquifolium
Rhododendron
Rubus tricolor
Skimmia japonica, and cultivars

Windy (not coastal) sites

Given some shelter (*see p.127*), it should be possible to establish these shrubs without too much difficulty in an exposed garden. Some, such as *Brachyglottis*, *Escallonia* and *Hebe*, suit coastal sites but by no means all.
Brachyglottis 'Sunshine' (formerly *Senecio*)
Calluna vulgaris, and cultivars
Cassinia leptophylla subsp. *fulvida*
Cistus
Cotoneaster (low-growing species such as *C. adpressus* and *C. dammeri*, *C. horizontalis*)
Elaeagnus
Erica carnea, and cultivars
Escallonia
Fuchsia magellanica
Gaultheria mucronata, and cultivars
Genista (broom, low-growing species)
Hebe
Lavatera
Olearia
Ozothamnus ledifolius
Phormium
Pyracantha
Prunus spinosa (blackthorn)

LAVANDULA ANGUSTIFOLIA 'TWICKEL PURPLE'

SKIMMIA JAPONICA 'BRONZE KNIGHT'

Salix (willow), some
Sambucus racemosa (elder)
Spiraea
Tamarix
Ulex (gorse)

Fragrant flowers

Flowers laden with perfume add an extra, very pleasurable, dimension to the garden.
Abelia × *grandiflora*
Abeliophyllum distichum
Azara petiolaris
Buddleja
Chimonanthus
Choisya ternata (Mexican orange blossom)
Colletia hystrix

DAPHNE CNEORUM

Corylopsis
Cytisus battandieri (pineapple broom)
Daphne cneorum, *D. odora* 'Aureomarginata', *D. tangutica*
Fothergilla major
Hamamelis (witch hazel)
Lonicera fragrantissima, *L.* × *purpusii*
Magnolia stellata
Mahonia japonica
Olearia × *haastii*
Osmanthus delavayi
Philadelphus (mock orange)
Pittospotum tobira (Japanese mock orange)
Rhododendron Albatross Group, *R.* 'Polar Bear'
Roses, many
Sarcococca (Christmas box)
Syringa (lilac)
Viburnum (particularly winter- and spring-flowering varieties such as *V.* × *bodnantense* and *V. carlesii*)

Dry shade

If planted well and given care while establishing, these shrubs should succeed in tricky dry but shaded areas.
Aucuba
Cornus canadensis
Daphne laureola
Euonymus fortunei, and cultivars, *E. japonicus*, and cultivars
Fatsia japonica
Pachysandra

PROPAGATING PLANTS

PLANT PROPAGATION is an area of gardening often shrouded in mystery, believed for some reason to be extremely difficult and beset by problems. Taking cuttings, dividing plants and the various other common methods used can, however, be an easy and economical way to build up stocks of familiar and not-so-familiar plants. Similarly, seed-sowing (*see p.38*) should be a fairly trouble-free means of filling your garden with colour and productivity.

Q What is the difference between a nodal and an internodal cutting?

A Nodal cuttings are trimmed back so that the base of the cutting is just below a node, where the leaf or leaf stalk joins the stem. The reason for this is that the plant's growth-regulating hormones tend to be concentrated here, and so roots are produced particularly readily from this area. Internodal cuttings are taken so that the base is at some distance from a node – often anything up to 2½in (6cm) away but this is extremely variable – or perhaps midway between two sets of nodes. With a nodal cutting, the node (or pair of nodes on stems with opposite leaves) is inserted into the compost. With an internodal cutting, stem only is inserted.

You will find that most climbers and shrubs and some herbaceous plants such as diascias and violas root well from nodal cuttings. A few shrubs such as buddlejas, however, seem to root better from internodal cuttings.

Q Is there a best time of day to collect material for cuttings?

A It is best to collect the stems from which you want to make cuttings early in the day, before the temperature rises. This will ensure that they are plump and full of moisture. When collecting the material, put it into a clean, labelled, polythene bag. Wherever possible,

you should prepare the cuttings from the stems straight away but, if necessary, they can be stored in a cool place, out of direct sunlight, for an hour or two. If they are put in a bag containing plenty of air, they can be stored in a refrigerator for even longer. Cuttings are, however, much more likely to be successful if prepared immediately.

Q How is it possible to tell which part of a plant will make the best cuttings?

A The most successful cuttings generally come from plants which are vigorous and healthy and therefore produce plenty of new growth every year. The stems you choose should be sturdy and growing well. Contrary to what you might expect, excessively vigorous shoots often make poor cuttings as they are likely to have hollow centres and be inclined to rot. Where possible, take growth from non-flowering shoots. Do not use any stems which have been damaged or show even the slightest sign of pest or disease attack.

Q Should cuttings be pulled or cut from a plant? What is meant by a cutting with a heel?

A You should always cut the material to be used for cuttings from the parent plant using a sharp knife or very sharp secateurs, even

though you will be trimming it later. If you tear off stems you are likely to damage them and consequently the cuttings; if you use a knife which is not sufficiently sharp, you may crush the stems and important cells within. Remove more material than you actually need and then trim it back to make the cuttings when you are ready to insert them into the cuttings compost.

There is an exception, and this is when you take a heeled cutting. Then, the cutting should be carefully pulled away from the plant so that it comes off with a very thin piece of bark attached to it – the "heel". This forms the base of the cutting. If plants are known to be difficult to root, it is often worth trying a few cuttings with a heel, as the plant's natural rooting hormones tend to accumulate around this area and the cutting is more likely to succeed. This is a good method for ceanothus, chimonanthus and osmanthus. In addition, heeled cuttings are somewhat less likely to succumb to fungal diseases.

Q What is the best compost mixture to use for rooting cuttings?

A You can either buy a ready-mixed cuttings compost or create your own by mixing equal parts of finely chipped bark and coir (or peat). For cuttings that root best if given good drainage, you can make a compost using equal parts coir (or peat) and a mixture of finely chipped bark and medium-grade perlite. If you are in any doubt as to whether your compost will give adequate drainage, include some extra perlite or a similar material.

Q What is the difference between softwood, semi-ripe and hardwood cuttings?

A Softwood cuttings are usually taken from the shoot tip, where the growth has not started to toughen up at all and is still soft and flexible.

Semi-ripe cuttings are still fairly flexible, but the stems will have started to develop a distinct woodiness. The base of a semi-ripe cutting is usually quite hard and woody, while the tip is still growing strongly and so is fairly soft. Semi-ripe cuttings are usually taken from mid- to late summer or very early autumn at the latest.

Hardwood cuttings are completely woody and are usually taken between the end of autumn and midwinter, once the growth is completely mature and woody. They generally have no leaves on them, unless of course they have been taken from evergreen plants. Hardwood cuttings usually need to be larger than softwood or semi-ripe cuttings because they are much slower and less ready to root. The increased size provides them with stored food reserves.

Q What is the best way to prepare a semi-ripe cutting from a shrub such as box?

A Remove any sideshoots from the main stem and carefully slice off the soft growth at the tip of each cutting using a sharp knife. Also remove the lowermost pairs of leaves. Rooting is generally stimulated if you make a shallow cut on one side of the

stem, at the base, removing a sliver of bark in the process. Insert the cuttings into pots of well-drained cuttings compost. You can root several cuttings in each pot but make sure that they do not touch each other. A pot is generally the easiest place to maintain ideal conditions for rooting but, if necessary (perhaps because you have very large quantities to deal with), you can try rooting the cuttings in an area of sand-covered soil that is protected by a cloche.

Q Is it necessary to use a hormone rooting powder or liquid?

A Most cuttings benefit from the use of a hormone rooting compound. Such compounds not only stimulate root production from the base of the cutting but also contain a fungicide which helps to ward off the sort of fungal root rots which can cause cuttings to fail. It is essential that you do not "overdose" the cuttings on rooting powder. After dipping the base in the powder, tap it sharply on the side of the dish to shake off any excess.

Q Why do cuttings go black and rot at the base?

A This is black leg, a problem which is likely to occur when growing conditions are slightly unhygienic and humidity and moisture levels are high. Black leg is caused by a range of fungi and bacteria and can kill cuttings.

Try to ensure that cuttings are inserted ino a really free-draining medium and that you regularly let air circulate around them. You should also only water cuttings with mains water, not water stored in a water butt, since this may harbour the sort of organisms which cause this problem.

Dipping the base of cuttings into hormone rooting powder containing a fungicide should help to ward off black leg.

Q When rooting cuttings in a flowerpot, how many cuttings can you put in each pot?

A This really depends on the size of the pot and the size of the cuttings. Whatever you do, you should ensure that the cuttings do not touch each other and will still not do so even if they put on a slight amount of growth while in the pot.

Q Why is it necessary to cut off some of the leaves or parts of leaves when taking cuttings?

A This is done for two reasons. Firstly, it often makes the cutting less inclined to wobble around in the compost. Any movement may inhibit rooting. And more importantly, perhaps, removing excess foliage helps to reduce the amount of moisture lost through leaves. Moisture must be retained if cuttings are to live and root.

Q Cuttings from plants with hairy leaves seem to rot off very quickly. How can this problem be overcome?

A The humid environment that is needed for most cuttings to root does, unfortunately, provide too much humidity for the healthy growth of many furry or silver-leaved plants. It is essential that you provide these with good aeration, perhaps removing any cover for a short period daily. You may also find that the cuttings root better in a cold frame than in a greenhouse, because air circulation is likely to be better and the atmosphere cooler and drier.

TYPES OF CUTTINGS • HORMONE ROOTING COMPOUNDS • SIGNS OF BLACK LEG

Q Is it possible to root cuttings without the aid of a propagator?

A It is certainly possible to root cuttings from many kinds of plants without a propagator. Some can be rooted in a "nursery bed" or in a cold frame in prepared soil in the frame or in trays or pots of compost. Others can be rooted perfectly well in pots or trays on a windowsill indoors. In place of a propagator, you can cover a pot with a clear polythene bag to create a miniature cloche effect. Use three or four slim canes to prop up the bag and keep it clear of the foliage. If leaves come into contact with the bag, condensation drip is likely to run onto them and encourage rotting.

Whether your cuttings are growing in a propagator or in pots with a polythene bag over the top, it is essential that air circulation is adequate or they are likely to rot. It is difficult to generalize about how often cuttings need to receive fresh air, but it is usually advisable to remove any plastic covering or propagator lid for a short period every other day.

Q What exactly is a "nursery bed" and what is the best way to make one?

A A nursery bed is an excellent place to root semi-ripe cuttings of many types of plant and to grow on other plants you are propagating. It can easily be created in a spare patch of soil somewhere in the garden. Ideally, you should position it in a sheltered, semi-shaded spot, since cuttings do not root well in very bright sunlight or dense shade. In most gardens you will find that you get the best results if you improve the soil in the nursery area, perhaps by digging in some organic matter. Also remove all weeds, of course, especially perennial types, to give whatever young plants you will be growing there the best possible chance of surviving.

Dig the soil over thoroughly, removing all large stones, until you have created a fine tilth. Use a rake if necessary. Then mix some loam-free compost into the soil to a depth of 15–20cm (6–8 in). This should provide a good rooting medium for the cuttings. On heavier soils it is a good idea to incorporate some grit to improve drainage. The cuttings can then be inserted directly into the nursery bed and watered in. Cover the bed with a large cloche or something similar that will reduce problems of excessive water loss. The relatively humid environment that builds up beneath the cloche will help to encourage rooting.

Q Can rooted cuttings be planted straight out into the garden ?

A It is always best to grow cuttings on before planting them out into the garden. In some cases this may mean potting them on into larger individual pots; in others you may be able to move the young plants into a nursery bed (see previous question, left).

If planted out too soon, there is a risk that newly rooted cuttings may too easily be swamped by other larger and more vigorous plants nearby or perhaps even by rapid-growing, highly competitive weeds.

Q What is the best way to root hardwood cuttings?

A Hardwood cuttings generally root best if the base is dipped in hormone rooting compound. On those which do not root readily, you should also remove a thin sliver of bark from the base, as this too will help to encourage rooting. The cuttings can be rooted in large pots, but it is often easier to root them in a nursery bed or outdoor slit trench, especially if the soil is well drained. Most hardwood cuttings should be adequately rooted after about 12 months and can then be lifted carefully and transplanted into a nursery row. Kept well watered, these young plants should then be ready to be moved into their permanent positions after a further 12 months. Spiraea, willow (Salix), weigela and philadelphus are all suitable subjects.

Choose a site which is fairly sheltered for making a slit trench and weed the area thoroughly. In heavier soils, there is an increased likelihood of the cuttings failing or rotting, so improve drainage by pouring a thin layer of horticultural sand along the length of the trench. To open up the slit, drive a spade into the soil to a depth of about 15cm (6in) and ease it back and forth slightly. Cuttings can then be inserted along the length of the trench. Insert each cutting so that about three-quarters of its length is buried in the soil and the remaining quarter protrudes above the surface. Cuttings can generally be spaced quite closely – about 5cm (2in) apart. Firm the soil carefully around them and water them in well, particularly if the ground is dry.

Q What is layering and when and how is it done?

A A number of shrubs have fairly low-growing branches which, when they touch the ground, form roots. This is called layering and is a process which you can either allow to happen naturally or which you can encourage on plants such as cotinus, hazel (Corylus), snowberry (Symphoricarpos) and many climbers. To layer a stem, choose a healthy, low-growing shoot and carefully cut off the sideshoots and foliage to leave a 30cm (12in) run of clear stem. In approximately the middle of this length of stem, make a slanting cut towards the stem's centre. Tap a small quantity of hormone rooting powder into the tongue that you have created. Use a U-shaped piece of sturdy wire to secure the layer into the ground, pegging it so that the wounded side of the stem is facing downwards. Mound up about 8cm (3in) of soil over the stem. Drive a short bamboo cane into the ground close by and loosely tie the top of the stem to it. Tie it in several places, up to the tip if necessary, so that the new plant will have a straight, upright stem.

Layers can be made between autumn and spring. They usually take about 12 months (but sometimes up to two years) to form adequate roots before the new plant can be severed from the parent. Once severed, carefully lift the rooted layer out of the soil. Try not to disturb the roots in the process. The layer can then be potted up and grown on until it is well established and has developed a good root system.

Q What is air layering and what plants could be propagated in this way?

A This method is often used for indoor plants such as the rubber plant (*Ficus elastica*) or philodendron but it can also be used on a number of hardy shrubs such as daphnes or rhododendrons.

Ideally, choose a one- to two-year-old stem and trim off the leaves and sideshoots for a length of about 30cm (12in) about halfway between the stem's base and tip. Then use a sharp knife to make a sloping cut towards the centre of the stem. Tap a small quantity of hormone rooting powder onto the cut surfaces to encourage rooting. Keep the wound

slightly open with a small chip of wood or a little bit of sphagnum moss, then surround the area with plenty of sphagnum moss held in place with a sleeve of polythene tied at either end. Use black polythene to exclude light, as this helps to encourage rooting.

It may take anything up to 12 months for the layered stem to produce an adequate number of roots. You will need to check from time to time to ensure that the stem is still healthy and to see how the rooting process is progressing. Once a good root system has developed, sever the stem just below the wound, taking care to keep the roots intact. Plant the new plant into a pot or nursery bed as appropriate. Take care not to let the new plant dry out.

Q Can you suggest some plants which can be air layered ?

A There are many plants which respond well to air layering including akebia, azara, camellia, celastrus, clematis, corylopsis, cotinus, dogwood (*Cornus*), fothergilla, hydrangea, kalmia, lilac (*Syringa*), magnolia, parrotia, pieris, rhododendron, vines (*Vitis*), wisteria and witch hazel (*Hamamelis*).

Q What are root cuttings and how are they taken ?

A Root cuttings often work when other methods of propagation prove difficult or unsuccessful and, although you need to dig up the parent plant, remember you can always replant it afterwards. Root cuttings are most likely to succeed if taken from young, vigorous plants. Ideally they should be taken in early winter. Carefully dig up the parent plant. (If this is not possible, scrape away sufficient soil to expose a section

of root which you can sever and lift.) If the roots are heavily covered with soil, wash this off gently. Remove a few fleshy roots using a sharp knife, cutting them off close to the crown of the plant. Cut each root into pieces about 5cm (2in) long and make sure that you know which end is the top (ie, was nearest the soil surface) and which the bottom. They will need to be inserted in the pot in the same direction that they were growing. Using a sharp knife, carefully remove any fibrous side-roots. Insert the cuttings into pots of compost so that the top end of each just protrudes above the surface.

With fine-rooted plants remove the roots in the same way but cut them into 7.5cm (3in) sections and then carefully lay them on the compost's surface before covering them with a thin layer of compost.

Root cuttings can be left to shoot in a cold-frame or greenhouse. Most should be ready to pot on in spring.

Plants that are readily propagated from root cuttings include acanthus, anchusa, Japanese anemones (*Anemone × hybrida)*, clerodendrum, crambe, dicentra, echinacea, eryngium, catmint (*Nepeta*), phlox, *Primula denticulata*, robinia, romneya and sumach (*Rhus*).

Q What is meant by serpentine layering?

A Serpentine layering can be done between autumn and spring and is especially suitable for plants which have long flexible stems – clematis for example. Carefully take a stem down to ground level and lay it on the soil surface. Mound soil over the top so that the buds are just exposed. The stem may need to be held in place using a few U-shaped metal pegs. The buds will produce aerial shoots, and roots will form between each pair of buds, allowing you to produce several plants from a single, vigorous stem.

SUITABLE SUBJECTS FOR AIR LAYERING • ROOT CUTTINGS • SERPENTINE LAYERING

HERBACEOUS PERENNIALS

At one time a garden was scarcely a garden without a herbaceous border. Then perennials seemed to fall from favour, displaced by shrubs and other plants regarded as less demanding. True, perennials do need a certain amount of care – some staking, feeding and deadheading – but success often depends on choosing suitable varieties and good combinations. Now, herbaceous perennials are as popular as ever. You may decide to devote a bed or border to them alone but, for a well-planned display, other types of plant are often needed, particularly bulbs.

CRAMPED PLANTS
Plants are starting to crowd one another out. **1**

JUMBLED HEIGHTS
Badly placed small plants are hidden by bigger neighbours. **2**

FLOPPING STEMS
Flower stems fall or break and damage nearby plants. **6**

SHORT DISPLAY
Early-flowering perennials have started to die down, leaving ugly gaps. **5**

JARRING COLOURS
Some flower colours are brighter than expected and clash with each other. **4**

1 Plants are too cramped or too gappy

Plants that have become squashed or misshapen, because they have grown too close together, need lifting and respacing. Temporary gaps can easily be filled with annuals while newly planted perennials take time to grow.

Lift and divide

In an established herbaceous border where plants have started to outgrow their space, lifting and dividing clumps will reduce overcrowding and allow plants to achieve their natural shape. This also gives you the chance to remove the older, less vigorous parts (usually the inner sections of a clump) that will proably be flowering poorly. If possible, divide plants in spring or autumn, when they are not actively growing and so have the best chance of recovery. On light soils, autumn is the best time to do this, but on heavy soil it pays to wait until spring. Discard areas with unhealthy-looking top-growth or roots. Most herbaceous plants benefit from being divided and replanted from time to time – roughly every two to four years. Revitalize the soil before replanting by forking in some organic matter, such as well-rotted manure.

If the border is overcrowded simply because you have put in too many plants and they are not at a stage where they need dividing, you will either have to find another home for them or be ruthless and get rid of those you like least.

ROOM FOR BULBS
Gaps in borders in spring, before herbaceous plants have made much growth, make ideal spots for bulbs. The perennials' leaves will later mask the deteriorating foliage of the bulbs.

Ways of dividing herbaceous perennials

Clump-forming perennials that have plenty of basal shoots are generally easy to divide. Dig out the entire plant, taking care to minimize root damage, and shake off excess soil. The best method for many is to use two garden forks. Small clumps can sometimes be pulled apart, but dense, fibrous root systems often need to be cut using a spade or sturdy knife. Rhizomatous roots on plants such as irises also need to be cut; make sure each section has some roots attached.

SIMPLY PULL APART
Some clumps can be pulled apart and divided into several sections. Replant only the most vigorous.

SLICE WITH A SPADE
Plants with dense roots, like a hosta, can be sliced through. Each section must have at least one healthy bud.

BACK-TO-BACK FORKS
For many plants, insert two garden forks, back to back, then prise them apart. Repeat to form smaller sections.

Temporary fillings

A new border where the plants have been spaced to the correct planting distances may look positively bleak and gappy for the first year or two. An easy solution is to grow annuals or bedding in the gaps. Choose varieties with flower colours that mix well with the existing plants. Either sow seeds of annuals direct into the soil in early spring or, after the last frosts, plant tender bedding for a display within a few weeks. Try to avoid notorious self-seeders or you may have to spend several seasons weeding them out.

COLOURFUL STOP GAP
Iceland poppies, usually grown as biennials, will usefully fill a gap for a couple of seasons until more permanent plants fill the spaces.

Planting distances

When planting up a new border it is tempting to set everything too closely to avoid ugly gaps, but if the border is to look good in the long term, the correct spacing is essential. Planting distances should be given on the plant label or, failing this, check in a reliable reference book. It is not worth trying to guess, since a plant's potential to spread varies greatly, even between varieties of the same species. To calculate the correct distance when planting in groups, simply multiply the spread of the plant by two.

❷ Jumbled heights

Borders do not necessarily need to be arranged in a neat gradation of heights, but tall, dense plants at the front can obscure smaller neighbours behind and make it difficult to get in to weed and deadhead.

Planning for growth

It is essential that you take note of a plant's potential height when deciding what to grow and check that it will not hide its neighbours. Bear in mind that the flower stems of some plants tower above the leaves, though a lofty spike produced in autumn will not obscure low-growing spring flowers. If planting up a bed that can be viewed from all sides, keep most of the taller plants in the centre. However, a display often looks better for having a few unexpected "peaks" in it.

Move badly sited plants

Most herbaceous perennials do best if moved in early to mid-spring, especially on heavy soils or if the plant prefers a dry situation, or in autumn. Choose the future site in advance: dig it over and fertilize before you move the plant itself, and aim to replant as soon as possible to prevent the roots from drying out. Once replanted, water the whole area thoroughly to allow the soil to settle in around the plant's roots. Let neighbouring plants, whose roots may also have been disturbed, benefit from the watering, too.

Although the majority of herbaceous perennials can be divided or re-sited, a few seem to resent disturbance and may take several seasons to perform well after being moved.

DO NOT DISTURB	
Anemone x *hybrida*	*Dictamnus*
Alstroemeria	*Eremurus*
Astilbes	Hellebores
Dicentra spectabilis	Peonies

SUCCESSFUL MOVES
Check that the planting hole has adequate space for the roots. Backfill with soil, then water well (inset) and spread a thick mulch.

❸ How deep to plant

Planting depth should not cause too much anxiety, because most herbaceous perennials need the same sort of treatment. However, a few do have special preferences.

Simple rules to follow

Provided you have obtained your plants from a reputable source, they should have been planted in their containers at the correct depth and you can plant them out in the garden using this as a guide. If set too deeply, the plant's crown may deteriorate and be prone to excessive moisture build-up during wet weather. If planted too shallowly, the plant may suffer from drought very early on in a dry spell. If you use a bulky organic mulch on the flower bed, make sure that when this rots down it does not gradually build up on top of the plant's crown, eventually burying it too deep.

DEEP PLANTING
This suits plants that cannot tolerate drought, Solomon's seal (Polygonatum), crinum and crocosmias, for example.

JUST BELOW SOIL LEVEL
Hostas, lily of the valley and peonies are best planted with their crowns about 2.5cm (1in) below ground level.

SHALLOW PLANTING
Positioning the crown just above soil level suits plants needing good drainage such as sisyrinchiums and irises.

❹ Jarring colours

What goes with what is a matter of personal taste, but not all combinations have quite the effect that was hoped for.

The way to harmony

Without a doubt, it is best to go for what appeals to you, whether your taste is for the subtle or bold. Having said this, labels and descriptions can be misleading and what you planned as an eye-catching display may, on occasion, prove too garish. When buying, try combining plants in flower in your shopping trolley. If a plant has definitely been planted in the wrong place, cut a leaf and flower and carry them around the garden to see where they look best, or take them to the garden centre or nursery. Some gardeners find a colour wheel helps them to plan combinations.

THE COLOUR WHEEL

❺ Faded flowers or too short a display

It is a something of a challenge to create a border that will provide non-stop colour and interest from spring to autumn. Diligent deadheading does a lot to help, as does careful planning.

Deadhead regularly

Some plants have a naturally short flowering season however much care and attention they may be given. This is something that you should bear in mind when planning a border. Many plants, though, can be persuaded to flower for longer or produce a second, later flush of blooms by deadheading, especially when combined with regular watering and feeding. Remove

KEEP THE SEEDHEADS
Some plants, such as eryngiums, echinops, phlomis and sedums, cannot be persuaded to bloom a second time but instead produce seedheads that are worth preserving.

the flower as soon as it fades, before any type of seedhead starts to form. The plant then doesn't waste energy on forming seeds and instead continues to flower in the hope that it will eventually manage to do so. On soft-stemmed plants, pinching the flower out between finger and thumb should suffice. On tougher plants, use a sharp pair of scissors, secateurs or a knife, whichever makes it easiest to achieve a neat, clean cut.

CUTTING BACK TO A SIDESHOOT

REMOVING THE FLOWER STEM

WHERE TO CUT
Cut the old flower stems of plants such as delphiniums (left) down to ground level. On perennials like phlox and salvia (far left), cut back to a sideshoot to encourage more flowers lower down the stem.

Choose some plants with late summer in mind

It is all too easy to find that you have filled the garden with early-flowering perennials and, once these have finished, it is bereft of colour. To pick up ideas for late-summer perennials that will cheer up beds and borders, do some window-shopping by visiting gardens that are open to the public to see what is looking good at this time of year. Good garden centres, too, will have plenty of late-flowering plants at the forefront of their displays.

ASTER ERICOIDES 'WHITE HEATHER'

CROCOSMIA X *CROCOSMIIFLORA* 'STAR OF THE EAST'

AGAPANTHUS 'BLUE GIANT'

HELENIUM 'BRUNO'

TRICYRTIS FORMOSANA

RUDBECKIA FULGIDA 'GOLDSTURM'

⑥ Plants flop

For some plants to look their best in a bed or border, they will need some sort of staking.

What makes them sprawl

Some plants with a lax habit of growth will tend to sprawl. This may be just the effect you want, at the edge of a border or raised bed or on a bank. Elsewhere, though, if they are starting to ruin their neighbours, some sort of staking will be needed. The flower stems of some cultivars which have been bred to produce very large blooms also tend to flop, particularly after rain, which increases the weight of the flowerhead. You may find it pays to choose smaller-flowered, less showy natural species.

The problem of flopping stems is much more likely to occur where plants are given unsuitable growing conditions. If soil has been too heavily manured this may promote soft, weak growth, which is more inclined to flop in even only slightly windy conditions. Too much shade may also result in weak stems.

Leggy growth

If grown in a position where it does not get the light it needs, a normally vigorous herbaceous perennial can develop spindly flower stems and look extremely sad. Always check the label for a plant's natural requirements before buying. If you have succumbed to temptation and planted a sun-lover in shade and it is looking miserable, the only solution is to move it (*see preceding page*) to a spot where it will get more light and should soon develop a more compact habit.

Choose an appropriate method of support

Whatever sort of staking you use, try to get it in place as early as possible in the season, to minimize any damage to the plant and increase the chance of the support being concealed by the plant's foliage as it grows. Twiggy sticks are unobtrusive and work well for plants which are not too bulky.

Use a single cane for supporting a tall flower spike. Sink purpose-made supports quite deep into the soil, then raise gradually as the plant gets taller.

PURPOSE-MADE SUPPORT
Plastic-coated, galvanized wire, L-shaped sections are easily linked to form a support of the appropriate size for the plant.

CANES AND TWINE
Where sturdy support is needed – in windy spots or for a vigorous plant – loop twine around canes driven securely into the ground.

SINGLE CANE
Support a tall, heavy flower stem, such as a delphinium's, with a cane, tying in the stem at intervals as it grows.

TWIGGY STICKS
Some sticks pushed firmly into the soil around a plant merge into the background and are ideal for perennials with delicate foliage.

PESTS AND DISEASES IN THE HERBACEOUS BORDER

APHIDS Greenfly and blackfly colonize and feed on the flowers and foliage of almost any plant, causing poor growth, distortion and discolouration. In most cases they can can be removed with a strong jet of water, or use a suitable insecticide, preferably one which is aphid specific, such as primicarb.

EARWIGS These may nibble petals. They tend to hide in flowers, foliage or nearby plants in the day and come out to feed after dark. Pick them off by hand or treat with a suitable insecticide such as derris.

PEDICEL NECROSIS If a flower stem turns brown and flops just behind the flower bud, causing the bud to fail, this is due to pedicel necrosis. It is particularly common on peonies and poppies and is encouraged by excess feeding with nitrogen and a deficiency of potassium.

POWDERY MILDEW This can be especially troublesome towards the end of the season and when soil is dry. Early in the year, remove badly affected leaves and, if necessary, spray with a suitable fungicide. In late summer, it usually suffices to have

DAHLIA FLOWERS MAY BE EATEN BY EARWIGS

a thorough clear-up at the end of the growing season and remove all the affected leaves.
(*Other pests and diseases, see pp.178–85.*)

Herbaceous perennial chooser

Good foliage

Some perennials combine flowers and attractive foliage and some are worth growing for their leaves alone.

Acorus
Anaphalis
Alchemilla mollis
Aquilegia vulgaris, including 'Nivea' and 'Woodside Pink'
Arum italicum 'Pictum'
Astilbe
Bergenia
Brunnera macrophylla
Geranium × *monacense* 'Variegatum'
Grasses, many
Ferns, many
Heuchera, especially 'Pewter Moon', 'Palace Purple' and 'Snow Storm'
Hosta, many
Lupins
Lychnis coronaria
Phormium tenax Purpureum Group and *P. tenax* 'Variegatum'
Pulmonaria (lungwort), most
Sedum
Sisyrinchium striatum 'Aunt May'

Bees and butterflies

These perennials should all help to attract bees and butterflies to the garden.

Alcea (hollyhock)
Alstroemeria
Anchusa
Aster (Michaelmas daisy)
Campanula
Centaurea
Coreopsis
Cosmos
Delphinium
Digitalis (foxglove)
Doronicum
Echinops
Eryngium
Gypsophila, single forms
Lupins
Origanum
Monarda (bergamot)
Nepeta (catmint)
Oenothera
Polemonium (Jacob's ladder)

Rudbeckia
Salvia
Sedum spectabile, especially 'Brilliant', *S.* 'Herbstfreude' syn. 'Autumn Joy'
Sidalcea
Verbascum
Veronica

Damp soil

The following all grow best in a reasonably moist soil.

Astilbe
Caltha palustris (marsh marigold)
Cimicifuga
Dodecatheon
Euphorbia griffithii
Filipendula, many
Gunnera
Hemerocallis (daylily)
Hosta
Lysimachia
Mimulus, some
Monarda didyma (bergamot)
Nomocharis
Persicaria, some
Primula
Rodgersia
Schizostylis
Trollius (globe flower)
Zantedeschia (arum lily)

PERSICARIA AFFINIS 'DONALD LOWNDES'

TROLLIUS × *CULTORUM* 'EARLIEST OF ALL'

Shady corners

Several herbaceous perennials are suited to shade.

Aquilegia vulgaris
Arum italicum
Aruncus
Bergenia
Brunnera
Campanula latifolia
Cimicifuga
Corydalis
Dicentra
Dodecatheon
Epimedium
Euphorbia amygdaloides var. *robbiae*

PULMONARIA 'LEWIS PALMER'

Geraniums, many
Hellebores
Heuchera
× *Heucherella*
Hosta
Lamium
Meconopsis
Phlox paniculata
Polygonatum (Solomon's seal)
Pulmonaria (lungwort)

Flowers for cutting

These should last reasonably well in water.

Achillea
Centaurea
Gypsophila
Monarda (bergamot)
Phlox
Rudbeckia
Scabiosa (scabious)
Solidago (goldenrod)

Perennials for chalk

Many flowers grow well on chalk or limestone.

Anthemis
Achillea filipendulina
Bergenia
Catananche
Centranthus
Dianthus
Doronicum
Eryngium, some
Gypsophila paniculata
Helenium
Irises, most
Salvia nemorosa
Scabiosa caucasica (scabious)
Sidalcea
Verbascum

SEED SOWING & COLLECTING

RAISING YOUR OWN PLANTS from seed is one of the most satisfying parts of gardening. It is also an inexpensive way to to fill beds, borders and containers with fabulous splashes of colour and the vegetable plot with delicious things to eat.

When you consider what a packet of seeds can produce, it is excellent value, but you may also decide you want to collect and save seed from plants in your own or a friend's garden. If so, what is the best way to be sure of success?

Q *When is the best time to collect seeds, and how can you be sure not to miss the crucial moment before they disperse?*

A Ideally, seeds should be collected at the point where they would naturally be shed, when they are fully ripe. This may cause difficulties, because many plants eject their seeds at this stage, so it is necessary to keep a close watch. With particularly precious seeds, or plants that produce only a few seeds each year, loosely tie a paper bag around the seedhead so that the seeds will not be lost. Use paper, since polythene is likely to create humid conditions which cause seeds to rot. Collect seeds when the seedhead is dry. This means avoiding dewy mornings, and certainly do not collect shortly after rainfall.

Q *Once collected, how should seeds be stored?*

A Seeds need to be kept cool and dry and, in most cases, are best stored out of natural light. Putting them in old envelopes works well and gives you a good place to write the name clearly and, if necessary, any plant description or sowing details. It is essential to label seeds promptly. Although you may think you will remember what they are, a few months later you are likely to find you have forgotten. Many people successfully store seeds in film canisters, but the seeds must be thoroughly dry and free from moist plant debris or moisture will build up in the canister and cause them to rot. Whether in envelopes or canisters, the seeds can then usually be successfully stored either in boxes or in the refrigerator.

Q *What does it mean if seeds need to be "stratified"?*

A Stratification is the method used when seeds need to be given a cool period (to mimic a winter) before being brought to the temperature required for germination. For instance, the seeds of bells of Ireland (*Moluccella*) require a period of about 14 days where they are kept cold (putting them in a polythene bag in the refrigerator is perfect) and then a temperature of 18–21°C (64–70°F) to germinate. Seeds of other plants which need stratification include adonis, amelanchier, some types of campanula, cotoneaster, euonymus, meconopsis, peony, primula, trillium and viburnum.

Q *What is the advantage of buying F1 hybrid seeds?*

A Cultivars described as F1 are generally very vigorous and produce particularly large or attractive flowers, or an especially good crop in the case of vegetables. F1 hybrid seeds are produced by crossing two selected parent plants. This first generation of seeds – first filial or F1 – will produce plants which are of a uniform height and spread and tend to flower over a well-defined period. If you save seed from an F1 hybrid that you have grown, it is unlikely to produce similarly vigorous offspring.

Q *Can you suggest some plants which self-seed and produce similar offspring to their parents?*

A There are a number of plants which should do this fairly reliably including antirrhinums, borage, pot marigolds (*Calendula*), cornflowers (*Centaurea cyanus*), clarkia, foxgloves (*Digitalis*), California poppies (*Eschscholzia*), poached egg plants (*Limnanthes*), toadflax (*Linaria*), forget-me-nots (*Myosotis*), love-in-a-mist (*Nigella*), evening primroses (*Oenothera biennis*), common and opium poppies (*Papaver*), nasturtiums (*Tropaeolum*) and violas. However, you may find that colours do not always come true. For instance, white foxgloves might get pollinated by purple ones nearby, and the resulting seedlings will not all turn out white.

Q *Is it necessary to clean off all plant debris around seeds?*

A In most cases, any part of the seedhead which is attached to the seeds is best removed. However, anything which actually forms part of a seed, such as the dispersal wings on a maple seed, should be left in position. Provided the seeds are collected dry and kept dry, it should be fairly easy to gently rub them with your fingers to remove any loose pieces of plant material. Sometimes separating this from the seeds can be tedious, and it is often easiest to pass the seeds through a sieve with a suitable-sized mesh. Alternatively, if the seeds are not too small and lightweight, put them in a shallow dish and gently blow over the surface so that the fragments fly away and the seeds remain in the dish.

Q What equipment do you need to raise plants from seed?

A Hardy annual flowers and vegetables such as carrots and beans can be sown directly into well-prepared open ground. However, if you want to raise something a little more exotic or to avoid problems with slugs and birds, it will certainly help to sow into appropriate-sized trays or pots filled with a good-quality proprietary compost. In addition, if you invest in a small electrically-heated propagator, it will hugely increase the range of plants you can raise from seed. If you go one stage further, a cold frame or greenhouse enables you to grow on a wider range of plants, in larger numbers, than if you rely on using windowsills.

Q Do all seeds germinate best in the dark?

A Most seeds germinate well in the dark but a few, including busy Lizzy (*Impatiens*), begonia, coleus (*Solenostemon*) and primulas, need light in order to germinate. Sow these carefully onto the surface of levelled compost and then place a piece of glass or some taut clingfilm over the

top of the pot or tray. This will help to ensure that the surface of the compost does not dry out.

Q What can be done to deter cats from raking up newly sown areas of seed?

A There are numerous suggestions for how to keep cats away from seedbeds including: placing short, twiggy sticks over the area; scattering spiky prunings of plants such as holly; sticking in twigs tightly strung with twine; covering with a chicken-wire cage. There are several cat deterrent formulations on garden centre shelves, but most gardeners find these have little, if any, effect. It is often said that sprinkling a eucalyptus-based decongestant onto used teabags helps to keep cats away because they dislike the smell. You can also buy electronic deterrents which produce sounds that are inaudible to the human ear but unpleasant to a cat. These seem to work well but can be quite expensive.

Q What does "scarification" mean?

A Some seeds such as sweet peas (*Lathyrus odoratus* cultivars) and morning glory (*Ipomoea*) are often said to germinate better if scarified. This means that the seed coat is gently abraded (perhaps using sandpaper) or nicked with a sharp knife. However, with sweet peas, this is now generally believed not to make a great deal of difference.

Q Are there any annual flowers which actually prefer to be sown straight into open ground?

A You will find you get better results if you direct sow any of the following: agrostemma, anchusa,

borage, cornflower (*Centaurea cyanus*), California poppy (*Eschscholzia*), clarkia, *Cynoglossum amabile*, *Linum grandiflorum*, *Gilia capitata*, *Gypsophila elegans*, poached egg plant (*Limnanthes*), toadflax (*Linaria maroccana*), poppies, phacelia, scabious and silene. (*See also, p.42.*)

Q Is there anything that can be done to prevent seedlings on windowsills becoming leggy?

A If seedlings have insufficient light, they often become drawn and pale (etiolated). You can reduce this problem by placing them on windowsills that receive plenty of daylight. Standing the trays or pots on aluminium foil and creating a backdrop of foil-covered cardboard will increase light levels by reflection. Daily turning all the trays or pots will prevent seedlings from leaning towards the light and help to produce straight stems. If your windowsills are a little dark, consider buying a small light which mimics natural daylight and placing it near the seedlings.

Q Pricking out is tedious and time-consuming, and some of the seedlings always seem to get damaged. What is going wrong?

A Prick out seedlings only when they are large enough to handle easily. Pick them up using the seed leaves (the lowermost pair), never the true leaves or the stem. Making sure that compost is moist so that the roots can be eased out gently is also essential; prepare the fresh compost similarly. You can minimize the amount of pricking out needed by sowing many types of seed in trays of individual cells. Although these are more expensive than normal seed trays, the time, energy and wastage saved makes them well worthwhile.

ANNUALS & BEDDING

MANY GARDENS rely heavily on summer bedding, annuals and biennials for the vibrant colour these plants can supply for much of the summer. Whether you grow them for use in hanging baskets, to liven up existing flower beds, or to create a seasonal display in a border of their own, it really is worth trying to keep them on top form for as long as you can. Although their lives may be confined to just one season, many annuals and tender bedding plants will keep flowering right up until the first frosts, making them a mainstay of the garden in late summer.

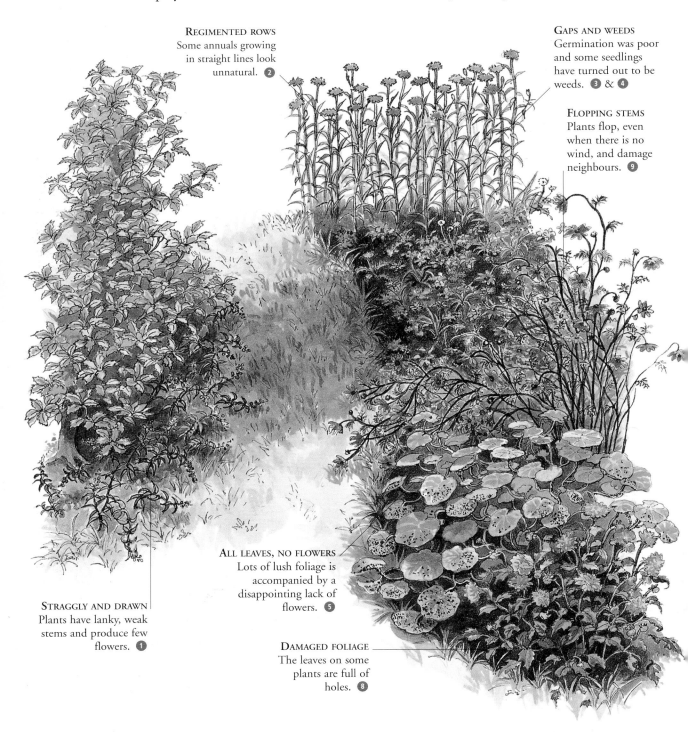

REGIMENTED ROWS
Some annuals growing in straight lines look unnatural. ❷

GAPS AND WEEDS
Germination was poor and some seedlings have turned out to be weeds. ❸ & ❹

FLOPPING STEMS
Plants flop, even when there is no wind, and damage neighbours. ❾

STRAGGLY AND DRAWN
Plants have lanky, weak stems and produce few flowers. ❶

ALL LEAVES, NO FLOWERS
Lots of lush foliage is accompanied by a disappointing lack of flowers. ❺

DAMAGED FOLIAGE
The leaves on some plants are full of holes. ❽

THE PROBLEMS

1. Plants have become straggly and drawn.
2. Plants have grown in unnatural-looking regimented rows.
3. Germination was poor and plants look gappy.
4. How is it possible to distinguish young seedlings from weeds?
5. There are lots of leaves but very few flowers.
6. Flowers didn't live up to expectations or match the photograph in the catalogue.
7. Plants stop producing flowers by the middle of summer.
8. Leaves of some plants are damaged by holes.
9. What can be done about plants whose stems flop or have droopy flowerheads?
10. Some bedding plants that were planted out in spring turned black and died.

See also:
Seed Sowing and Collecting, p.38; The Family Garden, p.106; In the Greenhouse, p.142; Weeds and Weeding, p.172; Pests, Diseases and Disorders, p.178.

❶ Plants are straggly and drawn

Most annuals and bedding plants need sunshine to grow into sturdy plants with plenty of flowers. In poor light under trees and shrubs or in the shadow of a wall or fence, the majority will get straggly and drawn. If light levels cannot be increased by thinning trees or shrubs, it's important to be realistic and choose plants that are suited to shade.

Choose the right plants

Try growing herbaceous plants instead because many of these are not so dependent on high light levels. Of the annuals, biennials and bedding plants to choose from, busy Lizzies (*Impatiens*) are some of the best performers in shade, and are available in a wide flower-colour range. Foliage colour can also vary from bronze in some hybrids to yellow variegations in others. Pansies (*Viola* cultivars) flower quite well in part shade as do small bedding begonias (*Begonia semperflorens*), some foxgloves (*Digitalis*), *Exacum affine*, *Mirabilis jalapa* and tobacco plants (*Nicotiana*). If you opt for perennials, look for those with interestingly patterned or textured foliage. Many ground-cover plants grow well in fairly shady spots, as do plenty of bulbs.

BUSY LIZZIES
(*IMPATIENS WALLERIANA*)

MIRABILIS JALAPA

PANSIES
(*VIOLA* CULTIVARS)

Encourage stems to branch

Pinch out bedding plants to encourage them to produce plenty of sideshoots and develop a good, bushy shape. Nip out the growing tip on the central stem between finger and thumb while the plant is still small. On slightly bigger plants that have already started to get lanky, you can take out the top few centimetres of stem, cutting back to a leaf joint, but it is important to leave sufficient foliage for the plant to recover – at least six leaves.

PINCH OUT SHOOT TIPS

Reduce the competition for light

Spacing plants slightly further apart than the label or seed packet suggests may help to prevent legginess. If grown too closely, plants tend to become drawn and spindly because the plants are competing with one another for light, moisture and food. Where necessary, thin out the display you have created, using the leftovers to fill gaps elsewhere. You will also often need to thin self-sown seedlings which, if left to grow in thick clumps, will produce rather weedy plants. With many biennials, such as foxgloves (*Digitalis*), the seedlings you remove are often extremely useful for transplanting to other areas of the garden (*see below*).

1 LIFT SEEDLINGS for transplanting carefully, using a trowel or hand fork, retaining as much soil as possible around the roots. It helps if the soil is fairly moist.

2 REPLANT THEM where they are to flower, giving each seedling plenty of space to develop. Firm in gently and keep well watered until established.

② Straight rows look unnatural and regimented

Unless you are trying to achieve the sort of display more usually seen in a municipal park, it usually looks best if plants are arranged in a naturalistic way, and not in straight rows organized with military precision. Plant young bedding in informal clusters or groups rather than lines. Odd numbers usually look better than even.

Create informal drifts

If direct-sown in rows in regular, straight-edged blocks, annuals look rather too formal. Try drizzling horticultural sand along the soil surface to create curving, uneven outlines for the sowing areas, and make the areas of unequal size. If the seeds are sown in straight lines within the outlines (a good way to make weeding easier, as the weeds will grow in haphazard fashion), the seedlings may initially appear regimented. However, once the plants have been thinned out and started to grow away, the effect gradually diminishes, so there is no need to panic. It also helps to vary the direction of the rows within adjacent sowing areas.

Broadcast the seed

An alternative to sowing in rows is to broadcast sow, scattering the seed so that as the seedlings appear they will naturally look less organized and regimented. This method also makes it possible to mix seed of different suitable species randomly if you are aiming for a completely mixed look. But do remember that doing it this way will make maintenance, especially weeding, much more difficult, unless you are confident you can distinguish between newly emerged weeds and the annuals you have sown. (See also the traditional "stale seedbed" technique described opposite.)

PATCHWORK PATTERN
When annuals such as cornflowers and pot marigolds are sown in uneven-shaped drifts it is possible to create a charming naturalistic effect that also leaves little room for weeds to flourish.

OUTLINES FOR INFORMAL DRIFTS
When sowing in drills, first mark out curving, irregular-shaped sowing areas using sand. Scallop patterns work well.

BROADCAST SOWING
Prepare the soil by raking to a fine tilth, then scatter the seed as evenly as possible. Lightly rake again (inset) to cover the seed with soil.

ESSENTIAL DIFFERENCES

Annuals
These are raised from seed, grow, flower, then set seed and die within one year. Hardy annuals survive winter outdoors without protection and are often grown from seed sown direct into the soil in autumn or spring. Half-hardy annuals will die outside if temperatures freeze unless given suitable protection.

Bedding plants
These may be annual, perennial or biennial in nature and are usually planted out as small plants and left to flower for one season. Most are tender and generally treated as annuals, although they could be overwintered in a suitably protected environment. There are a few hardy bedding plants such as wallflowers.

Biennials
These are raised from seed, often for a spring or occasionally a summer display. They grow into non-flowering plants in the first year and then, in their second year, produce flowers. Once a biennial has flowered it will die, but occasionally perennials are grown as biennials, for example hollyhock and foxglove.

❸ More gaps than plants

If plans for a brilliant border fizzle out because seeds fail to grow where you sowed them, there can be a number of causes.

Soil disturbance

A strong jet of water, from a hose perhaps, or a heavy downpour of rain can cause seeds to be washed out of the area or washed into clumps. Water newly sown seed gently, using a watering can with the rose attached, and avoid using a hose or sprinkler. Animals and birds can also disturb seeds before they have had a chance to germinate – for instance a cat using the area as a snoozing place or scratching up the soil, or birds taking a dust bath. Put chicken wire or canes strung with taut cotton or twine over the area to deter both cats and birds.

Are seeds being stolen?

Birds and occasionally mice may eat seeds before they have a chance to germinate. Bird scarers or lengths of cotton held taut between twigs or small canes positioned around the sown area should keep most birds away. The cotton threads must be kept taut so that birds cannot become

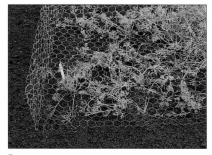
PROTECT SEEDBEDS WITH CHICKEN WIRE

entangled. Once the seedlings have appeared, the scarers or cotton and twigs can be removed.

The results of stale seed

Store seed carefully and check the use-by date on packets, since seeds that are either no longer fresh or which have been stored in unsuitable conditions may fail to germinate or have a low rate of germination. Store packets of seed in a cool but frost-free, dry place.

Prepare the soil well

A very infertile or dry soil can result in poor or gappy germination or early failure of the young seedlings. Improve the soil before sowing by incorporating plenty of well-rotted

organic matter and ensure that it is kept adequately moist while the seeds are germinating and the seedlings are still young. Preparing the soil well before sowing, by removing large stones and breaking down large clods of earth to give a fine texture, will also help to prevent poor germination.

Thin seedlings in stages

Direct-sown seedlings are best thinned out in stages. If you try to save time and do it in one operation, you may over-thin, and a disease or pest – slugs and snails, for example – may attack or damage the remaining seedlings leaving you with too few.

BEFORE SOWING RAKE THE SOIL TO A FINE TILTH

❹ Distinguishing between "weedlings" and seedlings

Once you have been gardening on the same patch of land for a few seasons and weeded regularly, you will be able to recognize young weeds, even when tiny. But at first, it's often a problem, particularly when seedlings start to emerge in ground that has recently been sown with annuals. Which are the plants you want and which should you be pulling out?

Sow in lines

Make it easier for yourself by sowing direct-sown annuals in drills or straight lines rather than broadcast sowing them. Then, anything which comes up in between or away from

SOW IN DRILLS WITHIN MARKED-OUT AREAS

the lines of seedlings can be weeded out. Unless you have very bad luck, the number of "wanted" seedlings should easily outnumber the weeds, and of course the seedlings will all look very similar whereas there will probably be quite a variety of weeds.

Try a traditional technique

Minimize the problem by preparing the soil well before sowing. It is essential to remove all weed growth, including the roots and rhizomes of pernicious perennial weeds. If you can plan ahead, the so-called "stale seedbed" technique works well. Prepare and weed the area thoroughly several weeks before you intend to sow. Dormant weed seeds in the soil will then germinate to produce flushes of weed seedlings which can be hoed off at regular intervals before you sow your flower seeds. The flower seedlings should all look alike. Also, weed seedlings usually grow faster than flower seedlings.

⑤ All leaves and no flowers

When annuals produce a mass of leaves with a distinct lack of flowers it could be due to poor light levels but the answer usually lies in the way they have been cultivated.

Inappropriate fertilizers
Plants which are given too much food, especially excess nitrogen, tend to produce lush, leafy growth at the expense of flowers. Avoid excessive feeding, particularly with high-nitrogen fertilizers, manures and so forth. Feed instead with a high-potash fertilizer (such as tomato food) which should stimulate flowering. Some plants, such as nasturtiums, are especially prone to producing more leaf than flower, and it is worth looking for varieties bred to hold their flowers well above the foliage.

Off with their heads
If plants stop flowering after their first flush, they may be persuaded to bloom again if deadheaded promptly.

Is the soil too dry?
Keep the soil adequately moist, as dry soil may inhibit flowers from forming and developing. If necessary, mulch around the bases of the plants, once they have made sufficient growth, to help the soil to retain moisture. It is important that ground is mulched while it is moist.

ENCOURAGING NASTURTIUM FLOWERS
Avoid over-feeding with nitrogen, which promotes foliage growth. However, this variety, 'Alaska', has attractive marbled leaves.

⑥ Flowers haven't lived up to expectations

Browsing seed catalogues is one of the pleasures of a winter's day, the seductive pictures conjuring up beds and borders full of glorious flowers all summer long. But in reality, once growing in your own garden, the flowers don't always look quite so spectacular. In some cases this may not be your fault at all, since plants are likely to have been photographed while at their peak and when growing under perfect conditions.

Natural variation
Even within a single packet of seed there may be a fair degree of variation in flower colour. This is especially true with very dark or near black flowers. If you want to save your own seed, rogue out any plants with pale flowers, if possible before any cross-pollination has had a chance to take place. Fragrance may vary too – for instance, white-flowered tobacco plants (such as *Nicotiana alata* and *N. sylvestris*) have a much better scent than some of the other colours.

Spoilt by the weather
Very wet weather will often spoil flowers, either preventing them from forming or damaging the petals once open. It may also encourage grey mould which will then kill off the developing buds or opened flowers. Remove damaged or infected flowers promptly. Many new varieties have been bred for improved weather resistance, especially among plants such as petunias, so check through catalogue recommendations for wet-weather tolerance.

Effects of soil and sunlight
The conditions under which plants are grown, such as soil type and levels of sunlight, and of course how well they are fed and watered, may sometimes also influence flower colour. Try to ensure that the conditions you give plants are as close as possible to those recommended on the seed packet or plant label, and that plants are properly fed and watered.

BLACK AND WHITE
For finest fragrance, choose white tobacco plants. If grown from seed, inky black violas (which may survive for a couple of seasons) often throw up pale-flowered plants.

NICOTIANA SYLVESTRIS

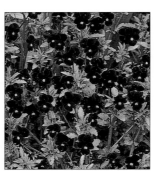

VIOLA TRICOLOR 'BOWLES' BLACK'

SURFINIA PETUNIAS STAND UP WELL TO WET WEATHER

❼ Plants cease flowering in midsummer

Plants that stop flowering early in the season often leave the garden with a dearth of colour when it is needed most, in late summer. This may be a natural characteristic of some plants which have only a relatively short flowering period or start flowering early but also finish early. Check length of flowering time before deciding what to grow. Sometimes different varieties of the same plant are noted for their longer flowering period, so scrutinize catalogues.

Keep deadheading

Every annual's goal is to produce seeds and a new generation of plants. That done, it will give up flowering and eventually die. To prolong flowering, it is essential to prevent seedheads forming by deadheading regularly. In many cases this is simply done by nipping out the spent flower between forefinger and thumb.

Stagger sowing times

If sowing times are staggered, plants reach maturity and come into flower in succession. Many hardy annuals, such as love-in-a-mist, cornflowers, pot marigolds and poppies, will start to flower early the following summer if direct-sown into beds and borders in autumn. If you sow another batch of seed in spring, you can then produce plants that will flower later that same year and carry on the display. Half-hardy annuals could be sown in small batches every few weeks during spring.

PETUNIAS ARE EASILY DEADHEADED BY HAND

Poor growing conditions

With some plants, dry soil at the roots may curtail flowering. Pansies, for instance, have a much shorter season in a hot site than if given somewhere reasonably moist and cool. Insufficient feeding with high-potash fertilizer may also contribute to the problem. Water if the ground is excessively dry, mulch if possible, and give plants a regular feed.

PLANTS TO EXTEND THE SEASON

Agastache foeniculum	*Eschscholzia*
Amaranthus	(California poppy)
Arctotis	*Gaillardia*
Bassia syn. *Kochia*	*Gazania*
(burning bush)	*Helianthus*
Ornamental brassicas	(sunflower)
Calceolaria	*Nemophila*
Calendula (pot	*Nicotiana* (tobacco
marigold)	plant)
Callistephus chinensis	*Rudbeckia*
(China aster)	*Salvia*
Chrysanthemum	*Tagetes*
carinatum	*Tithonia*
Cosmos	*Tropaeolum*
Dahlia, bedding	(nasturtium)
Dianthus	*Zinnia*

ADVANTAGES AND DISADVANTAGES OF SELF-SEEDING

RANDOM EFFECT
Where patches of annuals are allowed to self-seed, it is possible to create an almost meadow-like effect. Many of the bright, clear colours seem designed to look good with one another.

FOR THE MOST PART, the way in which many annuals and biennials self-seed around the garden is a bonus. They often manage to find the perfect corner or scatter themselves among perennials where they make effective but unexpected combinations. Thin out those that have germinated too thickly and don't let them swamp precious perennials, especially if these have been newly planted. Self-sown seedlings of biennials such as honesty (*Lunaria annua*) can often be transplanted. Watch out for the really rampant self-seeders. Some of the annual grasses fall into this category. Their seedheads can be so pretty it is hard to steel yourself to cut them off but quaking grass, for

example, can self-sow itself as thickly as a lawn. Look out too for tap-rooted biennials such as *Eryngium giganteum* (Miss Willmott's ghost). Once growing strongly in among the crown of a perennial, it can be difficult to uproot.

HONESTY SEEDS

QUAKING GRASS (*BRIZA MAXIMA*)

8 Foliage is full of holes

Slugs, snails and caterpillars are the usual suspects when leaves get eaten, but sometimes other creatures may be responsible, or leaves may be damaged by hail or really heavy rain.

Eaten by flea beetles

If the foliage looks as if it has been peppered by very fine shot, flea beetles may be the culprits. These tiny, shiny beetles, usually striped or black in colour, jump into the air when disturbed. Wallflowers, stocks and nasturtiums are among the most likely flowers to be attacked. Unless plants are otherwise weakened or are very small, they should shrug off the damage. Consider using a suitable insecticide if the problem is extreme.

Hail and rain damage

Leaves sometimes get slashed or badly marked if it hails or rains heavily shortly after planting out, especially if the young plants still have rather soft foliage. Protect with a temporary covering of horticultural fleece and avoid planting out when extreme weather conditions are forecast.

COMMON PESTS AND DISEASES

- **POWDERY MILDEW** This causes a white deposit on leaves, stems and even flowers, and occurs particularly in dry conditions, often seriously reducing a plant's general vigour. Avoid wetting the foliage but try to keep the plant adequately moist at all times. Remove affected growth promptly or spray with a suitable fungicide such as carbendazim or buprimate with triforine.
- **OTHER LIKELY PROBLEMS** These include slugs and snails, rust, leaf spots, grey mould, aphids, caterpillars, viruses and downy mildew, *see pp.178–85*.

---

9 Floppy stems and droopy flowerheads

Flopping plants are inevitably going to be more of a problem in windy sites, but one or two annuals seem to have an inherent tendency to collapse – tall cosmos and tobacco plants, for example. Lanky plants are often more likely to flop, so pinch out growing tips early on to encourage branching.

Give some support

Twiggy sticks driven firmly into the ground among a patch of annuals will provide unobtrusive support. You can often use prunings from shrubs or trees. As plants grow away, the sticks should be hidden completely. Chicken wire laid over the ground to

SUPPORT PLANTS WITH TWIGGY STICKS

prevent seeds from being disturbed (*see p.43*) will afterwards support the plants as they grow up through it. Sometimes other plants will provide support, for instance a scrambling nasturtium will help to prop up a neighbour that is starting to lean over.

Less nitrogen, more potash

Avoid using excessive quantities of high-nitrogen fertilizer or too much manure as this may promote relatively weak flower stem growth. Feed the plants with sulphate of potash or use it to dress the soil before sowing or planting out. It should help to strengthen stems.

Heavy heads

If flowerheads flop but the rest of the plant seems to be growing well, the flower stems are probably not sturdy enough to support the weight of the blooms. Consider choosing varieties with single or slightly smaller flowers rather than very heavy doubles.

---

10 Blackened bedding

Most bedding plants are tender and will be affected by frost, which blackens leaves and, depending on its severity, may kill the plants.

Delay planting out

Most bedding plants sold in garden centres are tender and so, however tempting they look on the shelves in spring, do not risk planting them out until frosts are over. If bought before this, plants need to be kept in a well-lit, frost-free greenhouse or porch or on a windowsill. Home-sown bedding plants and half-hardy annuals, and many plug plants bought by mail-order, will also be tender and need to be treated in the same way. If an unexpected frost is forecast, cover plants with horticultural fleece. All greenhouse-raised plants, even from a garden centre, should be hardened off gradually. Place outside for several days, bringing them inside at night.

A BELL JAR PROTECTS TENDER PLANTS IN SPRING

Annual, biennial and bedding plant chooser

Dry, sunny sites
The choice is wide for conditions such as this.
Alyssum
Arctotis
Bassia syn. *Kochia (burning bush)*
Calendula (pot marigold)
Catharanthus roseus (Madagascar periwinkle)
Coreopsis
Cosmos
Dimorphotheca pluvialis
Dorotheanthus bellidiformis (mesembryanthemum)
Eschscholzia (California poppy)
Gazania
Petunia
Phlox drummondii
Portulaca grandiflora
Salvia
Senecio cineraria
Tagetes (marigold)
Tropaeolum (nasturtium)
Ursinia
Zinnia

Seaside gardens
The following all tolerate salty air.
Ageratum
Alyssum
Antirrhinum
Calendula (pot marigold)
Dorotheanthus bellidiformis (mesembryanthemum)
Fuchsia
Gazania
Lavatera trimestris
Portulaca grandiflora
Salvia
Senecio cineraria

Shady spots
Most annuals and bedding plants need sun to flower well; the following are good choices for shade.
Begonia, bedding and tuberous types
Calceolaria, some
Campanula isophylla, *C. medium* (Canterbury bells)
Fuchsia

BRACTEANTHA BRACTEATA

Impatiens (busy Lizzie)
Lobelia
Matthiola (stock)
Mimulus
Nicotiana (tobacco plant)
Solenostemon (coleus)
Tropaeolum (nasturtium)
Viola (including pansies)

Exposed, windy sites
These plants are low-growing or have stems that will stand a certain amount of buffeting.
Alyssum
Antirrhinum
Begonia, bedding types
Calendula (pot marigold)
Dahlia, bedding types
Dianthus barbatus (sweet William), *D. chinensis* (annual pinks)
Felicia
Iberis (candytuft)
Impatiens (busy Lizzie)
Lobelia
Matthiola (stock)
Nemesia
Pelargonium
Petunia
Phlox drummondii
Senecio cineraria
Solenostemon (coleus)
Tagetes (marigold)
Tanacetum parthenium (feverfew)
Tropaeolum (nasturtium), dwarf types
Verbena
Viola (including pansies)
Zinnia

BIDENS FERULIFOLIA

Dried flowers and decorative seedheads
To dry flowers, cut while flowers are young and hang upside-down in a cool place.
Ammobium alatum (winged everlasting)
Bracteantha bracteata syn. *Helichrysum*
Eryngium giganteum (Miss Willmott's ghost)
Limonium sinuatum (statice)
Lunaria annua (honesty)
Moluccella (bells of Ireland)
Nigella (love-in-a-mist)
Papaver somniferum (opium poppy)

Rhodanthe syn. *Acroclinum* (straw flower)
Tanacetum parthenium (feverfew)
Xeranthemum annuum

Flowers for cutting
These last well in water.
Agrostemma githago (corn cockle)
Antirrhinum
Centaurea cyanus (cornflower)
Chrysanthemum carinatum
Consolida ajacis (larkspur)
Gypsophila elegans
Rudbeckia hirta
Tithonia rotundifolia

Plants for pots
The following are useful for containers of all kinds.
Bidens ferulifolia
Ornamental brassicas
Helichrysum petiolare
Impatiens (busy Lizzie)
Lobelia
Pelargonium
Petunia
Sutera grandiflora
Torenia fournieri
Verbena

AGROSTEMMA GITHAGO 'MILAS'

BULBS, CORMS & TUBERS

SEEING THE FIRST FLOWERS of spring open from bulbs or corms planted the previous autumn is something that never ceases to thrill. There is no reason, though, why bulbs should be confined to spring. Provided you choose a good range, they can be used to bring colour and perfume to the garden in every season. They can sometimes be subject to various pests and diseases, but troubles are more likely to come from poor planting or not giving them the right kind of site or soil.

Q *What is the best way to buy bulbs? From a garden centre or by mail order?*

A Bulbs at garden centres can be an irresistible temptation. One of the good things about them is that you can choose the individual bulbs yourself – avoiding any that are undersized or not in good condition, for example, soft or showing signs of mould. If you are not familiar with the vast range of varieties on offer, most garden centre packs have useful colour illustrations and give basic planting instructions. However, the selection available from specialist mail-order suppliers and nurseries is always far greater and will include many of the less usual, often very beautiful, varieties. So perhaps the answer is to try buying a few bulbs from each source.

Q *When is the best time to buy bulbs?*

A It really depends on the flowering and therefore the planting time. A reputable mail-order supplier will not sell you bulbs at the wrong time of year, whereas it is often possible to continue to buy them in a garden centre for a little while after the best theoretical planting date.

As a rule, try to buy bulbs as soon as they are available. That way, you get the pick of the bunch and can choose the healthiest-looking bulbs and plant them promptly. The majority of bulbs are grown for spring colour and so are usually available from the end of summer until the end of autumn.

Q *Since most spring-flowering bulbs are best planted in early or mid-autumn, why is it recommended that tulips be left until the very end of autumn?*

A Tulips planted too early (that is, before the end of autumn) are more prone to a disfiguring, sometimes fatal, infection known as tulip fire, which causes the shoots to be distorted and covered with fuzzy, grey fungal growth. If flowers are produced, these are infected too and are often flecked with white. This fungal disease is generally only a problem if tulips are grown on the same site year after year, but it is nevertheless best to be on the safe side. If planted in early autumn, the infection is more likely to take a hold than if you plant later on. Tulips planted at the end of autumn will still flower at the correct time.

Q *Spring bulbs look marvellous while in flower but then turn into a real mess when the leaves turn yellow and flop. Is there a way of avoiding this?*

A Try growing your bulbs in open-mesh baskets (pond baskets work well and are readily available from garden centres). Plant the bulbs in the lowermost third of the basket, having first filled it with garden soil, then top up with more soil and plant the entire basket in the ground, making sure that the bulbs are at the specified depth. As soon as the flowers fade, remove the basket and place it in a sheltered, shaded spot, or plunge it into a less conspicuous part of the garden. Keep the plants watered and allow the foliage to die down unhindered. The bulbs can then be replanted in the basket, using fresh soil, at the appropriate time of year in exactly the same way, and the whole process repeated.

It is also usually a good idea to plant bulbs where their deteriorating foliage is less likely to be an eyesore, naturalized in relatively long grass for instance. In flower beds, try planting bulbs in among herbaceous perennials. By the time the leaves are starting to look unsightly, the neighbouring herbaceous perennials will have started to put on rapid growth, and this soon helps to mask the decaying bulb foliage.

Q *How long after flowering must the leaves be left on daffodils?*

A Unappealing though the foliage looks, you need to put up with it for a minimum of six weeks. This means neither cutting it off nor folding or tying it over. If it is not left to its own devices for this period the bulbs will not be able to bulk themselves up adequately to put on a good display of flowers the following season. While they are dying back, the leaves help to feed the bulbs. Even tying and folding causes problems because it restricts the flow of nutrients from the foliage back down into the bulbs.

Q What is the best way to succeed with lilies?

A Lilies are most likely to fail because of excess moisture accumulating around the bulbs. Unless soil is light, put a 2.5–5cm (1–2in) layer of grit or gravel in the base of each planting hole to encourage excess water to drain away. Planting bulbs on their sides, so that moisture is less likely to accumulate around the scales, is also a good idea. If you still find you have problems, try growing lilies in deep pots full of a very well-drained compost, making sure that each container is well supplied with drainage holes and has at least 5cm (2in) of broken crocks at the base.

Q After growing lilies in pots successfully for several years, this summer the plants have been eaten almost overnight. What is reponsible?

A The most common cause of serious damage to the foliage and even buds and flowers of lilies is the scarlet lily beetle. This beautiful red beetle is about 1cm (½in) in length but has a voracious appetite for lilies, fritillaries and a few other closely related plants. Both the adult and the young stage (which is a grub-like creature resembling a small, moist bird's dropping) eat away at the plants, completely devastating them in a matter of days.

Try to collect up and dispose of as many of the beetles and their larvae as possible. This may be difficult as they tend to fall off the plant when disturbed and, since they land on their backs with their black undersides uppermost, they can be hard to spot against dark soil. Try laying a white sheet on the ground beneath the plant then returning an hour or two later and tapping the lily sharply. The beetles should drop onto the sheet where they can be seen easily and collected up. It may also be possible to spray the infested plants with a suitable contact insecticide.

Q Can lilies be grown successfully in pots?

A Most lilies do well in containers but it is essential that they are given really good drainage, so use plenty of crocks in the base of the pot. Also check that the bulbs are kept well watered during dry weather. A mixture of a loam-based compost, such as John Innes No. 2, and a loam-free multi-purpose compost works well, especially if you add a small amount of grit.

Choose varieties that are relatively short, as tall lilies often need support when grown in a container and this tends to spoil the effect. A particularly good choice is *Lilium longiflorum* 'White American'. This relatively hardy cultivar of this species, which seldom grows to more than about 75cm (30in) tall, usually performs well for a couple of years or more and provides a breathtaking perfume all the time that its large, elegant white trumpet flowers are open.

Like any other plant grown in a container, lilies should be fed throughout the growing season if they are to perform well for more than one year. After a few years you are likely to find that they fail to produce flowers as reliably, and they can then

be discarded or, better still, hardy varieties can be planted into open ground. After a year or two, they should start to flower well again.

Q Is it true that some bulbs offered for sale have been dug up from their native, wild habitats? If so, how can you tell which they are?

A Sadly, the unacceptable, often illegal trade in wild or non-cultivated bulbs still goes on, although it does seem to be on the decline. Before buying, always check the packet for the words "grown from cultivated stocks" or something similar. If bulbs are sold loose this is harder to ascertain, but ask the supplier for written proof. In the UK, a booklet entitled the Good Bulb Guide lists nurseries and garden centres which have pledged not to sell bulbs that are not nursery-raised. It also lists suppliers who have promised that, if they do sell wild-collected bulbs, these will be clearly labelled, allowing you to make an informed choice.

Remember that natural habitats are often damaged in the process of taking bulbs from the wild (with the result that other plant and also animal species may be endangered), and that the people who collect them may themselves be very poorly paid and often put their own safety at risk. It is also suggested that wild-collected bulbs are not as good quality as their cultivated cousins.

Q How deep should bulbs be planted?

A Planting depth varies with the type of bulb but, as a very general rule of thumb, most need to be planted at a depth of three to six times their own height. Always check the instructions on the pack or, if bulbs are bought loose, on the header card by the display. Information about bulbs bought by mail order should either be given on the labels on their bags or in the catalogue.

Do not be tempted to save time and energy by planting too shallowly as plants will not do well in the long term. You are also likely to find that you keep digging them up when you plant other things. Where winter temperatures are low or the soil is very light, with a tendency to dry out in summer, planting on the deep side is advisable for many.

Q Why do some bulbs, especially daffodils, produce plenty of leaves but no flowers?

A The problem of "blindness" is most likely to develop when bulbs are perfectly healthy but have simply not got enough energy to produce flowers. Blindness is particularly common where naturalized bulbs have been left undivided and unfed for several years. In this situation, lift and divide the congested clumps, then replant in freshly prepared ground. This may be sufficient to shock plants into blooming the following year, but usually you need to keep them well fed and watered for a couple of years before they get back to full flowering capacity. Feeding at the base with a general fertilizer and through the leaves with a foliar feed is worthwhile.

Bulbs growing on a dry site, or even in a perfectly normal site in a very dry year, may fail to flower the following year, and in this case you should try watering regularly and mulching. If possible, improve the soil texture before planting new bulbs by digging plenty of organic matter into dry soil. Multi-headed and double-flowered narcissi seem particularly prone to turning blind. Although complete failure to flower is quite common,

sometimes the flower stems develop but bear dry, empty flowerhead cases at the top. This is caused in the same way as blindness and requires the same sort of remedy.

Occasionally, blindness may be due to a pest or disease attack, but where this is the cause, the foliage or general plant vigour is also invariably affected.

Q Some bulbs are described as needing lifting and storing over summer and early autumn. Is this absolutely essential?

A Several bulbous flowers such as tulips are generally more reliable if lifted once the foliage has died back in early summer and allowed to dry off. This is because in their native habitat, perhaps the Middle East or around the Mediterranean, the ground would be warm and dry at this time of year. If, instead, the bulbs have to sit through a cool, wet summer in very damp soil, they are likely to deteriorate.

Few people have the time to lift their bulbs each year and simply take the risk of losing a few. It is, however, worth trying to increase the bulbs' chances of survival. It pays to choose the best sites for the trickiest. If the soil is well drained or the bulbs are planted towards the top of a slope, they are less likely to rot because of wet, either in summer or winter. Incorporating plenty of grit into the planting area should improve drainage.

If you plant several varieties, you will also find survival rates vary, so do keep a note of what is planted where and how well it fares. Species tulips, such as *Tulipa sprengeri*, are often much tougher than their more highly bred relatives, and make a fabulous display when allowed to naturalize over a period of several years.

Those bulbs that do most of their growing in summer rather than winter – galtonia and eucomis, for

example – are generally lifted in autumn. Since these are often not fully hardy, they need to be stored in a dry, cool, frost-free place. If they are of borderline hardiness, you may decide to give them good drainage but take a chance and leave them in the ground all year.

Q If soil is either very damp or very dry, what is the best way to ensure bulbs succeed?

A In a garden where soil is on the heavy, damp side, forking in plenty of grit will help. Then add a 2.5–5cm (1–2in) layer of grit to the base of each planting hole. It is also worth restricting bulbs to the drier, better-drained areas of the garden, for instance slopes or the sunnier spots. In extreme cases you may need to avoid bulbs altogether or limit yourself to those that can be successfully grown in containers.

If soil is too dry, bulbs may fail to perform properly and in extreme cases may even die. Again, improving the soil is important, so dig in plenty of bulky organic matter (such as garden compost, leaf-mould or well-rotted manure) before planting. Where soil is exceptionally sandy, you could also take the precaution of placing a 2.5–5cm (1–2in) layer of moist garden or planting compost in the base of the planting hole. Whatever type of soil you have, always read labels carefully and ensure that you pick those bulbs most likely to thrive in your particular site.

Q What is the best way to create a natural-looking display of bulbs under a tree?

A Plants such as daffodils and narcissi, bluebells and crocus can look stunning if allowed to naturalize and gradually develop their own ever-expanding populations. It sometimes looks best to keep to one variety, but multi-coloured displays of crocuses can also look wonderful.

Try to grow the bulbs in the sort of situation where they naturally look at home. The most common choice is under a deciduous tree or group of large shrubs. Do not plant the bulbs in too ordered or regimented a fashion. Straight lines and equal spacing look completely wrong. Instead, decide where you want the display and scatter the bulbs over the whole area. Then plant each bulb where it has fallen, moving only those that are touching one another. If the area is grassed over, you can either use a bulb planter to make an individual hole for each bulb, or you can carefully remove the turf, fork over the soil beneath, work in a little general fertilizer, and then scatter the bulbs on the bare soil. Carefully replace the turf and water in well.

Q **Can the foliage of daffodils that have been naturalized in grass be mown off?**

A Daffodil leaves need to be left in place for a minimum of six weeks before being mown so, when planting bulbs, try to choose a place where the foliage can remain for at least this length of time or, better still, be left to die back naturally.

Q **What does "in the green" mean? It often seems to be used with reference to snowdrops.**

A The term simply means that the bulbs are in full leaf. The vast majority of bulbous plants are sold while virtually dormant but a few, most commonly snowdrops (*Galanthus*) and winter aconites (*Eranthis hyemalis*), are also available in winter "in the green". When

bought like this, usually from specialist nurseries, the plants do establish better. It is important to plant immediately on buying them and to set the bulbs at the correct depth in the ground.

Q **Anemones seem to have a high failure rate. What can be done to improve their chances of success?**

A Spring and early summer-flowering anemones are among the few corms that really do benefit from being soaked in water before planting. Soak them for about 12 hours, then, once they have swelled up, plant them straight away. You should then find that almost every one grows away well. Never soak them for too long and always plant them immediately after soaking or they may start to deteriorate.

Q **What is the best way to keep containers of bulbs looking good for as long as possible?**

A Plant densely, far closer than you would in open ground. Regular feeding and watering also helps and, of course, it is essential to position the container in a sheltered place (out of the way of damaging wind or frost depending on the type of bulb). Planting at varying depths in the container will prolong the display. For instance, two layers of daffodils, one set 5–6cm (2in) below the other, will give a staggered flowering period, with the deeper bulbs blooming a little later than those closer to the surface. You could also choose varieties with slightly differing flowering times. Growing a mixture of different types of bulb, say tiny iris, crocus and miniature daffodils, in the same container should also ensure a long show of flowers.

Q **Can bulbs grown in pots and tubs be left where they are year after year or do they need to be replaced annually?**

A There is no doubt that bulbs that are replaced annually give the best, most reliable display. However, they can be kept for several years in one container, and provided they are given adequate food (in the form of a general fertilizer or foliar feed) and water they still put on a good show. Where the contents of a container is changed every year, plant the old bulbs in flower beds and borders.

Q **Do bulbs need to be deadheaded in the same way as other garden flowers?**

A Yes. The vast majority of plants that produce flowers go on to try to produce seeds, an energy-consuming process. In bulbs, this uses up a lot of resources that would otherwise help to produce flowers the following year. Cutting the flower stalk at the base makes the neatest job but if you have no time you can nip off a faded daffodil flower, for instance, just behind the head including any swelling where seeds are forming.

Q **What is the best way to cope with bulbs that flop? Often it is just the foliage, but sometimes even the flower stems keel over?**

A It shouldn't be necessary to provide support for bulbs, but a few well-hidden, strategically placed canes and a loop of twine can work wonders. Excessive feeding, especially with high-nitrogen material such as manure, may cause weak stems. In exposed sites, both foliage and flower stems may flop, so it is best either to avoid growing bulbs or choose varieties with short, sturdy stems.

BULBS IN THE GREEN • WAYS WITH ANEMONES • DEADHEADING • FLOPPY STEMS

LAWNS

ALMOST EVERY GARDEN has a patch of lawn. In many cases it forms the garden's centrepiece, taking pride of place and many hours of mowing, edging and feeding. But even if your lawn would be more accurately described as "grass", and is simply a linking surface between flower beds and borders or a place where the children play and you like to sunbathe, it can be kept looking perfectly good with a small amount of maintenance. It helps if an appropriate type of turf or lawn seed was chosen in the first place, but scruffy lawns are seldom beyond repair.

TOO MANY WEEDS
The grass is gradually being taken over by a variety of weeds. **4**

INFESTED WITH MOSS
Some areas of the lawn contain large amounts of moss. **3**

HUMPS AND HOLLOWS
The surface of the lawn is very uneven in parts. **5**

WORN PATCHES
Frequently trodden areas and those used for play are almost bare. **1**

RING OF TOADSTOOLS
A circle of small fungi has appeared in one part of the lawn. **9**

DISCOLOURED PATCHES
Grass appears to be dying or has turned varying shades of yellow or brown. **2**

BROKEN EDGES
The lawn's edges have become trampled and squashed. **8**

OVERGROWN EDGES
Grass continually grows into the beds and borders. **7**

Reinforcing the surface

Small areas which are likely to suffer constant wear and tear can be reinforced to a certain extent by incorporating rubber chippings (recycled from car tyres) into the soil before turf is laid or grass seed is sown. Alternatively, rubber or plastic mesh can be placed just below the surface (*see p.107*), for instance under grass beneath a child's swing or other play equipment. If you need to reseed the area, use a specially formulated mixture of tough grasses.

Ideally, however, children's play areas should be surfaced with other materials, such as round-edged bark chippings (often sold as playbark). These tend to be safer, better able to take impact without hurting the child and are also less inclined to be slippery when wet.

① Bare and badly worn patches

Using the lawn as a thoroughfare or for children's play not only wears away the grass, it may also compact the soil beneath, making it difficult for the grass to recover. Aerate lawns and, if necessary, replace worn areas with a different surface.

Lay stepping-stones

Frequently trodden areas of lawn may be under such constant attack that they soon wear thin. One answer is to lay stepping-stones. Set the stones, whether paving or timber, at or just below soil level to prevent them being hit by the blades of the lawnmower. If set on a bed of sand, they are easier to manoeuvre if they become displaced. Where a large area is used so much it has become badly worn, consider creating a proper hard surface for a path or patio. This will be less slippery and dangerous than worn turf.

Aerate compacted areas

Where turf is used regularly as a thoroughfare, the ground beneath becomes compacted. Soil particles get pressed together leaving insufficient space for air to circulate to plant roots. This affects growth, and the grass becomes thin and lacking in vigour. On heavy soil, compaction may also cause waterlogging in winter.

Compacted areas need to be aerated. This can be done either by driving in a garden fork to a depth of at least 10cm (4in) at 10–15cm (4–6in) intervals over the compacted area. Once the tines of the fork are in the soil, ease them back and forth gently to increase the size of the holes.

ACHIEVING A PERFECT FIT
Lay the stone in position and cut around it. Remove the turf to the depth of the slab plus a little extra and bed the slab on sand.

Aeration like this provides temporary relief, but for a longer term, more effective remedy, it is worth buying or hiring a hollow-tine aerator, preferably powered since this makes it easier to use. This will remove cores of soil at the correct intervals and to the correct depth. It is also possible to relieve compaction and improve aeration by using a slitting machine which allows air into the soil by cutting slits that penetrate the soil.

Top-dress after aerating

By applying a sandy top-dressing mixture after aerating, especially if you use a hollow-tine aerator, you can create semi-permanent cores of better-drained soil. Before applying the top-dressing, sweep up and dispose of all the cores of compacted soil. A good mix consists of six parts medium-fine sand with three parts sieved soil and one part peat. Apply it evenly over the area and use a stiff brush to work it into the holes.

AERATION
A garden fork can be used on mildly compacted areas, but a hollow-tine aerator does a much better job where the problem is severe.

A HOLLOW-TINE AERATOR

USING A FORK TO AERATE

❷ Discoloured or scorched areas

Discolouration or scorching can result from a number of causes, so it is important to investigate exactly what is creating the problem.

Adjust mowing heights

Set the height of the lawnmower blades according to the time of year and rate at which the grass is growing. If they are set too low, the grass will be cut too close, which may result in damage to its growing point at the base. Weak and often discoloured areas form as a result and, in extreme conditions, bare patches may develop.

Blade height is also determined by the quality of lawn you are trying to achieve. For the last cut before winter, mow a typical utility or family lawn to a height of about 4cm (1½in), and a high-quality lawn to 1cm (½in). In spring and autumn, cut a utility lawn to 2cm (¾in), and a high-quality lawn to 1cm (½in). During the summer months, a utility lawn should be cut to a height of 1–2.5cm (½–1in) and a high-quality lawn to approximately 8mm (⅜in).

If the lawn surface is uneven, scalped patches are likely to develop on the bumps. The only solution is to gradually level the surface by top-dressing the hollows in autumn and making an X- or H-shaped cut in each bump, peeling back the turf and carefully removing excess soil. After replacing the turf, tamp it down firmly (*see p.58*).

Effects of drought

Lack of water may cause patching or even overall discolouration of a lawn, particularly if it consists of fine lawn grasses and has been well maintained. Rougher or utility-type lawns are generally less severely affected or, if they are damaged by drought, recover reasonably quickly once conditions return to normal.

Excessive use of water on a lawn is generally regarded as extremely wasteful. However, if you do need to water the lawn, do it in the evening, so that there is plenty of time for the water to soak down to the grass roots before it evaporates. And give it a thorough watering. A light sprinkling may do more harm than good because it can encourage the grass roots to remain shallow or even grow towards the surface, where they will be more susceptible to drought.

During dry summers, provided the lawn is mown fairly frequently, it is worth detaching the box from the mower. If short clippings are left spread evenly over the lawn they will act as a miniature mulch.

A DRY LAWN USUALLY RECOVERS AFTER RAINFALL

Is the dog the culprit?

Animal urine, particularly from bitches or vixens, causes serious scorching and may kill off areas of turf. If you catch the animal "in the act", pour large quantities of water over the area immediately to dilute the urine and its harmful effects. This should save the grass. In the long term, however, try to keep dogs off the lawn, since repeated doses of urine will ruin it.

Wherever grass does get killed, you will need to cut out the whole patch of lawn, preferably to at least 2.5cm (1in) below the surface, and replace it with fresh soil as well as a fresh piece of turf (*see below*).

Replacing scorched or damaged areas in a lawn

Dead or badly damaged patches in the lawn can be repaired by returfing or reseeding. If the new turf you buy looks glaringly different from the surrounding lawn, cut the replacement from a less conspicuous part of the garden and put the new turf there instead. Reseeding is best done in spring or autumn.

1 REMOVE THE DAMAGED patch. Cut out a neat rectangle by using a half-moon edger against a plank (*see p.59*) and undercut using a spade.

2 FORK OVER THE SOIL to encourage the new piece of turf to root, and apply a fertilizer. Lightly tread the surface of the soil to firm it.

3 LAY THE NEW PIECE of turf over the hole and trim it to fit using a half-moon edger. Check that it will lay level with the rest of the lawn.

4 PRESS THE TURF into place and firm it down. Water it in thoroughly and keep the area damp until the turf has rooted well.

Seek the pest

Chafer grubs and leatherjackets can cause discoloured or dead patches to develop largely because they chew the roots of lawn grasses. To check if leatherjackets are the culprits, water the grass well in the early evening and place a sheet of black polythene (a bin liner, for instance) over the damaged area. When you lift the polythene the next morning, you should see the leatherjackets accumulated on the surface. They are legless, greyish-brown and up to 5cm (2in) long. If you can cover all affected areas, or indeed the whole lawn, in this way and systematically collect up and dispose of the larvae, it will greatly decrease the problem.

Chafer grub damage is particularly common on lawns on sandy soil but, unfortunately, by the time the damage is noticeable, the grubs are too large to control with insecticides. However,

INSECT PESTS
Leatherjackets are the larvae of crane flies. They are more commonly found in poorly drained lawns or in gardens in coastal areas. Chafer grubs are the larval stage of various types of beetle.

LEATHERJACKETS

CHAFER GRUB

APPLY FERTILIZER EVENLY
Even distribution is easiest to achieve by using a spreader, but if some parts receive a double dose because the rows overlap, brown stripes result. Cut off the fertilizer flow when turning at the ends.

SIGNS OF FERTILIZER SCORCH

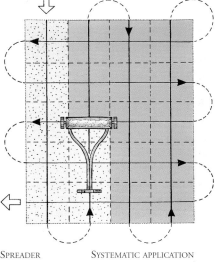
SPREADER   SYSTEMATIC APPLICATION

if a suitable insecticide, such as one based on pirimiphos-methyl, is applied in midsummer, the larvae should still be young enough to be controlled to a reasonable extent.

Fertilizer scorch

Excessive use of fertilizer, or applying fertilizer which is not then watered in quickly enough by rain or irrigation, will cause scorched patches. The precise amount of fertilizer needed depends on the kind used, the time of year and soil type, so it is essential to follow the instructions on the pack carefully. As well as applying fertilizer at the

required rate, you must also spread it evenly over the lawn surface. With care, you can do this by hand, but using a fertilizer spreader is easier and more accurate. This will need to be calibrated according to the type of fertilizer you have chosen and the instructions on the pack. To ensure even coverage, divide the fertilizer into two equal batches and then apply half of it as you push the spreader up and down the length of the lawn and the other half when pushing it at right angles across the lawn.

If rain is not forecast shortly after the fertilizer has been applied, water the area thoroughly and evenly with a sprinkler or hose, so that the fertilizer dissolves fully and does not cause scorching. Ideally, apply fertilizer just before rain is forecast so that you avoid wasting water.

Inadequate feeding

Discoloured or bare patches, particularly on lawns on very dry or poor soils, can result from an inadequate feeding regime. If this could be the cause, begin feeding the lawn regularly (in spring, summer and autumn) and apply a top-dressing in autumn. In addition, if lawn grasses are growing very poorly, mosses and broadleaved weeds are likely to invade causing further stress and competition for the few available nutrients (*see overleaf*).

QUICK CLUES TO CAUSES OF DISCOLOURATION

• **ANIMAL URINE** Roughly circular brown patches, sometimes with a deep green perimeter, are usually caused by a dog, cat or fox.

• **COMPACTION** If the whole lawn or large areas have turned yellow or brown and grass is sparse, check for compaction by testing how easily the surface can be penetrated by the tines of a fork (*see previous page*).

• **MOWER REFUELLING** When brown patches appear soon after mowing, it could be that you have spilt fuel while refuelling the mower on the lawn.

• **FUNGAL PROBLEMS** In damp weather in autumn, small yellow or brown patches accompanied by a white or pale

pink mould indicate the presence of snow mould (*see p.60*). Bleached-looking patches covered with red threads on a fine-grade lawn in late summer are a sign of red thread disease (*see p.60*).

• **LEATHERJACKETS** Irregular brown patches, which may spread rapidly, and flocks of birds pecking at the grass usually indicate the presence of leatherjackets, the most common lawn insect pest (*see above*).

• **FERTILIZER SCORCH** Brown stripes or patches appearing soon after applying fertilizer are a sign of uneven application, fertilizer overdose or lack of watering in (*see above*).

❸ Infestations of moss

Many different sorts of moss can invade a lawn but, generally speaking, moss is most likely to be a problem in areas that are excessively shaded or damp. In addition, a lawn that is under some form of stress or that has been poorly maintained is more likely to suffer from moss.

Let in the light

Consider pruning or thinning out overhanging trees to allow more light through (*see p.10 and p.121*). It may be possible to cut shrubs back without spoiling their shape.

Using moss-killers

Chemical moss-killers do a good job if applied exactly according to the instructions on the pack. It is essential that the moss is killed off completely before you attempt to rake it out. Raking out live moss may actually spread the problem. Bear in mind that using a moss-killer is a short-term answer and that unless you solve whatever encouraged the moss in the first place (excessive moisture, shade or compaction), it is likely to return.

Better maintenance

A good feeding and maintenance regime will encourage dense, vigorous grass growth and so make moss

SCARIFYING
Use a spring-tined rake (above) to remove moss and thatch. A special scarifying rake will cut more deeply into thatch.

SCARIFYING RAKE

colonization less likely. In autumn, scarify the lawn. This means raking it thoroughly with a spring-tined or scarifying rake which will remove large quantities of thatch (dead grasses and other debris) as well as any remains of moss. Scarification helps to aerate the lawn but you may need to take other measures against poor drainage and compaction (*see p.53*).

Use a specially formulated lawn fertilizer to feed the lawn and choose one which is suitable for the season when you wish to apply it – autumn is the most important time to feed.

WHICH WEEDKILLER?

LAWN WEEDKILLERS are available in various formulations, best suited to different situations. The one you choose will obviously need to include chemicals that, between them, will control all or most of the weeds in your lawn and also suit the lawn's size.

• **GRANULAR WEEDKILLERS** can be used on a lawn of any size but are particularly useful on medium to large lawns. Like any weedkiller, they must be applied evenly, at the specified rate.

• **LIQUID OR POWDER FORMULATIONS** are diluted with water, according to instructions on the pack, and applied with a sprayer or watering can with a dribble bar. They suit any size lawn.

• **SPRAYERS AND DABBERS** that are bought off the shelf ready to use are excellent if you have only a tiny lawn with a few weeds, or if you just want to spot-treat one or two weeds on a larger lawn, but using them over large areas is time-consuming and expensive.

DABBERS WORK WELL ON INDIVIDUAL WEEDS

LAWN MAINTENANCE CALENDAR

Spring
Once the grass starts to grow, lightly rake to remove debris, but do not try to remove moss or thatch. Make the first mowings, keeping the cut height to maximum. Lower the height gradually as the season progresses. Repair damaged patches (*see p.54*). Reseed new areas if necessary. Use a roller to level out lawns affected by frost heave and attend to humps and hollows (*see p.58*). Apply a feed and dig out dandelions before they have a chance to set seed.

Summer
Mow the lawn regularly, keeping the cut to a suitable height. Raise the blades in long, dry spells and decrease mowing frequency as appropriate. Irrigate if necessary. Aerate areas suffering from compaction (*see p.53*) and feed the lawn early in the season with an appropriate seasonal fertilizer while weather is moist. If using a weedkiller, apply it while the soil is damp. Keep edges trimmed.

Autumn
Reduce mowing frequency and raise the height of the cut. Brush away wormcasts first. Sweep up fallen leaves (and make leaf-mould if possible). Remove moss and thatch by scarifying and aerate compacted areas. Apply an autumn lawn feed. Brush away toadstools and treat any other fungal diseases (*see p.60*). Rectify humps and hollows and repair damaged patches. This is the time to plant bulbs that you want to naturalize in grass.

Winter
Continue to brush leaves from the lawn as necessary, but keep off the lawn in frosty or extremely wet weather. Put down boards if there is no way of avoiding wheeling a wheelbarrow across it or walking on it. Service the lawnmower.

④ Too many weeds

If a lawn is in poor condition because it has suffered from drought, compaction, waterlogging, has been mown too close or inadequately maintained, weeds can easily become a problem. Then, it is just as important to get the lawn back into good shape as it is to deal with the weeds. On large lawns, weedkillers are often the simplest solution, but chemicals aren't the answer for all weeds.

Using weedkillers

There are plenty of proprietary weedkiller mixes on the market, most of which contain more than one active ingredient. This means that they should be able to control a fairly wide range of weeds. Check the packet carefully before buying to ensure that the combination of chemicals in the product will actually control all, or most of, the weeds in your lawn. Some weeds are particularly resistant to weedkillers (speedwell, for instance) and may need several applications or might even not be killed at all. In this case, hand-weeding is the only option.

Always follow the instructions carefully when using a weedkiller: most are best applied in early summer when both lawn and weeds are growing rapidly. Then, the weeds will quickly take up the chemical and the lawn grasses should swiftly grow back and fill the spaces they have left.

Applying lawn fertilizer a few weeks before using weedkiller should also speed the grass-regeneration. Do not apply weedkiller in extremely hot, windy or gusty weather as this can encourage spray drift or contamination of other plants.

Dig weeds out if you can

Hand-weed where few weeds are involved or you prefer not to use chemicals. Hand-weeding is also useful for dealing with weeds that seem to shrug off all attempts to kill them with weedkiller. Those which form rosettes of foliage close to soil level – daisies and dandelions, for example – are particularly troublesome because lawnmower blades simply pass over them and do not weaken or mow them off.

Hand-weeding is especially appropriate for weeds with deep roots, such as dandelions. The best way to tackle these is using an old kitchen knife. Insert the blade under the rosette of foliage and cut out a long tube of soil containing the root. It is essential to try to remove dandelion and dock roots in their entirety as any little piece (or worse still, pieces) left in the soil will have the potential to grow into a new plant.

Dealing with weed grasses

Patches of coarse, often rather long grasses will not be controlled by normal lawn weedkiller mixtures

TAP ROOTS
An old kitchen knife makes a useful tool for digging out the entire length of root of tap-rooted weeds such as dandelions and docks.

which are formulated to control broadleaved weeds. The best way of coping with tough grasses is to rake or fluff them up before mowing to ensure they get sliced by the mower blades. Regular mowing often causes them to die out. Alternatively, use a sharp knife to slash the surface of the patch at 2.5cm (1in) intervals.

Meadow conversion

You may decide that you do not want to spend too much time weeding the lawn. Then it is better to learn to live with certain lawn weeds, particularly those such as speedwell which are difficult to control, and others such as daisies which many of us consider rather pretty. In extreme cases you may decide to encourage the growth of these weeds and turn your lawn into a miniature wildflower meadow. You could buy a few small plug plants of other flowers which would grow in this type of meadow, such as cowslips, and incorporate them into your old lawn.

Some common lawn weeds

BROAD-LEAVED PLANTAIN
The rosette of leaves tends to smother grass beneath. Dig out like a dandelion or spot-treat.

CREEPING BUTTERCUP
A common weed on moist clay soils. It spreads by runners. Dig out or use a weedkiller.

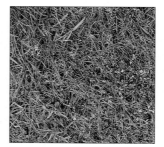

LESSER YELLOW TREFOIL
An annual weed that is easily spread by not using a box on the mower. Weedkillers are effective.

SLENDER SPEEDWELL
Weedkillers are not very effective, and you will probably need to dig this out by hand.

⑤ Humps and hollows

Apart from looking unattractive, any bumps in an uneven surface are likely to get scalped when mown. Unless the problem is extreme, it can be sorted out within a single season. Slight dips can be given the "quick fix" treatment. If drainage is also very poor, check that buried debris is not causing part of the problem and, where necessary, remove it.

Quick fix

Brush a sandy top-dressing mixture, composed of six parts medium-fine sand to three parts sieved topsoil, over the lawn, making sure that all the hollows are filled. The grasses should then be able to grow up through the top-dressing and create a level surface. This is best done in autumn but it can also be carried out in spring.

The corrugated lawn

Lawns that are always mown in the same direction using a motor mower may develop a ridged, corrugated appearance, sometimes known as washboarding. Over time, the vibrations of the mower have a rippling effect on the soil surface. Top-dress and make sure to alternate mowing direction with each cut.

Levelling a very uneven surface

It is quite easy to level out small bumps and hollows. This is a job for spring or autumn, when the grass will quickly regrow to hide the joins. After opening up the turf, add or remove soil as necessary. When you are satisfied that you have achieved the correct level, brush a sandy top-dressing mix *(see Quick fix, above)* into the surface and water well to encourage the cuts to knit back together and make a seamless join.

1 CUT A CROSS-SHAPED slit in the turf across the centre of the bump or hollow, using a half-moon edging tool or sharp spade.

2 PEEL BACK THE TURF carefully, opening out the four corners to allow access to the ground beneath. Lightly fork the soil over.

3 FILL HOLLOWS WITH a sandy loam or topsoil mixture or remove soil from any bumps until the correct level is achieved.

4 CAREFULLY REPLACE the turf in position, firm it, check that the level is correct and top-dress and water well.

⑥ Molehills, anthills and wormcasts

Hummocks of soil disfigure a lawn, but a simple yet surefire method for deterring moles is still to be found.

Determined moles

There is no easy way to deter moles, and in certain seasons they seem to be more prevalent than others. There are various potential remedies on the market, including ultrasonic devices (although these rarely seem to have any effect), mole smokes and traps. It is possible to buy humane traps. However, traps are not easy to set, and it is generally best to employ a professional mole catcher. It is important to remove the soil from molehills regularly since once it is dispersed over the lawn, the turf grasses may suffer, and the fine soil produced by the moles also acts as an excellent seedbed for weeds.

Dealing with anthills

As with molehills, soil from anthills should be removed promptly. There are numerous chemical preparations on the market which will kill ants. However, it may be difficult to get adequate chemical into the nest to eradicate them. If necessary, open up the nest first using a fork. If you do not wish to use chemicals, you could try to expose the nest and pour large quantities of boiling water directly into it. Anthills tend to be a seasonal problem, from late spring until late summer, and are more prevalent on sandy soils. They may loosen soil so much that the grass dies out and are certainly not the best place to sit.

Brush away wormcasts

The very fine soil in wormcasts is even more likely to produce a seedbed for weeds. It is best to disperse the casts regularly by brushing the surface of the lawn with a besom or broom. In particular, brush before mowing, so that the mower does not smear them into a slippery mess.

7 Overgrown edges

Trimming the lawn edges can immediately make an unkempt garden look tidy, but regular trimming is time-consuming. The corrugated plastic barriers designed to be sunk into the ground are sometimes not particularly successful at preventing grass spreading into borders and could be a hazard, for instance to tumbling toddlers.

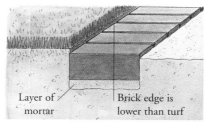

EDGING OF BRICKS
Lay a mowing strip at the edge of the lawn, setting the bricks on mortar, at a level slightly below that of the lawn itself.

Make a mowing strip

A mowing strip of bricks around the edge of a lawn is the best way of preventing grass from invading neighbouring borders. Ideally, a brick strip should be laid at the same time as the lawn is laid or sown, but it can also be installed later around an established lawn. Such a strip will help to protect the lawn from general wear and tear and people squashing the edges as they walk over them. This is something which frequently happens if the lawn is walked on while wet or when you are working on flower borders nearby.

8 Uneven or broken edges

When large weeds are removed from a lawn edge, or border plants flop over and prevent light reaching the grass, a tatty edge may result. Or the edge might get battered and broken by general wear and tear.

Restoring a straight edge

To create a really good straight edge, use a half-moon edger along the entire length, taking care to hold it vertically. Use a plank or line (made from two canes and string or twine tied tautly between them) to give a straight edge to work to. A plank usually works best and also helps to prevent compaction if you use it to stand on while edging. Since turf is constantly trying to encroach into adjacent beds and borders, there is no need to worry that regular edging will gradually make the lawn smaller.

USE A HALF-MOON EDGER AGAINST A PLANK

Ways of repairing a broken edge on a lawn

It is easy to repair small areas of damage, either by the method shown below, or by cutting out a square of turf that includes the damaged area and simply turning the square around so that the newly cut edge lies flush with the existing lawn edge and the bare patch is contained within the lawn. Firm and water it in well. Then fill the bare patch with a sandy top-dressing mixture (six parts sand: three parts topsoil) and sow it with a grass seed that matches the lawn. Make sure that the seed is kept well watered to encourage rapid germination.

1 CUT OUT A RECTANGLE of turf containing the damaged area using a half-moon edger or sharp spade. Slide the piece forward.

2 ALIGN A PLANK with the existing edge and lay it across the damaged area so that the broken part can be neatly sliced off.

3 CUT AND FIT a new piece of turf into the resulting gap. Test for depth (*inset*) and add or scoop away soil as necessary to make it level.

4 TAMP THE PIECES in place with the back of a rake once you are satisfied that they are level and fitting well. Water in thoroughly.

9 Toadstools in the lawn

The occasional toadstool is not a problem but large numbers may signal trouble if they appear in rings or rows.

Fairy rings

If rings of toadstools appear on a lawn, and if the lawn itself has a ring of dark green grass and a ring of dead or dying grass nearby, this suggests a fairy ring infection.

Brush up the toadstools as soon as you see them, preferably before they open and disperse their spores. Unfortunately, the infection also spreads underground in the form of an extensive white mycelium which causes the lawn to die out. There is no easy cure. Wait until the ring increases to such a size that it reaches the edge of the lawn and then dies

TOADSTOOLS FORMING A FAIRY RING

out, or dig out the entire area that might be infected. This means digging out a circle of turf to at least 45cm (18in) either side of the fairy ring and to a depth of at least 45cm (18in). Take care not to allow pieces of the fungal growth or anything associated with the ring to remain and don't drop any soil onto the lawn.

Dispose of the soil in the dustbin or well away from the garden. Then returf or reseed the area. If the ring is large, this is difficult, so many people simply wait for the rings to disperse.

Rows of toadstools

Where toadstools appear in lines, this usually indicates that they are growing on tree roots. The only long-term solution is to excavate beneath the toadstools and try to remove the root. Since this is usually dead, it is unlikely to do any harm to the tree. However, if the toadstools are on live roots, be careful not to remove too much root or the tree and its stability could be damaged. Toadstools growing from living roots may indicate that the tree is under attack from honey fungus (*see p.14*) and could be unsafe.

10 Fungal problems

Some patches on the lawn may be due to fungal infections.

Red thread

This often occurs in a year following a very dry summer, since turf that has not been fed is more prone to the infection. It is also encouraged by poor aeration. Patches of bleached or slightly orange-red grasses develop. If you look closely you will see dark pink gelatinous strands among the blades. These turn slightly fluffy and pale pink with age. The grass is rarely killed but will be weakened. Improve maintenance, especially feeding. A high-nitrogen feed such as sulphate of ammonia is the best remedy.

Snow mould

This is most likely in autumn or during mild spells in winter, when small patches of brown, dying grass appear, gradually getting larger. In damp weather, they may be covered in a pale pink to white fluffy fungal growth. The fungus is encouraged by compaction, excessive dampness and poor aeration, and often appears if the lawn has been walked on after snowfall. Try to avoid treading on the grass during cold or wet weather, and carry out routine maintenance such as spiking and other forms of aeration. If the problem is severe, the lawn can be treated with a suitable fungicide such as one containing carbendazim.

LAWN FUNGI
Red thread (far left) won't kill a lawn but does spoil its appearance. Snow mould (left) is a cold-weather problem.

11 Autumn leaves

Fallen leaves may be irritating on flower beds and drives, but they are potentially very damaging on lawns. Once gathered, they can be turned into beneficial leaf-mould (see p.12).

Removal methods

For small areas, a spring-tined rake and wheelbarrow are the only two tools you need, but if you have a large lawn, consider investing in a leaf vacuum cleaner which sucks up the leaves. Its collection hopper will make dealing with leaves easy and fast. Or you could use a leaf-blower to drive the leaves into heaps which can then be quickly collected up, or a leaf-sweeper. Try to make sure that any machine you choose will pick up wet as well as dry leaves.

LEAF-SWEEPER
A leaf-sweeper has rotating brushes which gather and collect the leaves in a large bag.

⑫ The only answer is to replace the lawn

If a lawn has got into such bad condition that it isn't worth the time and energy needed to restore it, it would be better to replace it. But first you need to kill the old lawn off, along with any weeds.

Remove the old lawn

One way of killing off the old lawn is to cover it completely with heavy-duty black polythene. Weigh down the edges or insert them into the soil. The polythene must exclude all light and will need to stay in place for probably a minimum of 12 months.

A far quicker method is to spray off the old lawn with a weedkiller based on glyphosate. This chemical will kill both grass and weeds, including their roots and, because it is inactivated on contact with the soil, you can safely sow or replant a new lawn once the green growth is dead. Weedkiller of this sort is best used in summer when the grasses are growing rapidly. If you spray towards the end of summer you can sow or turf the area in early autumn.

Alternatively, you could skim off the lawn (divided first into manageable-sized pieces) and the soil immediately beneath it and compost it. If you have room to stack the pieces soil-side up they will eventually compost down into useful loam. (If you intend to plant any trees, this is the ideal material to add to large planting holes. And if you put it through a sieve, it makes an excellent top-dressing for lawns.) The main disadvantages are that you will lose some valuable topsoil from the lawn area and sections of tap root of pernicious perennial weeds such as dock and dandelion may well be left in the soil and will resprout.

It is possible to incorporate the remains of the old lawn into the soil, but this may result in an uneven surface later on as clumps of grass rot down. There is also a tendency for pieces of old lawn to keep coming to the surface.

Prepare the soil well for the best results

You will need to dig over the area before laying new turf or sowing grass seed. On large areas, a powered cultivator will make the job a lot quicker and easier. Use the opportunity to remove large stones and any remains of roots.

Next rake the soil. This will also remove many of the weeds and help to re-level the site. Treading over the surface to firm it gently is essential since it will allow you to create an even, level surface which should not subside to leave hollows. Once this is done, fill in any hollows and level off any bumps and use the rake to gently fluff up the uppermost surface. This will create a good seedbed for sowing grass seed.

Ideally, leave the area for a few weeks so that any dormant weed seeds have a chance to germinate and you can hoe them off before sowing seed or laying turf. A dressing of a complete fertilizer will help to get your new lawn off to a good start. Spread this evenly over the whole area at the rate indicated on the packet.

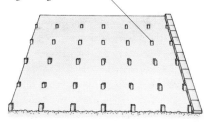

Pegs at regular intervals

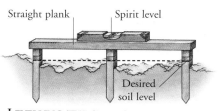

Straight plank — Spirit level

Desired soil level

LEVELLING THE SURFACE
Arrange a grid of marker pegs and check the level in all directions using a spirit level. Even out the soil surface accordingly.

Sowing seed

Choose seed that is suitable for the site and intended use, for example a mix for shade or for a utility lawn. Make sure that the seed is sown evenly and that you use a rake to cover it with a thin layer of soil. Try not to disturb it. Unless rain falls within a few, days you will need to gently but thoroughly water the whole area and continue watering as necessary to keep the ground moist until the seed germinates. Cotton held taut between a system of twiggy sticks or canes should help to keep birds from eating the seed.

Laying turf

Lay turves in a brickwork pattern so that joints are staggered. Brushing a sandy top-dressing into a newly laid lawn will help it knit together well. To ensure that the turf is firmly in contact with the soil beneath, tamp the entire area down with the back of a rake. Water regularly to encourage rapid rooting and establishment.

If you cannot lay turves on delivery, you can store them, rolled up, for up to three days. After this, they tend to turn yellow and are best unrolled, laid on a sheet of plastic and kept watered.

MARK OUT THE AREA TO ENSURE EVEN SOWING

STORE TURVES ON PLASTIC IF WORK IS DELAYED

BUSH & CLIMBING ROSES

ALMOST EVERY GARDEN contains at least one rose, often many more. Whether grown as bushes, standards, climbers, ground cover or in containers, roses are immensely popular – not surprising given their breathtakingly beautiful flowers, especially when laden with sweet perfume. Sadly it has to be said that some roses are not easy to keep healthy and vigorous. But despite being prone to a range of pests and diseases, these glorious flowers remain a firm favourite. How, then, can you keep the problems to a minimum and the enjoyment at a peak?

BUSH AND SHRUB ROSES

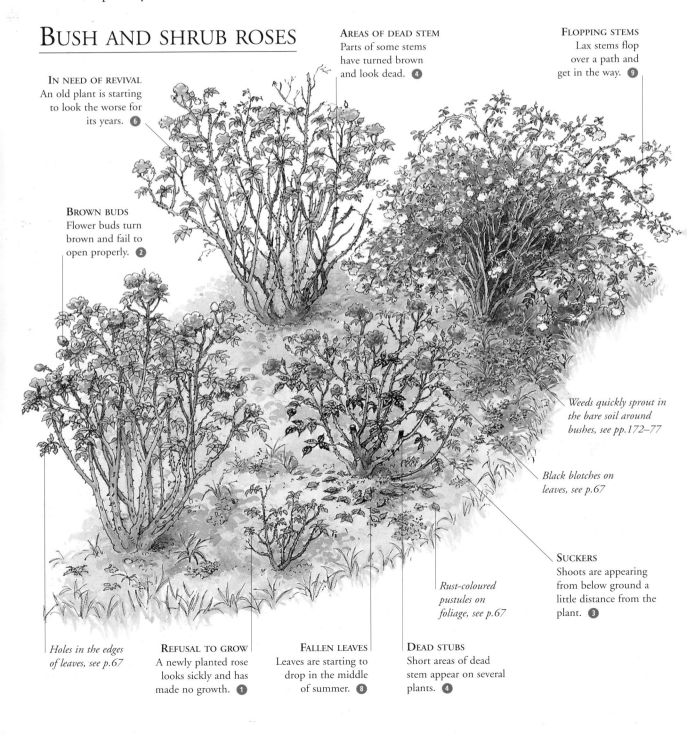

AREAS OF DEAD STEM
Parts of some stems have turned brown and look dead. **4**

FLOPPING STEMS
Lax stems flop over a path and get in the way. **9**

IN NEED OF REVIVAL
An old plant is starting to look the worse for its years. **6**

BROWN BUDS
Flower buds turn brown and fail to open properly. **2**

Weeds quickly sprout in the bare soil around bushes, see pp.172–77

Black blotches on leaves, see p.67

SUCKERS
Shoots are appearing from below ground a little distance from the plant. **3**

Rust-coloured pustules on foliage, see p.67

Holes in the edges of leaves, see p.67

REFUSAL TO GROW
A newly planted rose looks sickly and has made no growth. **1**

FALLEN LEAVES
Leaves are starting to drop in the middle of summer. **8**

DEAD STUBS
Short areas of dead stem appear on several plants. **4**

1 Why is a new rose refusing to grow?

If a new rose fails to take, although it was well planted, didn't suffer attack by pests and the ground was kept adequately moist, the problem may lie in the soil.

Rose replant disorder

This disorder, also known as rose sickness, is only likely to affect roses that have been planted in a bed previously occupied by roses. The precise cause is not fully understood, but it is thought that the problem is due to a combination of nutrient stress and the build-up of soil-borne fungal pathogens and nematodes.

It can be difficult to identify unless you know the history of what has been growing in the bed. Affected roses, if removed promptly and the soil washed from their roots, should grow well once replanted in fresh soil.

Ideally, try to avoid the problem in the first place. Never replant a rose bed with new roses unless the soil has first been changed to a depth of at least 45cm (18in). If simply planting an individual rose, removing a 45cm (18in) cube of soil should suffice. Feeding with lots of well-rotted manure or a high-nitrogen fertilizer may help to reduce the symptoms.

2 Petals go brown and buds fail to open fully

This is known as balling and occurs when the outermost petals get wet and are then dried and scorched by strong sun.

What can be done?

Once damaged in this way, the outer petals create a tight "jacket" around the inner ones, preventing the flower from opening. The bud may also then become infected with grey mould. Apart from avoiding watering buds directly in sun, little can be done to prevent this. Very double varieties seem slightly more susceptible, so perhaps take this into account when choosing what to grow. It is possible to pick off the outer petals so that the flower can open out, but this is very fiddly and not always successful.

3 What are suckers and what should be done about them?

Most roses are propagated by grafting the cultivar (bred for its flowers and other attributes) onto a "rootstock" (a good, vigorous root system that will keep the plant growing strongly). Sometimes, however, a rose will send out a shoot from below the point of the graft, from the rootstock, and this is called a sucker.

How to identify suckers

Rose suckers appear from beneath soil level, whereas all the normal growth develops from above soil level. Suckers usually have noticeably different leaves from the rest of the plant. These may look like the leaves on a wild rose, are often more extensively serrated, and may be composed of a different number of leaflets – often seven or nine compared with five or seven on the "grafted" plant. They are also generally a yellowish or paler green.

Prevention and removal

Some roses seem to be more prone to suckering than others but, wherever possible, try to avoid damaging the base of a rose when hoeing or weeding nearby, since suckers often develop from a point of injury. Remove suckers as soon as you notice them. Pull them away from the rootstock if possible, since cutting, like pruning, usually only serves to make the sucker grow more strongly.

REMOVE SUCKERS PROMPTLY
Scrape away soil from around the sucker and pull it away from the rootstock. This will remove any dormant buds that have formed where the sucker joins the rootstock.

❹ Areas on some stems are brown and dead-looking

Part of a stem, often at its tip, or sometimes the whole stem all the way down to the ground, may turn brown and dead-looking. This can be due to one of a number of causes and needs to be dealt with.

Canker disease

Various fungal infections may cause stems to turn brown, shrivel, then die back completely. In extreme cases the whole plant may be killed. As soon as these symptoms are noticed, prune out any brown areas, cutting back into healthy wood (*see below*). Dispose of the prunings by burning or putting them in the dustbin. Do not leave them near the plant as they may harbour disease-causing fungi. Plants which are under some sort of stress are generally more prone to canker attack, so ensure that the rose is being looked after properly.

Frost damage

After frost, stems and young foliage become discoloured and may die back. This is almost impossible to avoid, but affected stems should be removed, cutting back to a vigorous outward-facing bud. If the damaged growth is left on the plant, it may become colonized by secondary organisms such as grey mould or by canker, causing more serious problems.

Injured stems

If a stem turns brown it could be because the base was inadvertently damaged while you were hoeing or digging nearby. The wound itself may have been sufficient to cause the stem to die or secondary organisms such as grey mould or canker fungi may also have gained entry, even via a small point of injury, and caused the die-back. Prune out the dead stem.

ROSE CARE

- **ROSES ESTABLISH** particularly well if planted as bare-root specimens during the dormant season, but take care not to allow the root system to dry out.
- **PLANTS PREFER** a fairly heavy soil so dig in plenty of bulky moisture-retentive organic matter before planting.
- **MULCHING** to a depth of 5–8cm (2–3in) with compost or well-rotted manure helps to feed the rose and keeps the soil moist. Mulch moist ground in autumn or spring.
- **APPLYING ROSE FERTILIZER** after pruning in spring should encourage vigorous new growth.

Dead stubs are usually due to stems having been cut too far from a bud. Or a rough cut may have damaged tissue and allowed disease to enter. Prune out affected parts and improve techniques.

Improve your pruning techniques

Good pruning helps to keep a plant healthy and vigorous and often improves flower quality. It is essential to make clean cuts – a rough cut will heal slowly and may allow disease to enter – and to cut to an outward-facing, vigorous-looking bud, or the stem may die back, in some cases right to the crown of the plant. Use secateurs for stems up to 1cm (⅜in) in diameter and loppers for those up to 2.5cm (1in) wide. Anything bigger requires a pruning saw. Cuts normally follow the direction of the bud or leaf in order to avoid trapping moisture and fungal spores, except sometimes in renewal pruning (*see overleaf*) when a straight cut may be best.

Dead, rotting wood harbours disease

Crossing stems chafe and may create entry points for infection

Dead stub

REMOVE DAMAGED GROWTH
To maintain a plant's health, prune out all dead, damaged or diseased stems or areas of stem. Remove, too, stems that may rub and damage others or that crowd and clutter the centre.

HEALTHY WOOD
A good cut should reveal only white healthy tissue with no sign of discolouration.

CUT TO A BUD
To avoid die-back, cut to about 5mm (¼in) above a bud or leaf-joint. Use sharp secateurs and take care not to damage the bud or stem, since wounded tissue may become infected.

GOOD AND BAD CUTS
A good cut, just above a bud, should follow the slope of the bud. Water that collects in a poorly angled cut may cause rot, and too high a cut, which leaves a snag or stub, usually causes the stem to die back to a lower bud.

CORRECT CUT

CUT TOO HIGH

BADLY ANGLED CUT

⑤ The flowering season is disappointingly brief

Length of flowering may vary with variety, but in many cases, deadheading will help to extend the season. Check, too, that poor pruning is not the cause of a poor display.

DEADHEAD TO ENCOURAGE NEW BUDS TO FORM

PRUNE BLIND SHOOTS

Cutting back to a lower bud may stimulate the development of a flowering shoot

Deadhead regularly

As soon as flowers start to fade, remove them so that energy is not wasted when the plant starts to produce hips. Cut back to a healthy leaf two or three leaves lower down the stem. Regular deadheading invariably prolongs flowering of most roses. Some varieties have a second, late summer or early autumn flush of blooms and this, too, is improved if deadheading was thorough during the main flowering season.

Choose varieties carefully

It helps if you can choose a range of varieties of rose so that, between them, they cover the earliest and latest flowering periods. It is also worth looking out for roses described as "repeat flowering" as these should produce a first particularly flamboyant display, followed by a second flush of flowers at the tail end of the season. This second flush is not as long or as good as the first but it is a real bonus. Some of the older roses (*see below*) have a relatively short

flowering period, although their beautiful flowers and fragrance more than make up for this.

Blind shoots

Shoots that produce no flower buds at all are usually caused by seasonal variations, and there is little you can do to prevent the problem. However, it is worth checking whether the rose is being properly pruned, fed and watered, and, if not, taking measures to improve growing conditions.

Hips prolong the season

Growing roses that produce hips makes an attractive way of extending the season. Then, deadheading is not such an issue. The rugosa roses, for instance 'Fru Dagmar Hastrup', 'Schneezwerg' and 'Scabrosa', have

glossy, round hips, sometimes the size of cherry tomatoes. *Rosa moyesii* has flagon-shaped hips. Interesting but less spectacular are the purple-black hips of *R. pimpinellifolia*, while native roses such as *R. rubiginosa*, the sweet briar, also put on a good show if you have a suitable spot for them.

SPECTACULAR HIPS ON *ROSA MOYESII*

Length of flowering may depend on rose type

MODERN BUSH ROSES
Most modern roses (such as 'Sexy Rexy', above) have been bred to produce repeat flowers that follow on from the first big flush, sometimes until late in the year.

ENGLISH ROSES
'Graham Thomas', above, is typical of these roses, in which breeder David Austin has combined repeat-flowering qualities with the look of an old-fashioned rose.

OLD-FASHIONED ROSES
Unfortunately, a drawback of many of the lovely old Damask, Gallica, Moss, Alba and Centifolia roses is that they have only a single flush of blooms.

WHAT'S IN A NAME

- **HYBRID TEA** These roses are characterized by their large flowers, often present for much of the season.

- **FLORIBUNDA** Also known as cluster-flowered, these are perpetual-flowering modern bush roses whose blooms are carried in clusters.

- **HYBRID PERPETUAL** This type of rose produces repeat flowers from early summer. Although they are bush roses, a few have such long stems that they can also be grown as climbers.

- **PATIO ROSES** These usually have small- to medium-sized flowers and are particularly well suited to growing in small spaces or containers.

⑥ Revitalizing an ancient plant

If a plant has been neglected or is past its prime, the simple solution is to remove it, but given the complications in replacing one rose with another (see p.63) and the fact that roses often respond well to renewal pruning, you may prefer to try to revitalize it.

Revival plan

A combination of good, regular pruning and general care, especially feeding with a rose fertilizer in spring and early summer and watering, should gradually improve the rose's health. However, some more drastic pruning will probably be needed.

Do this while the plant is dormant. With bush and shrub roses you can take a chance and, after taking out all dead stumps and stems and removing suckers, cut remaining growth back to within 5cm (2in) of the ground. Or, less drastically, carry out a programme of phased renewal (*see below*).

Pruning to reinvigorate a rose

1 REMOVE DEAD STUMPS to prevent rain collecting and causing rot to set in.

2 PRUNE OUT UNHEALTHY, old or spindly stems, cutting right back to the base.

3 CUT BACK SEVERAL of the older main stems to a suitable replacement shoot further down the stem. More old stems can be pruned out in succeeding years.

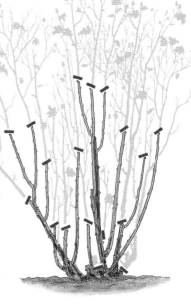

PHASED RENEWAL
Spread the work over two or three years, first removing suckers, stumps and spindly growth, and reducing the overall height of the plant by about a half to promote new growth. Prune out a few old main stems each winter until, gradually, they have all been replaced.

⑦ Rose in a pot looks miserable

Roses are invariably happiest growing in open ground, but they can be grown successfully in a pot. You need to choose a suitable variety, for instance one of the miniature forms or specially bred patio roses, and give it plenty of care and attention.

Check the container

If a plant is ailing, make sure that the compost is being kept adequately moist at all times and, if necessary, consider installing a trickle irrigation system. A larger pot may be the answer, and if so, repot in autumn or early

CONTROLLED-RELEASE FERTILIZER GRANULES

winter. Size of container depends on the size of the rose, but even a small plant will need a pot at least 30cm (12in) in diameter. Roses prefer a reasonable depth for their roots, so do not choose a shallow pot. It may also help if you position the pot so that it is partially shaded and therefore less likely to get hot, which accelerates the speed at which compost dries out.

Signs of hunger

Poor growth and discoloured foliage may be a sign that the plant is hungry – in the confines of a pot it will soon run out of nutrition unless it has been properly fed. Feed regularly with a suitable liquid fertilizer and consider using controlled-release fertilizer granules incorporated into the

compost. Some patio roses do not, in theory, require deadheading, but most will benefit from the regular removal of faded flowers, and this also helps to conserve moisture.

Winter root damage

Any plant in a pot is more prone to winter damage than if it were growing in open ground. This is especially true of root damage, particularly if the roots are close to the sides of the container. Either plunge the pot in a spare corner of ground at the start of winter or insulate it by wrapping it in hessian or bubble-wrap plastic. Lining the insides (not the base) of the pot with bubble-wrap before planting will also help to provide protection and will not show from the outside.

8 Premature leaf loss

If leaves start to fall early in the season, check if the plant is suffering from rose rust, powdery mildew or black spot (see below). Alternatively, the plant may not be getting sufficient water.

Suffering from drought?

Extremely dry soil may cause leaf loss, especially on fairly newly planted roses. Before planting, dig in plenty of bulky organic material to help the soil to retain adequate moisture in between periods of rain or watering. This is especially important on light, sandy soils and for plants in drought-prone spots such as close to a wall. Once planted, mulch to a depth of 8cm (3in) over the entire root area while soil is damp.

9 Lax stems flop over paths and other plants

Some roses have a naturally lax habit of growth so, if it's too late to alter your choice of plant or planting site, give a variety with annoyingly floppy stems some support. If relatively recently planted, you could move the rose to another spot where it will be less of a problem.

Methods of support

It may be possible to tie the stems together using wire or garden twine which should not be too evident if carefully positioned. A well-hidden short stake could also be used to support the plant either directly or using a system of twine or wires. Metal supports could be used but are really better suited only to young, small plants. Many hybrid perpetual roses have a very lanky habit and so could be grown as a climber instead and given the support of a wooden post, tripod or obelisk.

OFFER SUPPORT
A system of stakes and twine will help to keep the stems of a naturally floppy rose in place and need not be obtrusive.

SOME COMMON ROSE PESTS AND DISEASES

ALTHOUGH THE DAMAGE may look serious, the activities of some pests such as the leaf-cutting bee or rose leaf-rolling sawfly have little harmful effect in the long term and no action is needed. Black spot, rust and powdery mildew are, however, likely to prove more debilitating. Chemical sprays can be used against them but in the first instance it is better to try to choose disease-resistant varieties or improve cultivation, especially in the case of rust and powdery mildew (*see p.185*), so that plants are less likely to be affected. If infestations are severe, an insecticide can be used to control rose leafhoppers.

ROSE BLACK SPOT
This causes premature leaf drop and may seriously weaken the rose as well as spoiling its appearance.

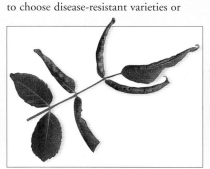

ROSE LEAF-ROLLING SAWFLY DAMAGE
Although this may make the plant look peculiar, it has little effect on its performance.

ROSE LEAFHOPPER DAMAGE
The fast-moving insects cause creamy mottling and often leave their cast skins beneath the leaf.

ROSE RUST
Orange or brown spores appear beneath leaves, which fall early, particularly in damp conditions.

LEAF-CUTTING BEE DAMAGE
The bee removes neat circles from leaf edges but this is highly unlikely to affect the plant's vigour.

POWDERY MILDEW
This fungus causes leaf distortion and early leaf fall; it may attack prickles, stems and flower buds.

CLIMBERS AND RAMBLERS

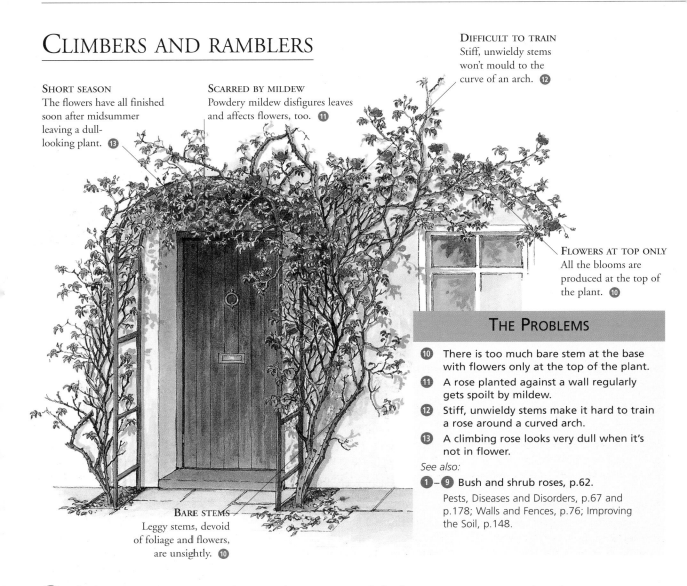

DIFFICULT TO TRAIN
Stiff, unwieldy stems
won't mould to the
curve of an arch. **12**

SHORT SEASON
The flowers have all finished
soon after midsummer
leaving a dull-
looking plant. **13**

SCARRED BY MILDEW
Powdery mildew disfigures leaves
and affects flowers, too. **11**

FLOWERS AT TOP ONLY
All the blooms are
produced at the top of
the plant. **10**

BARE STEMS
Leggy stems, devoid
of foliage and flowers,
are unsightly. **10**

THE PROBLEMS

10 There is too much bare stem at the base
with flowers only at the top of the plant.

11 A rose planted against a wall regularly
gets spoilt by mildew.

12 Stiff, unwieldy stems make it hard to train
a rose around a curved arch.

13 A climbing rose looks very dull when it's
not in flower.

See also:

1–**9** Bush and shrub roses, p.62.

Pests, Diseases and Disorders, p.67 and
p.178; Walls and Fences, p.76; Improving
the Soil, p.148.

10 Flowers appear only at the top, with bare stems at the base

*A plant with ungainly bare stems at
the base and flowers at the top is, to
some extent, in the nature of the
beast, although some roses such as
'Seagull' bloom relatively low down.*

Pruning and training

Annual pruning helps to encourage
new growth and prevent the build-up
of too many woody, poor-flowering
stems. Most climbers produce their
flowers on the current season's growth
so need to be pruned in early spring.
The best flowers are usually produced
on ramblers on the previous year's
growth, so prune these as soon as
flowering has finished, taking a
proportion of the stems back down to
ground level. Training shoots so that
they are close to the horizontal also
encourages flowers to develop.

Use camouflage

Since no rose will bloom right to the
base, grow a small shrub or herbaceous
perennial in front. Take care when
planting not to damage the rose's roots
and remember that plants in close
proximity need extra food and water.

A WELL-TRAINED ROSE
*A combination of good training and
attractive foreground planting overcomes the
problem of bare lower stems.*

⑪ Roses against a wall are regularly attacked by mildew

Dry soil encourages powdery mildew and roses trained against a wall are particularly susceptible.

Keep soil moist

Because foundations and bricks draw moisture from the soil, and the wall and overhang of roof tiles and guttering create a "rain shadow", a rose planted against a house wall is almost entirely reliant on your supplying it with adequate moisture.

Before planting, improve the soil over a large area by digging in moisture-retaining organic matter such as garden compost, well-rotted manure or proprietary planting compost. Make sure that the soil in the planting hole has been improved to an even greater extent. Water in thoroughly and keep well watered, particularly in dry or windy weather. Apply a mulch to keep soil and roots cool and minimize evaporation.

Improve air circulation

Poor air circulation, which often leads to the build-up of moist or humid air around stems and foliage, will also encourage powdery mildew disease. Careful pruning and training should help to keep the stems well spaced and so improve air circulation. Prune back nearby plants that could be making the situation worse.

Choosing varieties

Some varieties show more resistance to this disease than others, so check current catalogues from specialist rose

IMPROVE AIR FLOW BY REMOVING OLD STEMS

nurseries for relatively resistant roses. However, bear in mind that mildew resistance and susceptibility vary greatly with age of plant, area and growing conditions. On the whole, ramblers are more prone to powdery mildew than climbers.

⑫ Unwieldy stems

Where roses need to follow a curve, around an arch for instance, train young growth and opt for ramblers.

Flexible ramblers

Rambling roses are often more pliant and easier to train than climbers. Tie in stems as soon as they are long enough and while still young and flexible, and tie in further new growth at regular intervals. Where spiny stems are likely to cause problems, choose thornless 'Zéphirine Drouhin' or near-thornless 'Bleu Magenta'.

ROSA 'ZÉPHIRINE DROUHIN'

⑬ Dull when the rose is not in flower

Since roses are not the most attractive of plants when not in flower, ways of extending the season of interest are particularly useful.

Longest flowering period

Rambler roses generally have only a single flowering period, and this tends to finish soon after midsummer. Some climbers, however, have a second, later and somewhat smaller flush of blooms and so could be a better choice. Deadheading may also encourage them to produce further flowers. Several ramblers, often the most vigorous varieties, do though have eye-catching clusters of hips in the autumn. 'Rambling Rector' has good hips but will climb to 6m (20ft) and 'Kiftsgate' gets a great deal taller.

Combine climbers

Allow a late-flowering clematis, such as one of the viticella types, or another favourite climber to scramble through the framework created by the rose. Choose one whose flower colour and shape appeals to you and which will look good with neighbouring plants. It does not have to look good with the rose unless it is to be in flower at the same time.

GOOD PARTNERS
The annual climber morning glory (Ipomoea) should be at its peak when the rose has faded. Late-flowering clematis, such as 'Madame Julia Correvon', which are cut back hard in late winter, do not affect the pruning of the host rose.

IPOMOEA TRICOLOR 'HEAVENLY BLUE'

CLEMATIS 'MME JULIA CORREVON'

CLIMBING PLANTS

EVERY GARDEN contains vertical surfaces of some sort, be they house walls, garden fences, trellis, or a pergola. Having these structures helps to add new dimensions to the garden and each vertical surface, no matter how drab it currently looks, should be seen as an opportunity not to be missed. Clad with plants, even the ugliest wall or fence can become a thing of beauty. Well-chosen climbers can add colour, interest and, in some cases, a delightful perfume. Many climbing plants are well-behaved and require little beyond some general maintenance, although more rampant types – often those chosen to provide rapid cover – need to be kept in check.

WHEN TO PRUNE
The rules about when to prune a clematis are difficult to fathom. ❼

FLOWERS AT THE TOP ONLY
Most flowers appear at the top of the plant and trail over the neighbour's side. ❺

OUTGROWN ITS SITE
A rampant Virginia creeper is getting into gutters and under tiles. ❸

NO WISTERIA FLOWERS
A wisteria is growing vigorously but never produces flowers. ❶

AILING CLEMATIS
Although growing well until recently, several shoots are dying. ❹

REFUSAL TO CLIMB
A climbing hydrangea, planted last season, shows no inclination to climb. ❷

DRY SOIL
The ground at the foot of a wall is poor and dry and hinders growth. ❻

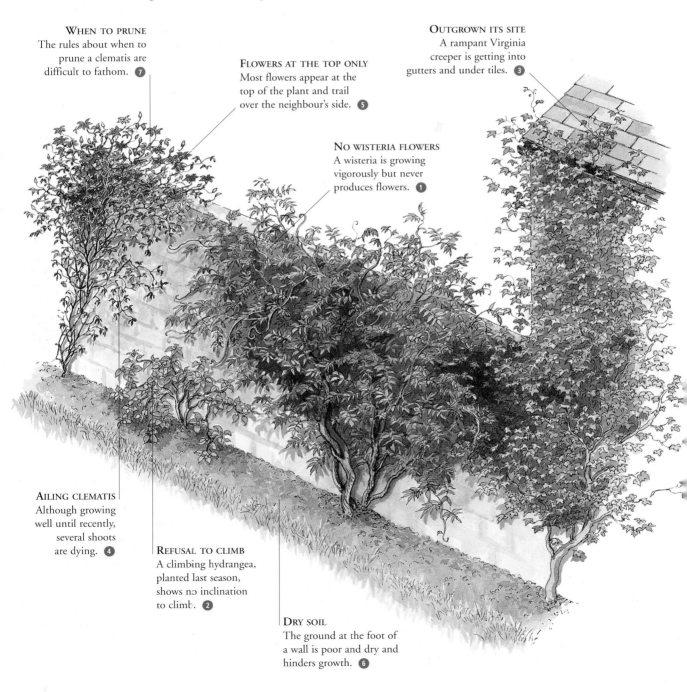

1 Why isn't a wisteria producing flowers?

A wisteria that fails to flower is a common and frustrating problem.

Be patient

Unless you pay a high price for a large plant, you may have to wait from four to 10 years for blooms, usually until the lower stems are at least 1.5cm (½in) in diameter. Ideally, try to buy a large plant that is bearing buds, flowers or seed pods. Otherwise, use annual climbers (*see p.75*) to brighten a fence or wall in the meantime.

Adopt a two-stage pruning regime

Gardeners, knowing that a wisteria should be pruned, sometimes get over enthusiastic and prune too severely at the wrong time of year. The correct regime is fairly simple and is carried out in two stages, in summer and mid- to late winter. In summer, cut back

Avoid seed-grown plants

A wisteria that has been grown from seed is much less likely to flower than one that has been grafted onto a rootstock. It may, unfortunately, be difficult to tell how a wisteria was propagated, particularly if it is already established in the garden. However, if you are buying a new plant from a garden centre or nursery, this is less likely to be a problem since it is relatively rare to come across seed-raised wisterias on sale today.

long sideshoots to five or six buds. If you want to extend the system of stems, just shorten last year's growth a little; this encourages development of side-buds and allows extension growth. In winter, prune the summer-pruned shoots back to two or three buds.

CLIMBER OR WALL SHRUB?

• **CLIMBERS** generally have a more open structure than wall shrubs and long, often lax, growth which will not stay upright without some kind of support. Given a system of wires or trellis, many hold themselves up by twining stems, tendrils and suchlike. Some need to be tied in to the support, a few are self-supporting (*see p.78*).

• **WALL SHRUBS** are often simply shrubs that are grown against a wall for the protection it gives them. Many wall shrubs need no support.

1 **SUMMER GROWTH,** which can be extensive with whippy shoots up to 2m (6ft) long, needs to be restricted to encourage flowering spurs to form.

2 **CUT BACK** long sideshoots to within 15cm (6in), or five or six buds, of a main branch. This is best done about two months after flowering.

3 **IN WINTER,** cut back the sideshoots pruned in summer to within 10cm (4in) or two to three buds of their base. These spurs will produce the flowers.

2 A climbing hydrangea refuses to climb

The climbing hydrangea is a self-clinging climber, yet often it seems reluctant either to climb or to cling.

Give a helping hand

Although this hydrangea (*H. anomala* subsp. *petiolaris*) develops aerial roots on its stems which help it to cling, you often find instead that at first it produces lots of whippy growths that grow away from the wall. Check that

there is no contamination of any sort on the surface of the wall or fence preventing the roots from clinging. Then do all you can to encourage the roots to cling by training the stems towards the wall and tying a few of them in to vine eyes or wires. To a large extent, however, it is a matter of time and patience and you usually find that plants start to cling well in about their third year.

METHODS OF SUPPORT

• **FOR LIGHTWEIGHT CLIMBERS** a system of strands of galvanized wire held taut between vine eyes can be used. The tendrils on plants such as passion flower, or the twining leaf stalks on clematis, will wind around the wires.

• **HEAVY CLIMBERS** need more substantial support, such as trellis.

• **CHECK TIES** regularly to ensure they are not constricting expanding stems or chafing them.

❸ Can an overgrown climber be drastically cut back?

If allowed to develop a congested mass of woody stems, flowering climbers produce fewer blooms, and really vigorous plants will force their way into guttering and under roof tiles. Many climbers respond well to renovation. With some the job can be completed in one season; others need more gradual treatment.

WHERE TO BEGIN
Tangled growth is often best sheared away (left) before unravelling main stems, but with honeysuckles (far left) simply cut all stems at 60cm (2ft) from the ground.

To prune or not to prune
On the whole, you can prune climbers fairly hard, in some cases right back to just above ground level, and in others back to the main framework of stems. However, it is not worth risking this if the plant is showing any signs of ill health or stress. Instead, reduce its size gradually, over a period of at least two years. After cutting back, make sure the plant is kept adequately watered during the growing season and fed in early spring, to help encourage new growth and plenty of flowers. A general fertilizer applied at about 30–100g per square metre (1–3oz per square yard) should work well.

Gradual renovation
When renovating a climber over a couple of seasons, start by removing a large proportion of the woody, congested growth towards the top of the plant in the first spring and prune back 30–50 per cent of the main stems. You will need to unravel tangled shoots carefully in order to minimize damage to those that are to be retained. Where this is impossible, shear away some of the densest growth first. Remove particularly weak stems and any which are dead, diseased or dying. New basal shoots which appear should be trained in to the support, arranging them so that they fill the gaps. Repeat the process

the following spring and you should be left with a plant that is in much better condition and more likely to produce attractive fresh growth that will flower well.

More drastic methods
A few climbers can be completely cut back to within 30–60cm (12–24in) of soil level. This is usually best done in early spring, so that there is plenty of time for new growth to be produced during the same year. Climbers that can be treated in this way include campsis, ivy, most honeysuckles, vines, Russian vine (*Fallopia baldschuanica*) and potato vine (*Solanum crispum*).

❹ A clematis has started to look decidedly ill

If a clematis looks poorly, it is not necessarily due to clematis wilt.

Look for slugs and snails
The most common cause of a clematis suddenly dying back, particularly a young plant, is an attack by slugs or snails. These graze away the surface of the stems causing sudden, extensive deterioration. This is less likely to happen once stems have become tougher and woodier, but in an area where slugs and snails abound, take precautions.

Clematis wilt
This fungal disease is usually seen as a wilting of the terminal shoots, particularly on young stems, and a darkening of the leaf stalks where they join the leaf. Large-flowered hybrids,

THE SYMPTOMS OF CLEMATIS WILT

particularly 'Jackmanii', seem most prone. It may be possible to save the plant by cutting all the affected stems back hard into healthy growth, below ground level if necessary. A deeply planted clematis – set in the ground at least 5cm (2in) deeper than it was growing in its pot – has the best chances of survival.

Poor cultivation
Lack of moisture can also cause wilting. If the root ball was dry at planting time, water will subsequently often not be able to penetrate the compost and reach the roots. Clematis also need good feeding with a general fertilizer in early spring.

Slime flux
Occasionally, large, usually woody stems may be injured, often as a result of winter damage or pest attack. Sap leaks from the stem and becomes colonized by a range of secondary fungi, yeasts and bacteria. This causes thickening and discolouration of the sap, leading to a problem known as slime flux. It is essential to cut out infected stems promptly to reduce the risk of further contamination.

❺ Flowers appear only at the top and the neighbour gets the benefit

Most of us grow climbers to decorate our own walls and fences, not to benefit our next-door neighbour, so it is annoying when plants produce all their flowers at the top. With some climbers it is an inherent problem and there is little you can do other than grow an attractive shrub near the base to mask bare stems. But, in many instances, climbers can be encouraged to flower lower down.

EARLY TRAINING
Fan out young stems, keeping some as near horizontal as possible, to encourage good coverage of the wall or fence and a wealth of flowers on the lower parts of the plant.

Train stems horizontally

If possible, train some of the stems into a horizontal position, or at least close to horizontal, as this often stimulates the production of flower buds. These lower stems should then bear some blooms. Train stems while they are young and supple, after planting and when new growth has been made after pruning.

Put up trellis

If you put up trellis along the top of the fence or wall, you can train the stems so that they produce their flowers in your garden rather than in your neighbour's.

Improve pruning techniques

Where few flowers at all are being produced, check that you have been pruning correctly, as in some cases if growth is removed at the wrong time of year you could be reducing the plant's flowering potential. You might in fact be cutting out the stems that would have produced that year's flowers. It could also be that because too much old growth has been left on a climber, it fails to produce new stems of the kind that would produce flowers. If plants such as late-flowering clematis are not pruned sufficiently in early spring, the new flowering growth simply grows as an extension of the old stems – at the top of the plant.

Wrong climber for the site

If the majority of a climber is in shade on your side of the fence, but its head is in sun, most of the flowers are likely to form towards the top of the plant. Check that the climber is suited to the position and if not, either consider moving it if it is not too old or replacing it with something more appropriate.

❻ Plants fail to grow in the dry soil at the base of a wall

In constantly dry soil at the foot of a wall or fence, plants need extra help if they are to thrive.

Rain shadows

Wall foundations and bricks at or just below soil level tend to draw moisture from the soil. On house walls the problem is exacerbated by overhanging roof tiles and guttering. Unless rain falls at just the right angle, soil stays dry, so it is essential to remember that a climber close to a wall is likely to suffer from drought-related problems.

Moisture conservation

Improve the soil before planting by incorporating lots of organic matter, such as well-rotted garden compost or manure. In addition, you could add a proprietary planting compost or leaf-mould. It is essential to improve a really large area, not just the planting hole. Water in the plant thoroughly and make sure it receives adequate water, especially in the first few years while getting established. Covering moist soil with a 8cm (3in) layer of mulch will also help to retain soil moisture. Do make sure that when improving the soil and mulching, you do not let the soil level or mulch get too close to the damp-proof course.

Shade the roots

Some climbers, in particular clematis, enjoy a fairly sunny position on the whole, but to thrive, need a cool, moist root run. Where plants are growing against a fence or wall, provide shade at the base. Mulching will help, but a covering of large, flat stones, pebbles or tiles is better. If the site is also naturally dry but has sufficient sunlight, consider choosing a climber listed as being suitable for a wall or fence that receives sun for much of the day.

COOL ROOTS
A few old roof tiles placed around a climber's stems will shade the roots and also help to conserve moisture.

❼ When and how should a clematis be pruned?

How and when to prune depend on clematis type, so keep the label both as a reminder of what you bought and because it is likely to give instructions. If you inherit a clematis on moving house and have no idea what it is, make a note of when it flowers so that you can fit it into one of the pruning groups below.

Pruning after planting

This may sound severe but in the first spring after planting, cut all stems back to about 30cm (12in) above ground level, to just above a pair of vigorous-looking buds. If left unpruned, plants may not produce sufficient stems for a good display of flowers. Once established, the amount of pruning needed depends on the group to which the clematis belongs.

Group 1: minimal pruning

Vigorous and small-flowered clematis that flower early in the year, from late winter to late spring, need no regular pruning. Generally, you need to cut these back only if they have outgrown their position or if they have become very congested. In this case, prune after flowering, taking out any dead, diseased or damaged stems at the same time. This group includes *Clematis alpina* and its cultivars, *C. armandii*, *C. cirrhosa* and *C. macropetala* and cultivars. If a *Clematis montana* gets out of hand, renovate it gradually over a couple of seasons (*see p.72*).

LIGHT PRUNING
Prune stems on group 2 clematis by about a third, back to a pair of healthy buds.

Group 2: light pruning

Large-flowered clematis that flower in early summer, sometimes with a second, lesser flush in late summer, need light pruning. The flowers for this group are produced on sideshoots from growth made during the previous season, so these clematis need to be pruned in early spring, before the new shoots start to grow. Cut stems back by roughly one-third, to just above a pair of vigorous-looking buds. At the same time, cut out all unhealthy or damaged stems. Common examples of clematis in group 2 include: 'Daniel Deronda', 'Duchess of Edinburgh', 'Henryi', 'Lasurstern', 'Marie Boisselot', 'Nelly Moser', 'Niobe', 'The President' and 'Vyvyan Pennell'.

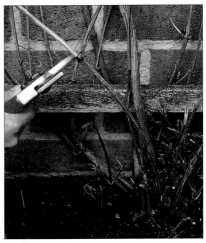

HARD PRUNING
Group 3 clematis are pruned to strong buds fairly close to the ground in early spring.

Group 3: hard pruning

Large-flowered hybrids and smaller-flowered species clematis that bloom in late summer fall into this group (group 3). These clematis flower on stems produced during the current season, so need to be pruned hard in early spring, before the new growth starts to develop. All the previous season's stems should be cut back to a vigorous pair of buds 15–30cm (6–12in) above ground level. Once the new growth appears, tie it in to the support. Examples of group 3 include 'Comtesse de Bouchaud', 'Ernest Markham', *C. florida*, 'Gipsy Queen', 'Hagley Hybrid', 'Jackmanii', 'Perle d'Azur', *C. tangutica* and cultivars, 'Ville de Lyon' and *C. viticella* and cultivars.

❽ The leaves on an actinidia are a disappointing colour

Actinidia kolomikta is grown for its flamboyant green, white and pink foliage, but sometimes the leaves fail to live up to the promise.

Maturity brings rewards

If the foliage remains an unexciting plain green or the leaves show only small amounts of variegation, this may simply be because the plant is still young. Generally, *Actinidia kolomikta* seems to colour up best when it has been planted for a few years. In addition to this, if the soil in your garden is fairly chalky, the colours are usually less intense. For a plant to be happy, it needs to be in an acid, neutral or only very slightly alkaline soil, which is moist but also well drained.

A MATURE ACTINIDIA COLOURS UP WELL IN SUN

Climbing plant chooser

Self-clinging climbers

These have all developed some means of clinging to a vertical surface so do not usually need a support system of wires or trellis or regular tying in.

Campsis grandiflora (may need some support)

Hedera colchica, H. helix H. hibernica (ivy), including many variegated cultivars)

Hydrangea petiolaris syn. *H. anomala* subsp. *petiolaris* (climbing hydrangea, may need initial support, *see p.71*)

Parthenocissus henryana, P. quinquefolia (not smooth surfaces), *P. tricuspidata* 'Veitchii'

Pileostegia viburnoides (may need initial support)

Schizophragma intergrifolium (may need initial support)

Climbers for sun

These grow best in a position that faces the sun.

Actinidia kolomikta

Akebia quinata

Humulus lupulus 'Aureus' (golden hop)

Passiflora caerulea (passion flower)

Solanum crispum 'Glasnevin', *S. jasminoides* 'Album'

Trachelospermum asiaticum, T. jasminoides (not fully hardy)

Vitis 'Brandt', *V. coignetiae*

Wisteria

A good scent

Some useful choices for pergolas and arches and on walls by windows and doors.

Clematis armandii

Lathyrus odoratus (annual sweet pea)

Lonicera japonica and cultivars, *L. periclymenum* including 'Serotina' and 'Graham Thomas'

Roses, many including 'Zéphirine Drouhin', 'Paul's Himalayan Musk'

Trachelospermum asiaticum, T. jasminoides (not fully hardy)

Wisteria

Suitable for clay

These either prefer or will tolerate the conditions created by a clay soil.

Campsis grandiflora

Celastrus scandens (oriental bittersweet)

Clematis, many

Euonymus fortunei

Hedera (ivy)

Humulus lupulus 'Aureus' (golden hop)

Hydrangea petiolaris (climbing hydrangea)

Lonicera (honeysuckle)

Parthenocissus (Virginia creeper)

Vitis coignetiae

Wisteria

Fast cover

These can be useful for quickly hiding an ugly wall, but some are rampant and may easily get out of control.

Calystegia hederacea

Clematis montana, C. montana var. *rubens*

Fallopia baldschuanica (Russian vine)

AKEBIA QUINATA

LONICERA PERICLYMENUM 'SEROTINA'

Lathyrus grandiflorus, L. latifolius (everlasting pea)

Parthenocissus quinquefolia, P. tricuspidata 'Veitchii'

Vitis coignetiae

Annual climbers

In their native habitat some of these are perennial, but in northern temperate gardens they are generally grown as annuals.

Cobaea scandens (cup and saucer plant)

Convolvulus tricolor

PILEOSTEGIA VIBURNOIDES

Eccremocarpus scaber (Chilean glory flower)

Ipomoea lobata and *I. tricolor* 'Heavenly Blue' (morning glory)

Rhodochiton atrosanguineus

Thunbergia alata (black-eyed Susan)

Tropaeolum majus (climbing nasturtium), *T. peregrinum* (canary creeper)

Cool or shade

These climbers appreciate a spot out of direct sun.

Akebia quinata

Berberidopsis corallina (mild areas only)

Celastrus scandens (oriental bittersweet)

Clematis alpina, C. macropetala, and many large-flowered clematis including 'Jackmanii Superba', 'Hagley Hybrid', 'Comtesse de Bouchaud', 'Perle d'Azur'

Euonymus fortunei

Lonicera japonica 'Halliana', *L. periclymenum* 'Serotina'

Schisandra chinensis, S. rubrifolia

WALLS & FENCES

GARDEN BOUNDARIES such as walls and fences are a necessity but because, in themselves, they are often not particularly exciting they are all too easily forgotten – until they become a problem or eyesore that cannot be ignored. A little regular care should make them last considerably longer; house walls, of course, always need to be kept well maintained. When planted with climbers and wall shrubs, walls and fences act as a marvellous backdrop to the garden as a whole and give a degree of privacy while screening off unwanted views.

THE PROBLEMS

1. Areas of brickwork have crumbling mortar and need repointing.
2. What is the best way of removing stains and white patches?
3. Can climbers, such as ivy, damage brickwork?
4. A wall shrub flops forward instead of growing neatly up against the wall.
5. An ugly concrete wall spoils the garden.
6. What is the best way to camouflage an unsightly drainpipe?

See also:

7–9 Fencing problems, p.80.
    Climbing Roses, p.68; Climbing Plants, p.70.

WALLS AND BRICKWORK

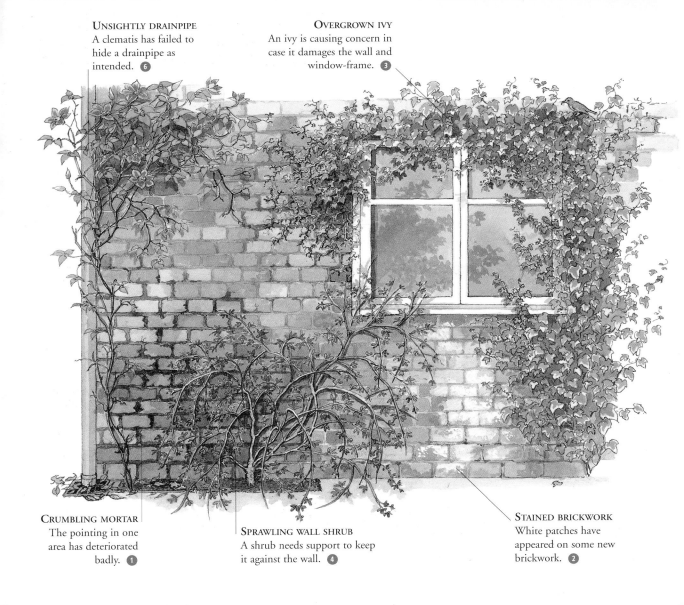

UNSIGHTLY DRAINPIPE
A clematis has failed to hide a drainpipe as intended. 6

OVERGROWN IVY
An ivy is causing concern in case it damages the wall and window-frame. 3

CRUMBLING MORTAR
The pointing in one area has deteriorated badly. 1

SPRAWLING WALL SHRUB
A shrub needs support to keep it against the wall. 4

STAINED BRICKWORK
White patches have appeared on some new brickwork. 2

❶ Crumbling mortar needs repointing

Repoint brickwork as soon as you notice that mortar has become loose or the wall may deteriorate rapidly. If there is any loss of stability in the wall, seek professional help.

Remove loose mortar

Try to allocate time to remove all loose pointing in one go and start work on the repointing straight away so that the mortar beneath is exposed for the shortest period possible. It is essential, however, to poke or chip out every scrap. It is better to remove too much than too little. The tip of a bricklayer's trowel makes a good tool for the job. Alternatively, use a screwdriver or narrow chisel and club hammer. Be sure to protect your eyes with goggles. Also take care not to damage the bricks.

Mix and match

CHECK POINTING Make sure mortar is sound before attaching plant supports. Screwing in vine eyes or trellis fixings will make crumbling pointing worse and access is difficult once plants are in place.

Pointing is made from a combination of sand and cement and sometimes lime. On old walls lime is a particularly common ingredient. It is important to try to make a mix that matches the existing

pointing, although you will need to take ageing into account. A typical mixture uses about three parts of soft sand to one part cement, with lime added as necessary, but recipes vary greatly. Since the colour changes as mortar dries, mix up a sample, let it dry, match it to the existing mortar and then adjust if necessary. The shade of sand used (it can be much yellower from some sources than from others) can considerably affect the ultimate colour.

Smooth application

Use a pointing trowel that is small enough to manoeuvre easily to apply new mortar and spray the area with a mister, since mortar adheres best to a damp surface. You may find you need to wear gloves because of the caustic effects of cement. Firmly press the pointing mixture into the gap between the bricks, smoothing it off and giving it a recess so that water does not accumulate on the bricks. This

POINTING TOOL

POINTING TROWEL

SAND AND CEMENT

• **SAND** Soft, or builder's sand, which is fine grade and salt free, is the type to use in masonry mortar. Use coarser sharp sand, plus aggregate, in concrete for setting fence posts in the ground.

• **CEMENT** When mixed with water, cement, which contains limestone, acts as the bonding agent in mortar and concrete. Masonry cement, designed for better workability, should be used in masonry mortar for brickwork.

usually means angling it so that it slopes downwards, or running an old piece of copper piping or garden hose along it to create a concave finish. You can also use a specially designed pointing tool (*below left*) which will give an inverted V-shape finish.

Clear off any excess mortar from the brickwork immediately and, for the strongest joints, cover with a plastic sheet for up to four days so that the mortar cures slowly.

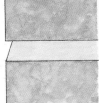

POINTING PROFILES
The finish on pointing generally needs to be angled or shaped so that it will direct rainwater away from the bricks.

❷ How can patches and stains be removed?

Deposits of white salts, called efflorescence, sometimes develop on new brickwork. Algal stains can also mar a wall's appearance and may signal a damp problem, although they sometimes help to age new brickwork allowing it to blend in with older nearby buildings.

Efflorescence

Avoid scrubbing this off with water, which often makes the problem worse, and instead use a dry wire

brush. Check, too, whether there is any obvious source of excess moisture around the wall that is aggravating the problem.

Algal stains

Use a stiff brush and water or, if necessary, a proprietary cleaner recommended for use on brickwork. A power washer can be used if the problem is extreme, but take care not to damage the surface of the bricks, thereby increasing their porosity.

Some bricks are tougher than others, so test the washer on a small area first. Old bricks that have lost their protective outer finish may be damaged by a very strong jet of water; if need be, use the washer on its lowest setting.

PERSISTENT STAINS If algal patches persist after cleaning, check that there is not a problem with leaking or blocked gutters and down-pipes or some other cause of damp.

❸ Will ivy damage a wall?

Whether climbers damage walls depends on the state of the wall and the type of climber.

Self-clinging climbers

If a wall is in good condition with sound mortar and pointing, climbers should not pose a problem. But if pointing is damaged, self-clinging climbers like ivy can increase the rate of deterioration. The aerial roots produced by ivy and climbing will undermine crumbling mortar, as will the adhesive pads on Virginia creeper (*Parthenocissus*). As long as tendrilled or twining climbers, such as passion flower and honeysuckle, have a good support system attached to a well-maintained wall, they should not cause any problem unless they get too large and heavy for their support.

If you remove a self-clinging climber, some roots tend to remain on the wall. They will eventually fall off but you can speed up the process by using a stiff yard broom or scrubbing brush.

AERIAL ROOTS ON IVY STEMS

VIRGINIA CREEPER'S ADHESIVE PADS

SELF-CLINGERS
Ivy's tenacious aerial roots should not harm sound brickwork but they can leave disfiguring remains. The pads on Virginia creeper also cause little damage except to loose mortar.

Vanishing windows

Any kind of climber on a house wall needs to be kept well maintained and trimmed so that it does not start to obscure windows and doors or block aeration bricks or vents. Around windows, take stems well back past the window-frame, since many climbers can work their way in between wood and wall. Cut them at varying lengths for the most naturalistic effect. Scrub the glass to remove plant debris or the remains of aerial roots or suckers.

FIVE-STAR ROOST

IF YOU ARE KEEN to attract birds to the garden, a dense climber provides a good roost. But if their droppings or noise becomes a nuisance, there may be little you can do to discourage them without drastically cutting back the climber or replacing it with something less to their liking. You may be able to put netting over the plant which allows the outer leaves to grow through and hide the netting yet prevents the birds from perching on the sturdier stems.

❹ Shrubs and climbers need some form of support

Most wall shrubs and climbers, apart from those that have developed self-clinging mechanisms, need a support.

Methods of support

To a large extent, type of support is determined by type of plant. A lightweight climber such as clematis may receive sufficient support from a few strands of wire and vine eyes but a larger, heavier plant such as wisteria needs something much stronger, such as a secure framework of heavy-duty wires or trellis. Tendrilled climbers may need tying in at first but will then be able to support themselves adequately. You may need to tie in some of their stems to position them where you want them. Plants which have no means of clinging will need tying in regularly. The support should be in place before planting, even if it

will take a year or two for the plant to make much use of it. If you compact the soil while putting up the support, dig it over thoroughly before planting.

Putting up trellis

Attach wooden battens at least 5cm (2in) thick to the wall using rawlplugs and screws, and then attach the trellis to these. This will help a little air to circulate around the plant. To make future maintenance of the wall easier (important on painted walls) attach the trellis to the battens using hinges at the base and hooks and eyes at the top. If regular access to the wall is unnecessary, simply screw the trellis to the battens, preferably using brass screws which will not rust. This latter method gives sturdy support. The base of the trellis should be about 30cm (12in) above ground level.

HINGED TRELLIS
For easy access to the wall, attach trellis using hinges on the bottom batten and hooks and eyes at either end of the top batten (inset).

5 An ugly wall could do with a makeover

Ugly expanses of wall can dominate a garden, but given a transforming coat of paint, innovative decoration or a lush covering of foliage, they will contribute to the setting.

Coat of colour

Before starting work, clean the surface thoroughly, brushing away any dirt, flaky patches or algal deposits. Allow the wall to dry before painting and prime it according to the paint manufacturer's directions. For the most lasting effect, choose paints designed specifically for use on masonry or concrete (although the specially formulated outdoor emulsion paints now available in a wide range of colours are useful for small areas and special effects). If in doubt, seek advice from the supplier.

Painting a wall can dramatically influence the way a garden looks so do take time to choose an appropriate colour. It is often worth painting a tester patch. Remember that bright colours may appeal this season but not be so much to your liking the next, and consider how the colour

SHELL WORK
Mellow earthy tones create a warm, relaxing ambience. The shells have simply been set into the stucco rendering while it was still slightly soft.

relates to other surfaces nearby and to neighbouring plants in their various stages of growth during the seasons.

Murals, stucco and mirrors

If you really want to liven up a blank concrete wall, consider painting a mural. If well done this can hugely enhance the feel of a garden. Or use mirrors (*see p.125*) to add a new dimension. Another way of disguising concrete is to render it with a coat of stucco, a mixture of fine sand and

cement, which can then be painted, scored with a pattern or studded with some kind of decoration such as a mosaic of glass or ceramics, shells or other found objects.

Disguise with plants

Don't forget that the appearance of most walls can be improved with a good selection of climbers or wall shrubs and their support system can help to decorate, or disguise, the wall (*see Climbing Plants, pp.70–75*).

6 An unsightly drainpipe needs camouflage

Climbers often fail to hide a drainpipe simply because they have no proper support or an inappropriate plant has been chosen.

Go for evergreens

Where possible use an evergreen climber, or, with deciduous climbers, fit some sort of mesh at the base and top of the drainpipe so that there is no risk of it becoming clogged with fallen leaves in autumn. You may decide to do this regardless of the type of climber you plant since it will ensure that leaves or debris do not become a problem.

Try, too, to choose a climber with a reasonably bushy habit of growth at its base. Many, such as clematis, are naturally leggy near the ground.

Construct a support

You can cover the drainpipe with a sleeve of chicken wire. If you anchor it well to the wall, especially at the base and top, you can grow a

lightweight climber up it which will eventually hide the pipe. It is also possible to buy purpose-made trellis kits which will fit around the pipe, or create your own trellis structure.

1 ASSEMBLE AND FIT the trellis around the pipe as indicated on the pack. Plant the climber a short way from the wall to reduce rainshadow problems.

2 TIE THE STEMS into the trellis using a figure of eight. This allows room for the stem to expand and move slightly without chafing.

FENCE PROBLEMS

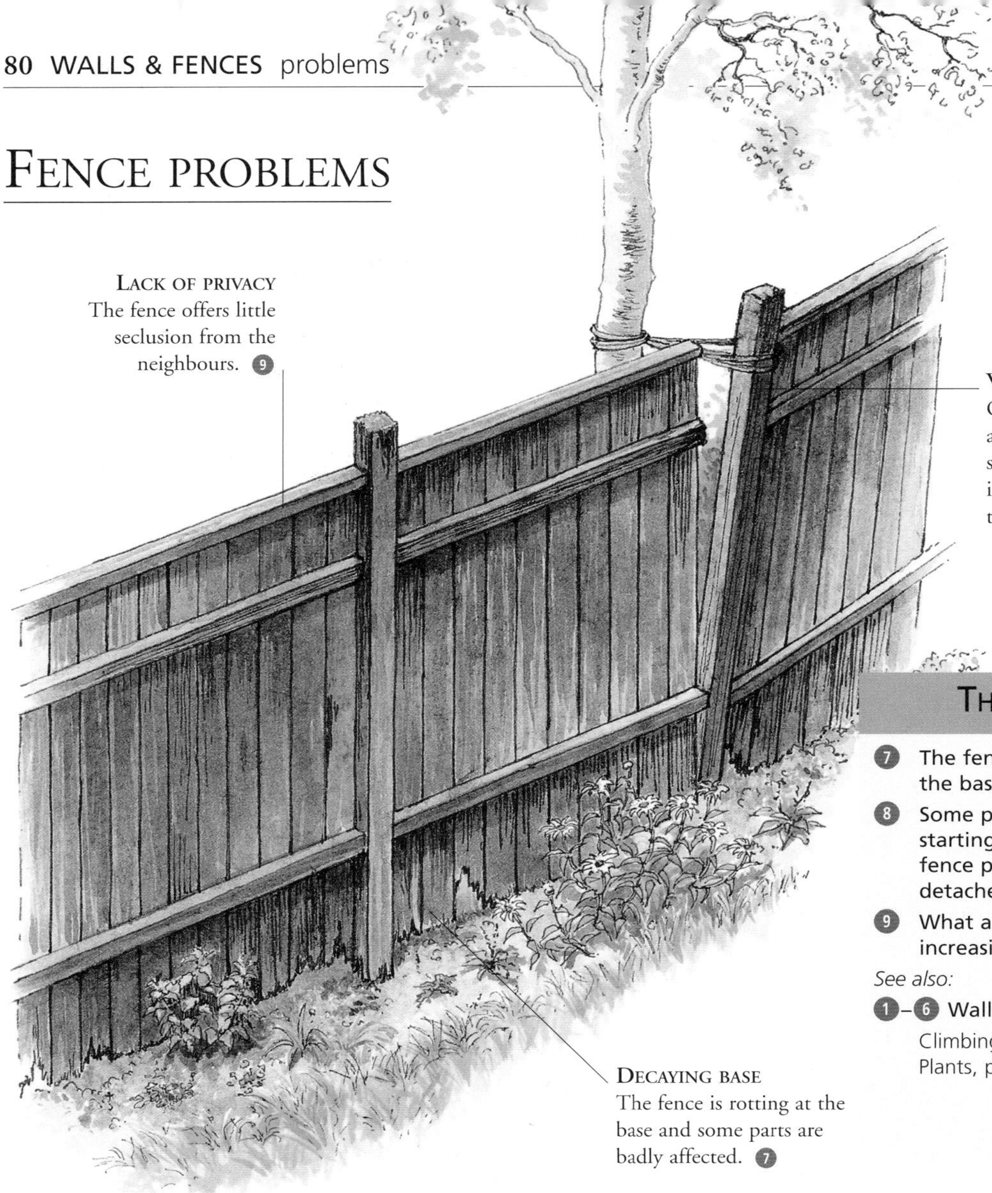

LACK OF PRIVACY
The fence offers little
seclusion from the
neighbours. **9**

WOBBLY POSTS
One or two posts have rotted
and adjacent parts of the fence
sag badly. Neither household
is sure who is responsible for
the repairs. **7** & **8**

DECAYING BASE
The fence is rotting at the
base and some parts are
badly affected. **7**

THE PROBLEMS

7 The fence is starting to decay at
the base.

8 Some posts are wobbly and
starting to rot at the base, and
fence panels have become
detached.

9 What are the options for
increasing privacy?

See also:

1–**6** Wall problems, p76.

Climbing Roses, p.68; Climbing
Plants, p.70.

7 Fence is decaying at the base

*If the soil level is allowed to build up
around the base of a fence, decay is
almost inevitable.*

Clear the soil
Check regularly that neither soil nor
mulching material is in contact with
the base of a fence or the moisture
will soon cause panels to deteriorate.
If left for too long, you may have to
replace an individual panel or, at
worst, the whole fence. Try to keep air
circulating at the base of any fence.

Fit gravel boards
To a large extent, the problem can
be avoided if you fit gravel boards
between the posts before attaching the
fence panels or boards. (They can also
be fitted to an existing fence but this
is a more tricky task.) Gravel boards
keep the base of the fence from
touching the ground without leaving
a gap through which next-door's dog
can squeeze. If they rot, they are
reasonably easy and inexpensive to
replace. Extremely durable concrete
gravel boards are also available.

Renew preservatives
Fences need regularly treating with a
timber preservative. Modern solvent-
or water-based formulations are
generally preferable to creosote, which
can be toxic to plants and poisonous
if ingested.

WHO IS RESPONSIBLE?

BOUNDARIES ARE a classic cause of
dispute between neighbours. In most
cases, a fence between two properties is
owned by one household. If you are
not sure whether a fence is your
responsibility or your neighbour's, you
may have to check the deeds. This is
certainly worth doing before moving
into a new property, especially if fences
or walls are in poor condition. Usually,
if you look towards the back boundary
of a property, the fence to your right is
your responsibility and the one to your
left belongs to the left-hand property.
If the fence clearly has two different
faces to it, for instance, if it is a close-
board fence with arris rails, the rails are
usually fitted on the owner's side, to
give easy access for repair.

8 Wobbly posts and sagging panels

Wooden posts, though attractive, are prone to rot. Keeping their bases out of contact with damp soil prolongs their life.

Use a concrete spur

Where a wooden post has already started to rot, it may be possible to remove the rotten section and attach the remainder of the post to a concrete spur (which will have pre-drilled holes) using sturdy bolts. The concrete spur can then be reset in the ground in concrete. This is a good method as it keeps the post away from moist soil and prevents further rot. Or you could replace the entire post and attach it to a concrete spur.

You can, of course, simply replace the post and set it in a concrete foundation, having dug out the remains of any previous foundations. A hardcore base beneath the concrete will aid drainage and should help to prolong the life of the post. However, posts set in concrete do not tend to last as long as those on concrete spurs and are less easy to renew.

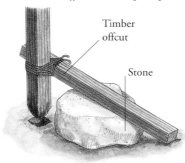

REMOVING A ROTTEN POST
To exert extra leverage when removing an old post, lash a timber offcut near its base. Using a large stone as a pivot, press down on the offcut to lever up the post.

Timber offcut

Stone

Metal supports

As an alternative to concrete foundations, you can use a spiked metal post-support. Protect the top of the support with a piece of wood as you drive it into the ground using a sledgehammer. Insert the post into the socket at the top and nail it into position if necessary. In stony ground, where the metal spike may bend or twist, you can set the post-support into concrete.

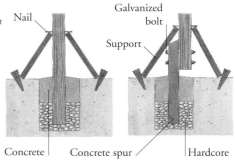

Nail

Galvanized bolt

Support

Concrete | Concrete spur | Hardcore

REPLACING POSTS
When setting a post into concrete or bolting it to a concrete spur set in the ground, hold it in place with wooden supports and check it is truly upright using a spirit level.

Re-attach the fence

The method by which you re-attach the fence boards or panel to the post depends on the type of fencing.

You will either need to reinsert the fence panel into a pre-cut groove in the post or, on close-board fencing, slot the chiselled ends on the arris rails into pre-cut holes in the post. It is also possible to buy metal brackets into which you can hang the fence panel.

9 Lack of privacy

If your garden is easily overlooked, you may want to raise the height of the fence without introducing excessive shade. If you decide on a taller fence, however, check any legal restrictions first.

Add trellis

Trellis sections fitted to the top of a fence are one of the simplest ways of increasing privacy, particularly when planted up with climbers. To attach trellis, you can use a wooden batten nailed onto the existing fence post and then nailed either directly to the trellis or preferably onto a wooden extension of the post. Use galvanized nails which will not rust and, if you are using a post extension, remember to replace the post-cap at the top to give it a finished look.

Alternatively, you can buy metal post extensions. These are in the form of metal sleeves which fit onto the top of the existing fence post and act as a link point, allowing you to slot the post for the trellis into the sleeve. There is a disadvantage in that the post extension is clearly visible and there will be a gap between the fence and the trellis. However, if you plant some climbers, both will be hidden once the climbers start to grow.

TRELLIS FIXING
A metal plate drilled with screw holes makes it easy to add an extension to a fence post to which trellis can then be attached.

Make it decorative

You can buy trellis in various shapes and designs, for instance with a convex or concave top, which can be used to create an ornamental effect. Once the trellis is in position, you may also decide to make the fence, trellis and posts blend together well by using a coloured wood stain.

High fences

Before replacing a fence with a taller one, or even adding trellis, check with your local authority that it will not be above the legal limit for your area. In most cases the maximum height of fences between gardens is 1.8m (6ft). At present, this does not apply to hedges, which could be an alternative, but high hedges that block light tend not to help good neighbourly relations.

SITE CLEARANCE

YOU MAY BE LUCKY and have just inherited a garden that has been beautifully maintained until the moment the previous occupants moved out. But in many cases, part if not all will be in a serious state of neglect. Alternatively, with a newly built house, you may find you have a hastily levelled plot with a thin scraping of topsoil and a lot of debris. Anything can be tackled – although sometimes the order you do it in helps – and, with time, made into a garden.

Q *When an area resembles a bombsite, what are the first things to do before trying to turn it into a garden?*

A Rubbish will invariably be buried beneath the surface, as well as lying on the ground. Try to make a thorough job of unearthing it all at the start, since anything left is likely to find its way to the surface sooner or later. You may well need to hire a skip. This will be useful for disposing of non-biodegradable material, large shrubs, tree stumps and so forth.

First remove the major pieces of debris (get someone to help with heavy items). Then, starting in one area, make a thorough clearance. If you begin at the far end, you will be encouraged to keep on working and finish the areas easily visible from the house. If you do it the other way round, you may be tempted to slow down or give up.

Make sure you have sturdy old clothes to work in that are loose and comfortable and get a thick pair of gloves to protect your hands.

Q *If a large tree in a garden needs to be removed, how should you best go about it?*

A Check that the tree is not covered by a Tree Preservation Order or growing in a Conservation Area. Your local council should be able to advise you on these or any other restrictions. Once you are sure that the tree can be felled ask for advice and quotations from several reputable local tree surgeons. The felling of a large tree is a specialist, potentially dangerous job that you should not attempt yourself.

Q *What is the best way to dispose of toxic waste?*

A If you uncover nasty things such as chemical containers and car batteries, your local council should be able to advise on which materials they can dispose of and which need to be taken away by a contractor. Try to avoid moving hazardous waste yourself. If you have no alternative, make sure your skin is well protected, and wear safety goggles and chemical-resistant gloves (available from good garden centres).

Q *If large areas of the garden are thick with weeds, what is the best way to clear them and which chemicals are suitable?*

A Woody weeds such as brambles are best treated with a proprietary brushwood killer, but take care because some of these products remain active for a considerable time and may contaminate the soil. Annual weeds can be hoed off, but perennial weeds may need a systemic weedkiller, such as one based on glyphosate, unless you have time to dig them out (an operation you may need to repeat in subsequent seasons if the weeds regrow). Follow the instructions on the weedkiller packet carefully. Glyphosate tends to be most successful if applied to weeds in full growth.

Q *How can the risk of weedkiller contamination be minimized?*

A Always follow the instructions carefully and apply the product in the manner and at the rate specified on the pack. Avoid using weedkillers in very hot or windy conditions, which are likely to cause drift and contamination of other plants. A watering can with a dribble bar is usually the best means of application. This makes it easy to direct the chemical accurately and, because the droplets are larger than if applied through the rose of a sprayer, they are less inclined to drift. Keep a sprayer or watering can for weedkillers only and label it clearly. Like other garden chemicals, weedkillers can be very useful and save a lot of hard work and time, but they must be used with care and never indiscriminately.

Q *What is the best way to clear very weedy areas without using chemicals?*

A Organic methods of weed control tend to take considerably longer than using chemicals and usually involve a lot of hard physical work, particularly if there are deep-rooted perennial weeds. You can dig the area over thoroughly and remove the weeds, roots and all, by hand, but this is a lengthy process. Some organic gardeners like to use the smothering method, where weedy areas are covered with old carpet, black polythene or similar material. The weeds die off due to exclusion of light. This works quite well but it may take a considerable time to eradicate the more pernicious weeds. Or you could leave some parts of the garden under a weed-smothering cover while you get on with digging the weeds out of other areas.

Q *Should dead trees and tree stumps be removed?*

A Although it is sometimes advocated that you leave dead trees or tree stumps *in situ* and use them as scrambling frames for climbers or roses this is not a good idea. A dead tree may look delightfully "rustic" but if it is of any size it may shed limbs or the tree itself may fall. There is also an increased risk of encouraging honey fungus, which may build up in the roots and stump and then spread to other plants in the garden. (*For methods of removing stumps, see p.13.*)

Q *What can be done in the garden of a newly built house which has little, if any, topsoil?*

A A skimpy or sometimes even non-existent layer of topsoil is an all too common problem. Buy in some good-quality topsoil from a reputable supplier. Make sure that it is of the pH (acidity) that you need. Most topsoil is sold as "screened" which means that it has come off a development site and large lumps of debris have been removed, although it

often still contains a fair quantity of crushed concrete and brick rubble. Obviously this should be avoided if possible. When spreading the topsoil, take care not to cause problems of water run-off by raising the soil level and watch that you do not build up levels to anywhere near the damp-proof course.

Q *Does it matter what time of year a site is cleared?*

A Ideally, major clearance should be done when soil is dry to minimize the damage caused to it. Working on wet soil, particularly if it is at all heavy, will cause compaction.

Q *What is the best way to deal with compacted soil?*

A Make sure you are not going to cause any more damage to the soil yourself before you try to resurrect it. It is essential that you try to break up the existing compaction by thorough digging and the incorporation of plenty of bulky organic matter. If this is not possible, perhaps because it is large, you could consider hiring a mini-excavator. Because these machines are tracked they produce relatively little compaction. However, since they make deep digging so much easier, you will need to take great care not to mix subsoil with topsoil.

Q *The soil in one area of the garden is devoid of plant life. What action is needed?*

A If nothing at all is growing, not even weeds, there may be some sort of contaminant in the soil. Do a mini-test by taking two small flowerpots and filling one with soil from the suspect area and the other

with soil from a known healthy area. Sprinkle some lettuce seeds over the surface of each, water gently and cover with a clear polythene bag. If there are any contaminants in the soil, the seeds will either not germinate in that pot or the seedlings will become distorted, die or show other symptoms of distress. The pot of healthy soil can act as your control. If you need to know more precisely what is wrong, you could have the soil analysed but this can be expensive and it may be impossible to identify the exact contaminant.

Q *Once trees or old hedging have been removed, is extra soil preparation needed?*

A Yes. Trees and large shrubs that have been in place for a long time, especially if grown closely together as for hedging, will have exhausted the soil of nutrients. Dig the area over thoroughly and try to remove all remaining roots. Then incorporate lots of bulky organic matter, such as well-rotted manure. Do not rely on chemical fertilizers alone. Although they will introduce nutrients they will do nothing to improve the soil's texture.

Q *Are powered cultivators useful or can they sometimes damage the soil?*

A These machines can be useful but it is worth bearing in mind that on heavier soils they tend to fluff up the top layer and smear the lower levels, sometimes forming a virtually impenetrable layer, or pan, which will impede drainage. They will also chop any bindweed or ground elder roots left in the soil into small pieces. Since each piece will grow into a new plant, any weed problem you have will be made considerably worse.

PATIOS, PATHS & STEPS

AREAS OF HARD-STANDING such as patios and terraces are becoming increasingly popular, while paths and steps form necessary links between house and garden and also between areas of the garden itself. But once constructed, these features are often taken for granted and may be neglected to the extent that they become unsightly and even dangerous. Some basic maintenance should keep them in good repair but if you can lavish a little extra attention on these areas, they can be transformed into something that is functional yet an attractive part of the garden, too.

PATIOS AND TERRACES

SLIPPERY PAVING
The patio gets dangerously slippery, especially in winter. ❶

FULL OF WEEDS
Weeds sprout from between paving slabs and next to walls. ❷

STAINED SLABS
Some areas of the patio have got badly marked, mainly by the barbecue. ❼

FACELIFT REQUIRED
The patio needs a makeover to turn it into a more attractive place to sit. ❽

UNEVEN, BROKEN SLABS
Cracked slabs and an uneven surface are creating a hazard. ❸

1 Slippery paving

The most likely cause of a slippery patio is a layer of algae, especially in winter and if the surface has stayed damp for a long time. If possible, cure the cause of the dampness first. Dealing with the algae is easy. (For slippery timber decking, see p.88.)

Seek the cause

Investigate first what is making the patio is wet. Unless causes and solutions are found, the problem will only return. Check that gutters and downpipes are not damaged or blocked and consequently spilling water onto the area. Also make sure that nearby drains are not clogged with leaves or debris, or leaking in any way. The patio should have been constructed with a slight camber so that water runs straight off the surface. If not, there is no easy remedy without rebuilding. If the damp-proof course on the house or garage has been covered in any way, either by the patio or by soil in a border, this too could be causing problems, not only to the patio but also to the building.

Banish algae

Algae can usually be brushed off most surfaces using a stiff yard broom or, in small areas, a scrubbing brush. Plain water is often sufficient. If you use a proprietary patio cleaner, check any limitations regarding the types of surface on which it can be used or its safety near plants. Cleaners are not usually a good idea if they are likely to run off into garden ponds where they may harm fish and wildlife. Once clean, check the surface regularly and try not to let the algae build up again.

Smooth slabs

York and other types of stone with a very smooth surface have a tendency to become very slippery in wet weather. If this could be dangerous, choose a style of paving with a rough surface.

SAFETY FIRST
A light sprinkling of sharp sand scattered over the surface of the paving will help to prevent an area from becoming dangerously slippery after periods of rain.

2 The patio has too many weeds

Although certainly possible, hand-weeding from gaps between paving slabs is difficult. Weeds with tap roots, such as dandelions, are especially tricky to pull out.

Using weedkillers

When choosing a weedkiller, make sure it is labelled as suitable for use on hard surfaces such as paving. Check, too, that it can be safely used on your particular type of slab, as some chemicals may cause discolouration. If necessary, test a small patch first. Use an accurate method of application. A dribble bar fitted to the end of a watering can works well if you have a large area to treat. If there are only one or two weeds, which you cannot remove by hand, try a spot-weeder which allows you to treat individual weeds without any risk of contaminating nearby plants.

Chemical-free methods

Individual weeds can often be eased out using an old kitchen knife with a strong blade or, from gravel, with a hand fork. If there are a lot of weeds, you could try using a special weed-burning apparatus. These are rather like small flame-throwers and will safely burn off weed top-growth. The larger, professional types work well but inexpensive models tend to prove much less efficient. Pernicious weeds will need to be burned off regularly until so weakened they die out. Take care not to ignite any landscape fabric that may be laid beneath gravel.

DEALING WITH A DANDELION
A dribble bar is ideal for large weeds. The length of bar can often be adjusted according to the size of area, or weed, to be treated.

❸ Uneven surface and broken slabs

A broken, uneven surface can be dangerous, looks messy and allows water to accumulate, in turn attracting slippery algae. Individual slabs can often be replaced, although new slabs may need to be cut to size. Or you might instead be able to turn cracks and gaps into planting spaces.

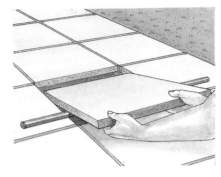

Lift and replace slabs

Rather than re-laying the entire patio, try lifting individual broken, damaged or sunken slabs. If you can't find suitable-sized replacements of the right colour and texture, the answer may be to remove a selection of slabs, including some undamaged ones, and create a pattern using a mixture of old and new. Save any old unbroken slabs in case you need further replacements at a later date.

Level up the hardcore or sand and soil mixture in the gaps and re-firm it before replacing the slabs. Carefully

ROLL IN A REPLACEMENT
Supporting the slab with a pole, pipe or broom handle helps to ease it into place without damaging it or surrounding slabs.

ease each new slab into position, check with a spirit level and leave for a couple of days, then check again that it is still level. Once you are satisfied that it will not sink unevenly, replace the mortar, taking care not to splash it on the surrounding surface. Clean any spillages promptly, while the mortar is still wet, using a stiff brush and water. Place a piece of wood between hammer and slab to protect the slab when tapping it into place, or use the hammer handle.

Cutting replacement slabs to fit

Wear protective clothing – eye goggles and gauntlet-style gloves. The easiest way of cutting is to use an angle grinder and, for several slabs, it is well worth borrowing or hiring one. However, the odd slab or two can be cut by hand. To ensure a comfortable fit and allow for any uneveness on the cut edge, make the replacement slab marginally smaller by cutting 6mm (¼in) to the inside of the measured lines.

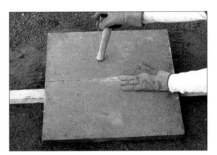

1 MARK BOTH FACES of the slab where you want to cut and make a final check that the measurements are accurate. Then score along the marks on either face using a bolster and straight-edge.

2 POSITION THE BOLSTER on the scored line and use a club hammer to tap it gently but firmly to create a groove 3mm (⅛in) deep. Repeat the process on the other face.

3 PLACE A STRIP OF WOOD under the groove – the wood and slab must be resting on a firm, flat surface. Tap with the hammer handle to one side of the groove until the slab breaks along the groove.

Camouflage unsightly cracks with low-growing plants

Where slabs have large cracks but the paving has not sunk, you can mask the cracks by sowing seeds into them. This looks perfect in an informal or cottage-style garden. Clean out the gaps so that the plant roots can tap into the soil below – they won't work their way through cement or mortar – then drizzle in some good quality top-soil, perhaps mixed with compost, and sow the seeds direct. You could use annuals such as Virginia stocks (*Malcolmia maritima*), candytuft (*Iberis*) or alyssum, or a herbaceous perennial such as *Alchemilla mollis*, which will rampantly self-seed itself and complete the job for you.

Alternatively, small, deep holes can be used to insert tiny plants of thyme, oregano or other creeping herbs. This works particularly well where corners of paving slabs have broken off. These plants thrive in dry conditions and release their aroma when walked on.

SOW SEEDS TO FILL SMALL GAPS IN PAVING

❹ A sunny patio is in need of some shade

A patio in full sun may be fine for sunbathing but, without any kind of shade, eating lunch outside can turn into an uncomfortably hot experience that is far from relaxing.

Use screens and canopies

For something more substantial or permanent than an attractive parasol, you will need to build a roofed structure to give overhead shade. A vertical screen will also help but will only give protection when the sun is not too high in the sky. Trellis, attached to sturdy posts, makes a decorative screen, arbour or pergola.

Or you can build a simple framework of uprights and cross-timbers and train climbers up and over it. A house wall often provides a useful point of attachment, especially if you can fix a sturdy batten to it and then use brackets to attach the cross-beams to the batten.

Make sure any structure is high enough for a tall person to stand comfortably beneath it, even when plants are trailing through the canopy, and that there is an adequate seating area for a table and chairs. Remember that people need room to move chairs a little way back from the table.

Foliage for shade

Rather than planting so densely that you create a wall of solid shade, use plants that cast dappled shade. Good climbers include ornamental vines such as *Vitis coignetiae*, the kiwi fruit (*Actinidia deliciosa*) or a fruiting grape vine such as *Vitis* 'Brant' (*see p.75 for other climbing plants*). Honeysuckle, if adequately thinned, will also provide light shade and a delicious perfume. You would have to make sure that its roots had sufficient space and that the lower portion, at least, was not in too hot an area, or it would be prone to attacks of powdery mildew.

❺ Ways of lighting the patio

Installing lighting extends the time and ways in which you can enjoy your terrace or patio. More practically, it also aids safety and security.

Candle and solar power

To work well, solar-powered garden lighting needs to be installed so that the solar panel receives as much sunlight as possible. In uncertain climates you may need some lights powered by mains electricity as back up. If you want temporary lighting in order to enjoy the odd evening meal outside, you can achieve attractive results using candles, storm lanterns or garden flares. Take care there is no fire risk. Using candles containing citronella oil helps to keep mosquitoes and other unpleasant insects at bay.

Installing electrical systems

Off-the-shelf low-voltage systems are readily available from DIY stores and garden centres and these are safe and relatively easy to install without a great deal of specialist equipment or cabling. For a good-quality, long-lasting system, however, it is usually advisable to employ a qualified electrician or even a specialist garden lighting designer. Unless guaranteed

A GENTLE GLOW
Glasses help to shelter candle flames from the wind and provide some safety protection.

ILLUMINATED WATERWORKS
A well-lit water-spout makes an even more dramatic focal point by night than by day.

safe for use in the garden as supplied, make sure that all electrical equipment is fitted with armoured cabling. This must be buried deeply – check local regulations for the depth – and fitted with some form of circuit breaker or residual current device.

Choosing lights

There are many different types of lighting available, perhaps to illuminate individual trees, light steps

to make them safer or create subtle lighting so that you can enjoy sitting out on your patio on warm summer's evenings. It is essential to check that the lighting you choose is suitable for the purpose you have in mind. At the same time consider lamp designs and whether you want the lamp itself to be a prominent feature of the garden, or whether you would prefer something that can be hidden among foliage instead.

6 Shabby or slippery decking

In wet weather wood can get really slippery, especially if a film of algae develops on the surface. With time, decking may also begin to look the worse for wear.

Clean it up

Use a stiff brush to scrub off any algae or moss. It is usually fairly easily removed, but use a fungicide if it proves particularly stubborn. While brushing, take the opportunity to check for any repairs that are needed, such as screws that have worked loose or timbers that have become rotten and need replacing.

Make it safe

Where areas of decking often remain damp for long periods, for instance by the side of a pool, the slippery wood could be dangerous. For a long-term solution, tack galvanized chicken wire over the surface, using U-shaped galvanized staples, to provide a secure foothold.

Choosing decking timber

If you are creating a new area of decking, choose a type of timber that is rot-resistant, for example, western red cedar, and if you use a soft wood make sure that it is tanalized (pressure-treated with preservative).

It may be tempting to purchase cheaper materials, but in the long run they are not good value.

Leave a slight gap between timbers to allow them to swell when wet without warping. Planks with grooves help to prevent slipping, but you need to keep the grooves free of debris or they will become just as slippery as smooth-surfaced timbers. If you use ready-made decking squares, for extra safety lay them so that the grain or grooves are at right angles in adjacent squares instead of all running in the same direction.

GO WITH THE GRAIN
When applying colour, brush in the direction of the wood grain. Here, alternating shades emphasize the angles in this stylish decking.

Apply colour

To revamp shabby decking, give it a good clean and, once the surface is completely dry, revitalize it with a coat of paint or wood stain. The non-slip paint designed for use on yachts has a grainy texture that will give a safe surface for a number of years. Or try one of the porous wood-stain treatments now available. These have the advantage that they allow moisture to escape from the wood and so greatly slow down the rate at which the stain lifts or the surface starts to deteriorate.

Apply any wood stain or other treatment with a good quality paintbrush and make sure that you apply it in the direction of the grain and give the number of coats suggested by the manufacturer. Colour does tend to wear away with a lot of use.

SAFETY CHECK
Ready-made grooved squares of decking create a subtle chequerboard effect that is also less likely to be dangerously slippery.

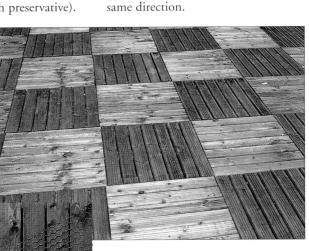

WIRED FOR SAFETY
Galvanized chicken wire tacked to a wooden surface gives a good foothold when the wood itself is wet and slippery.

UNDER THE DECKING
If installing new decking, cover the soil underneath with a thick layer of gravel which will prevent weed growth and also allow good drainage.

⑦ Stained slabs

Patios that are used regularly for eating and entertaining are easily stained, especially around a barbecue. Ideally, clean them before the stains get too ingrained.

Elbow grease required

A stiff brush or yard broom is usually sufficient to remove fat and other cooking stains, but if really stubborn, detergent or a proprietary patio cleaner should solve the problem.

Check the active ingredients on the label to ensure that any run-off will not damage plants or pond-life.

When cleaning fails

Badly stained slabs that cannot be cleaned may have to be replaced (*see p.86*). In this case, it is worth making some form of pattern that mixes old and replacement slabs, so that newly laid areas are less apparent. Try to incorporate some sensible-coloured slabs close to high-risk areas such as by the barbecue. Cooking stains are less likely to show up on multi-coloured paving than on slabs of a single colour, particularly pale grey. Alternatively, you may be able to cover up the affected areas with containers of small shrubs or brightly coloured bedding, but make sure they will not create a hazard or interrupt the flow of traffic between a seating area and barbecue.

⑧ Simple facelift required

New life can be injected into an old patio built of uninspiring materials and in a predictable shape. It is even possible to transform one that is just plain ugly.

Fittings and fixtures

Sometimes a terrace or patio looks dull purely because it consists of a large expanse of paving with little on it. Although you will probably want to retain a reasonable space for table and chairs, you can make it a much more pleasurable place to sit if you add plenty of containers brimming with plants. A small pond in a tub or a wall fountain will create a focal point, or introducing a particularly handsome pot, whether empty or planted, will have the same effect.

Changing shape

If the patio is a conventional rectangle or unappealing shape, alter it to something more exciting. It may be possible to do this by simply moving existing slabs to create a different shape and introducing some bricks or cobbles. If you have to add new slabs, avoid making it obvious which areas have been extended by mingling old with new. Work some new slabs into the centre of the patio and similarly use a few old slabs in the added-on areas. Remember that any new, extended sections must be laid on compacted soil and hardcore.

BOLD AND BLUE *Simply introducing some striking and colourful furniture can give a rather dull, ordinary patio its own special character and make it an inviting place to sit.*

Make spaces for plants

If you need to remove any slabs, the gaps created can be used as planting spaces, provided they aren't in an area where you need to walk or sit. Take out all the hardcore, sand and mortar and revitalize the soil by digging in

A COBBLED CORNER

plenty of planting or garden compost or well-rotted manure. If necessary, top up with some good-quality topsoil and make sure that the planting holes you dig are large enough to easily accommodate roots. As long as you choose plants that won't get in the way once full-grown, they will enhance an area and help to soften a large expanse of paving. Aromatic herbs are ideal on a sunny patio that is near the kitchen door or the barbecue.

Disguise with decking

Timber decking can be built over the top to conceal an ugly patio. Ensure that the support system for the decking is raised slightly above existing paving to prevent moisture from accumulating on the patio surface and accelerating the wood's deterioration.

PATHS AND STEPS

THE PROBLEMS

9 A concrete path has developed several cracks. Can it be repaired?

10 The edges of a path have broken and crumbled away.

11 Some steps are rather unsafe because they are not very easy to see.

12 A short flight of wooden steps gets extremely slippery in wet weather.

See also:

1–**8** Patios and terraces, p 84.

UNSAFE STEPS
Steps are not easily visible at night and have even caused problems in the day. **11**

CRACKED CONCRETE
Significant cracks have developed in a path and are getting worse. **9**

BROKEN EDGES
A path is crumbling away at the edges and needs repair. **10**

SLIPPERY STEPS
Wooden steps are dangerous in wet weather. **12**

9 Cracks have appeared in a concrete path

Cracked concrete needs repairing promptly, before water gets into the cracks in winter, turns to ice, expands and makes the damage worse.

Filling in

Generally, a crack or hole is worth repairing only if it is at least 1.5cm (½in) deep, otherwise the filling will simply fall out. Although hairline cracks need not be filled, do keep a watch on them and repair them as soon as necessary. When frequently used, cracked paths can quickly deteriorate beyond the point of repair, especially in frosty weather. Ready-prepared mixes, to which you simply add water, are available if the repairs are small and you want to avoid buying large bags of sand and cement.

Use an old chisel to chip away around the edges of the hole or crack, making sure that all loose or crumbling material is removed. As you do this, angle the chisel so that the base of the groove or hole becomes wider than the top. This will hold the filler securely in place and make it less likely to become dislodged. Brush out all loose material to create a clean, dry and dust-free surface. Paint the sides of the hole or crack with a PVC adhesive, then fill with concrete filler.

Protect newly repaired areas from rain or heavy dew by covering with polythene. If frost is forecast, some newspaper, hessian or even old curtains will provide some insulation.

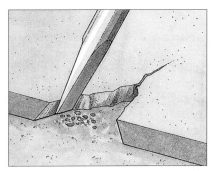

1 CHIP AWAY jagged edges using an old chisel or screwdriver, angling it to make the base of the crack wider than the top. Remove all loose material.

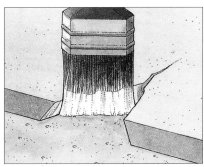

2 PAINT THE EDGES and floor of the crack with a PVC adhesive, which will enable the concrete filler to bond well with the path itself.

⑩ Broken and crumbling path edges

The edges of paths, steps or even patios can be subject to a lot of wear and tear and are often one of the first areas to deteriorate.

Mending concrete edges

It is essential that edges, particularly of steps, are well maintained, or they may become dangerous. On concrete paths, chisel away any loose or crumbling areas of concrete to leave a stable surface, and brush the area well to remove dust and small fragments. Wear tough gloves to protect your hands from chippings and, if you are creating a lot of dust, it is advisable to wear a mask. Protective eye goggles are essential. If necessary, replace and firm down

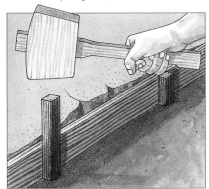

REPAIRING CRUMBLING EDGES
Use wooden pegs to hold a timber plank in place along the path edge and pour cement between path and plank.

any areas of hardcore, and paint the edges of the concrete with a PVC adhesive to help the cement to bond.

To make the repairs, put up a temporary timber edging, held in place by firmly driven-in wooden stakes. Pour cement mixture into the gap between the timber and path. Leave the timber in place until the cement has completely hardened, and remember to protect the area from footmarks, especially if pets or children are likely to go near. As with mending cracks (*see opposite*), protect from moisture and frost.

Repairs to paved paths

If paving tiles get damaged at the edge of a path, you may be able to lay replacement tiles after filling in gaps in the cement on which they have been laid. Put up some timber edging and follow the same procedure as for a concrete path.

Conceal with plants

If the crumbling edges are on a path, and in an area where they could not cause an accident, you could hide them by planting some well-chosen perennials. Plants with a creeping or sprawling habit will work best. Obviously, this is not an option on a flight of steps, where it would be extremely dangerous.

⑪ Poorly visible steps

Ensuring that steps are safe and easily visible if used at night is a high-priority job.

Install lighting

Installing some form of lighting is the best idea (*see Lighting a patio, p.87*). If it is not possible to supply electricity, solar-powered lights may prove to be the answer. Uplighters are useful by the side of steps and paths in open areas, otherwise attach lights to walls or other vertical surfaces.

Other safety devices

Painting the edges of the steps white or a very pale colour will make them much more visible, day and night. Before applying any paint, make sure the surface is good and sound and has been properly cleaned, or the paint will not adhere and could prove even more dangerous.
A handrail is often helpful, particularly where elderly people use the garden. Install a low-level handrail if children are finding the steps difficult to use safely.

> **SAFE DESIGN**
> Good proportions make steps safe and comfortable to use. Make sure the tread (where you place your foot) is sufficiently deep, and the riser (the vertical part) not too high.

⑫ Slippery steps and stepping stones

Any slippery surface is potentially dangerous but on a flight of steps it could be lethal.

Make timber steps safe

The surface of wooden steps may become extremely slippery in damp conditions, particularly if covered with a layer of algae. First check that there is no obvious source of water running onto the steps (for instance, from blocked gutters or leaking downpipes). Then you can try to improve the surface of the steps.

Scrubbing with a stiff brush and proprietary cleaner should largely solve the problem, but tacking galvanized chicken wire over the timber (*see p.88*) will create a surface that doesn't become slippery as soon as it rains.

In autumn, gather up fallen leaves from nearby trees and shrubs before they have the chance to turn to dangerous slush.

For the safest brick steps, build the treads from stable bricks. Their cross-hatching provides a non-slip surface.

Lethal stepping stones

You could replace stepping stones made from smooth slabs with a rougher textured stone, or perhaps create your own slabs by pouring cement into circular or square moulds and incising the surface with a rough-textured pattern once the cement is nearly set. Or you could press in twigs or deeply ridged leaves to create a textured ornamental effect.

Brush algae off tree-trunk stepping stones using a wire or stiff brush, or tack chicken wire over the top.

CONTAINERS

IF YOUR GROWING AREA consists mainly of a paved patio and whatever you can manage to fit on walls and windowsills, your gardening will be largely centred around containers of one sort or another. But even if you have a large garden, with ample beds and borders, the chances are that you will still enjoy growing a range of plants in pots, simply because they can look so good. Containers also allow you to grow plants which would not do well in your garden's natural soil. But you need to make sure the display – of both plants and containers – lives up to expectations.

POTS, TUBS AND PLANTERS

TOO LARGE TO POT ON
A bay tree has been in the same container for a long time but is too big to pot on. **5**

HOLE-RIDDEN LEAVES
Despite being planted in a pot, a hosta's leaves are full of holes. **10**

YELLOWING FOLIAGE
The leaves of an azalea growing in a concrete planter have turned an unhealthy yellow. **6**

ROTTING PLANTER
A wooden Versailles tub is starting to rot around the base. **4**

TOPPLED POT
On windy days, a plastic plant pot regularly ends up on its side. **12**

UGLY CONTAINER
A cheap pot is useful but could do with a facelift to make it more attractive. **2**

CRACKED CLAY
A terracotta pot has developed a crack during winter. **1**

HARSH ORANGE CLAY
A new clay pot would look better if it could be made more mellow. **8**

TENDER PLANT
A phormium needs some sort of winter protection. **11**

1 Terracotta pots crack and crumble

Clay varies in its resistance to frost depending on type, source and firing. Cracked pots can sometimes be repaired, but little can be done when clay flakes and crumbles.

Mend with wire

If a pot has cracked, it may be possible to repair it with some taut wire concealed beneath the rim. This will prevent more rim from falling away. You could also then hide the damage with a mosaic of broken tiles or china. Repairs are only worthwhile, however, if a pot is particularly large, precious or of great sentimental value since terracotta is now reasonably cheap and replacement not the frightening prospect it once was.

SIMPLE REPAIR
Tighten a band of wire under the rim by twisting the ends together, using pliers if necessary.

Check frost resistance

If you want to ensure that a terracotta pot remains in good condition whatever the weather, buy something that is frost-proof. Pots that are described as frost-resistant have a slightly more open texture and although they usually withstand a fairly cold winter, their survival is not guaranteed. If no indication at all is given, pots are likely to have little if any resistance to frost or harsh weather. Many of the more exotic ones fall into this category, especially if offered at fantastically low prices. This does not mean you should never buy them, but you need either to regard them as disposable or move them to a frost-free spot for winter. Tell-tale signs that may help you decide include:
• Terracotta pots made in the UK are more likely to be frost-proof than those made in the Far East and countries with a warmer climate.
• If flicked with your fingernail, a frost-proof pot has a more musical "ting" than the duller sound of frost-resistant clay.
• Frost-proof pots are generally the most expensive.

2 An ugly pot needs disguise

High-quality materials and good design often have a correspondingly high price tag. Cheap but useful pots, though, can be given a facelift. Or, in a group, they can be hidden by more attractive neighbours.

Natural camouflage

Use trailing plants such as creeping Jenny (*Lysimachia*), *Helichrysum petiolare* or ivy, and trailing forms of pelargonium, petunia, catmint (*Nepeta*) or fuchsia. They can be added to long-term plantings of shrubs or trees, or worked in with annual arrangements. Once they are growing well, an ugly container will disappear beneath a cascade of foliage and flowers.

Materials for a makeover

There are now a number of paints on the market which can be used successfully on outdoor containers, whether the pots are made from plastic, concrete or terracotta. You might be able to use a colour which will harmonize with plants or perhaps the colour of your front door, gate or garden furniture. Alternatively, paints can be used to create interesting designs, perhaps to complement a Mediterranean or Oriental theme. Simple designs are often more effective than elaborate schemes. Follow the manufacturer's instructions as to whether an undercoat is needed to help the paint adhere. It may also

be possible to conceal the pot with mosaic. Provided you use suitable tile adhesive you can create an individual design using glass tesserae, available from craft shops, or your own selection of pieces of china or tile.

STENCIL A MOTIF
A simple stencil adds character to a plain pot. Use a sponge to apply the paint.

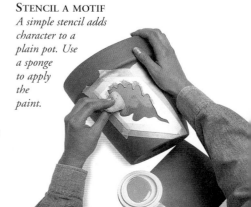

❸ Compost dries out rapidly and plants wilt

A plant in a container is much more susceptible to drought damage than one growing in open ground but provided it is watered as soon as it shows signs of stress, it should recover. If it is allowed to dry out regularly, general vigour, growth and flowering are likely to be affected. When a plant wilts, however, test the compost for dryness first, since there may be a different cause.

Check moisture levels

The best way to test compost for moisture is to insert a finger beneath the surface and check how dry it feels a few centimetres down. If a plant has wilted but the compost feels reasonably moist, check for other possible factors.

Material effects

Any pot made from a porous material, such as terracotta, tends to lose water through evaporation. Glazed or varnished containers, or those made from plastic or wood, lose far less moisture from their surfaces. In addition, dark-coloured containers absorb more heat than those of a pale colour. As a result, the temperature of the compost rises, moisture loss is increased and roots at the edge of the root ball may be damaged.

Planting tricks

Before planting up a container with a porous surface, you could line the inside with polythene or bubble-wrap plastic, taking special care not to obscure any drainage holes. Either material will greatly decrease water loss through evaporation, and bubble-wrap will also provide insulation against heat and cold and help to reduce possible

DAMPEN CLAY
Thoroughly moisten terracotta pots, inside and out, before planting up. This helps to prevent the clay from drawing water out of the compost, which then remains moist for longer.

Granules absorb water then release it later

ADD WATER-RETAINING GRANULES TO COMPOST

damage to roots on the edge of the root ball. You could also simply give the inside of a clay pot a coat of clear water-resistant varnish so that it loses its porosity. This may need renewing when plants are next repotted.

Ensure that you leave sufficient space between the pot rim and surface of the compost. This usually means a gap of 1–2.5cm (½–1in). Without it, moisture, whether from rain or watering by hand, will not have time to sink into the compost and penetrate to the roots before it starts to spill over the sides.

If you are planting up a long-term container with a shrub or small tree, it may be worth inserting a small pipe at planting time so that one end is

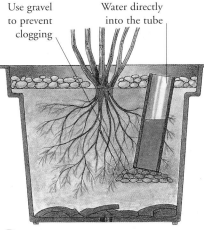

Use gravel to prevent clogging

Water directly into the tube

PIPED WATER
A tube or short length of hose will channel water to roots. A handful of gravel prevents it becoming blocked by compost at the base.

just above the compost surface and the other end is down by the roots. This allows you to direct the water to where the plant needs it most.

Water-retaining granules

Mixing moisture-retaining granules evenly into the compost helps it to retain water for a slightly longer period than normal. These granules are likely to be already incorporated into compost specially formulated for use in containers. This also generally contains wetting agents to make it easier to re-moisten if it dries out (*see also p.103*).

Mulch the surface

Adding a layer of mulch will help to conserve moisture. Ideally, the mulch should be decorative, perhaps pebbles, interestingly shaped stones, fir cones, seashells or even glass marbles. The compost must be moist when you add the mulch. Mulching also cuts down surface weed growth and helps to prevent vine weevils from laying their eggs in the compost.

Go automatic

If you have a collection of containers, or would like to cut down on time spent watering, consider installing a small automatic trickle irrigation system. Drippers release water into individual containers, though for large pots with lots of plants you may need two or more. If you can, get adjustable drippers which allow you to vary the flow. Such systems are not particularly expensive or difficult to install and are quite easy to camouflage.

Other causes of wilting

When leaves wilt, do not rule out the possibility of overwatering, since it can be a sign that roots have become waterlogged. Make sure there are sufficient drainage holes and that they are not clogged with compost or debris. Pest damage, including attack by vine weevil grubs (*see p.98*), is another likely cause.

④ A wooden container is getting shabby and disintegrating

Wood is one of the most sympathetic materials for plant containers but also needs the most care if it is not to deteriorate.

Buy treated timber

Before buying, check that a wooden container has been properly weatherproofed. It should have either been pressure-treated (tanalized) with timber preservative or painted or varnished on all surfaces, inside and out. An exception is when you buy half-barrels which have been used for storing sherry. The alcohol seems to act as a timber preservative and these barrels are also often made from hardwood that is less inclined to rot. Also check that the base has sufficient holes to allow free drainage and so make the container less likely to rot.

Fit a new base

If the rest of the container is sound but the base has started to rot, it may be worth fitting a new one. You will obviously have to use pressure-treated timber, cut it to shape and drill drainage holes. Use metal angle brackets to attach it to the sides.

Keep water from wood

If a wooden container is particularly precious, use a plastic pot for the actual planting and stand it inside the

LINE TUBS WITH PLASTIC TO PREVENT ROT

container. Putting a barrier between moist compost and wood should dramatically decrease the rate of deterioration. Make sure, however, that there is still free drainage. Alternatively, line the container with polythene, perhaps a black plastic bin liner. Again, puncture it with plenty of drainage holes, or you will be creating a miniature bog garden.

Find some feet

Stand containers on feet, if these are not an integral part of the design, to aid drainage. This helps to prevent debris accumulating around the base which impedes drainage and encourages rot. You can use decorative feet, specially designed for the purpose, or bricks. If tucked under the tub they need not be too apparent.

Barrel care

Although the wood used in barrels is usually pretty durable, the metal hoops do sometimes deteriorate. Periodically brushing down with a wire brush to remove rust, then painting with anti-rust paint followed by something more decorative, is the best solution.

When choosing a new half-barrel, try to get one that really has been used for storing alcohol since it is likely to last longer than an imitation designed purely for plants. Real barrels don't always have drainage holes so, if necessary, these must be drilled before planting up. Making the holes, even with the aid of an electric drill, can be difficult, and it may take one person to hold the barrel while another wields the drill.

BRUSH OFF RUST FROM METAL BARREL HOOPS

⑤ A shrub is too big and cumbersome to pot on

Given care and attention, most plants can be grown in containers, at least for a certain length of time. A large plant, though, needs frequent maintenance to keep it happy in a confined space, especially when both plant and pot are of a size that makes potting on tricky.

AVOID BACK STRAIN
Use a board fitted with castors, or a trolley or sack truck when lifting or manoeuvring large, heavy containers, and make sure that you get help if you need it.

Feed and top-dress

Regular pruning should keep the top-growth of a shrub or tree in check and also help to restrain root growth. Plants will also need to be fed and watered on a regular basis. Top-dressing every spring or autumn will allow you to grow a large plant in the same pot for several years, without potting on. Remove the top few centimetres of compost, along with any weeds and weed seeds that may be lurking in it, and replace it with a mixture of good fresh compost mixed

with a little general fertilizer. For the long term, incorporate some controlled-release fertilizer granules.

RENEW COMPOST
Take care not to damage surface roots when scraping away the top layer of old compost.

⑥ What makes leaves turn an unhealthy shade of yellow?

There are a number of reasons why foliage on plants growing in containers might start to turn yellow. It is important, therefore, to try to pinpoint the cause of the problem in order to find the remedy.

SIGNS OF LIME-INDUCED CHLOROSIS

Reaction to lime

An acid-loving plant that cannot tolerate a lot of lime in the soil may start to turn yellow if it has not been planted in lime-free compost. When plants are suffering from lime-induced chlorosis they generally show the most intense symptoms on the younger, smaller leaves. The old foliage remains a good green colour for much longer. The yellowing is also concentrated between the veins, so that the leaves may take on an almost striped appearance. When growing acid-loving plants such as rhododendrons, many heathers, camellias or pieris, use a lime-free compost, often labelled ericaceous compost. If you have used the wrong type, repot as soon as possible.

Poor nourishment

Occasionally general nutrient deficiency may cause yellowing of leaves, so it is important to feed container-grown plants regularly. Which fertilizer to use and the frequency of application depend on the type of plant, its size and that of its container, plus time of year. Generally speaking, feeds can be given during the growing period, mainly from early or mid-spring through to midsummer. Do not feed long-term plants such as shrubs too late in the season, especially with high-nitrogen fertilizers, since this may encourage soft growth that will be prone to damage by cold winter weather.

Controlled-release fertilizer granules are simple to add at planting time and should keep a plant correctly fed for about six months. These granules release most fertilizer when compost is moist and warm, just when the plant is needing it for growth, and least in cool and/or dry conditions. Liquid fertilizers are often the easiest to apply to plants in containers. However, these may be insufficient where a large, well-established plant has been growing strongly for some time, and you may need to apply an annual top-dressing.

Nutrient deficiencies

Deficiencies of nitrogen or magnesium cause yellowing in leaves (*see p.22*). Nitrogen deficiency, seen as a general bright yellow, is relatively uncommon in container plants and is easily put right by applying a high-nitrogen feed. Magnesium deficiency is more common, since magnesium is rapidly leached or washed from compost with regular watering. It is seen as a concentrated yellowing around the leaf edges and between the veins. The yellowing is invariably most serious on older leaves because, if in short supply, the magnesium is moved from these into the new growth.

Magnesium deficiency can quickly be cured by a foliar application of Epsom salts. Make a solution at the rate of 150–200g (5–8oz) salts to 10 litres (2½ gallons) of water, adding a few drops of washing-up liquid to act as a wetting agent. If you are also feeding plants with a high-potash fertilizer to encourage flowering, this tends to increase the likelihood of magnesium deficiency developing.

Avoid concrete containers

Concrete containers may gradually leach lime into the compost causing it to become more alkaline over a period of years. They are best avoided for lime-hating plants but one way around the problem is to line the container with polythene, puncturing it first with plenty of drainage holes.

Don't trust tap water

In hard water areas, tap water tends to have a high lime content. Initially this may not seem to have any adverse effect on lime-hating plants in containers, but over time it will gradually make compost more alkaline and plants may start to show signs of distress. The pH changes much more readily in the confines of a container because of the small volume of compost and the fact that the roots are confined within a small space. Wherever possible, water lime-hating plants with rainwater, but that said, do remember that it is better for a plant to receive some water than none at all. The effects of one or two waterings with hard tap water are unlikely to be of significance, whereas the effects of drought can be fatal.

Too much moisture

Excessive watering and/or poor drainage can result in leaf yellowing, which is generally widespread throughout the plant and accompanied by dramatic leaf loss. Check that there are sufficient drainage holes before planting and add more if necessary. It is usually possible to melt or drill holes in new containers (wear safety goggles). Also check that existing holes are not blocked.

DRILL DRAINAGE HOLES IF NECESSARY

7 The patio could do with some off-season interest

Many people use containers purely to house displays of summer flowers and for the rest of the year the pots are left empty. This is a wasted opportunity if you can see the patio or terrace from inside the house.

Underplant to add colour

Shrubs or small trees can be underplanted with seasonal displays of bulbs. Miniature varieties fit in particularly well and do not have a lot of deteriorating foliage to cope with after the flowers have faded. Bulbs such as snowdrops, early crocuses and winter aconites bring colour at the end of winter. With spring-flowering bulbs, the potential is huge, especially using the many varieties of miniature narcissi, crocuses and miniature iris, such as *Iris reticulata*.

Cyclamen are useful either side of winter. *Cyclamen coum* flowers from late winter and has lovely marbled or silver leaves. *C. hederifolium* flowers in autumn. Its leaves unfold later. Mix the bulbs with an ivy or periwinkle (*Vinca minor*) and perhaps some bedding plants such as pansies and primulas.

CLEAR HARMONY
In spring, narcissi bring fresh colour to a long-term planting. Later, they can be replaced by some summer bedding.

Let the show go on from autumn to spring

You can either plant up a few containers specifically to bring colour to the leaner months — for instance a mixture of spring bulbs or, for autumn, some dazzling pink nerines — or you can plan an arrangement containing some plants to extend the season of interest. Choose those with a long flowering season, such as gazanias and felicias, or that flower late in the year, such as dwarf rudbeckias. Deadhead them regularly and the display should continue until the first frosts. Small evergreen shrubs, such as variegated euonymus or box, are invaluable in winter for their leaf colour or because they can be clipped into neat shapes. Check that any variegated ivy you plan to use is fully hardy. Remember that in a deep pot, bulbs can be planted in layers, allowing you to fit plenty in and also extend flowering. Put the larger bulbs such as daffodils and tulips at the lower levels.

RUDBECKIA HIRTA
'RUSTIC DWARFS'

GAZANIA
'CHANSONETTE'

EUONYMUS FORTUNEI
'EMERALD 'N' GOLD'

HEDERA HELIX
'EVA'

OTHER CHOICES

LATE SUMMER AND AUTUMN

Coreopsis, some
Colchicum
Autumn-flowering crocuses
Hebe, some
Nerine, especially *N. bowdenii*
Pelargoniums
Sedum

WINTER AND EARLY SPRING

Bellis perennis (double daisies)
Box, especially *Buxus sempervirens* 'Marginata'
Ornamental brassicas
Erica carnea (winter heath)
Gaultheria mucronata (use small plants)
Hellebores, such as *H. foetidus*
Leucojum vernum (spring snowflake)
Winter-flowering pansies
Skimmia japonica 'Rubella' (use small plants)
Tulips

8 Harsh new terracotta needs toning down

Handsome though terracotta is, brand new pots can sometimes look stark and orange compared with the mellow tones of old clay containers covered with lichens.

Speed up the years

The quickest way to give a new pot the patina of age is to paint the surface with liquid manure (farmyard manure mixed with water) or plain yoghurt. Use a stiff brush and aim to get a fairly even coating all over the outside and inner rim. Both materials attract the growth of algae, then lichens and mosses. Apply the manure or yoghurt to a new pot before planting, since the dry surface will absorb the solution more readily than a pot that contains damp compost.

AGEING PROCESS
A coating of yoghurt helps to speed up ageing by attracting lichens and mosses to colonize the clay surface.

⑨ A death on the patio

When a plant suddenly collapses for no obvious reason, the answer often lies at its roots. Or the plant may simply have starved to death.

Vine weevil victim

The most common cause of plants in containers suddenly dying is attack by vine weevil grubs. Top-growth collapses because the grubs have eaten the plant's roots. Some gritty or scratchy mulches (which will also deter slugs and snails, *see below*) help to prevent the female laying her eggs in the compost, or you could also try a compost containing chemicals which are reckoned to keep vine weevils at bay for a year. These are particularly useful when planting up containers with annual bedding, but will obviously only provide a temporary solution for long-term plantings. The use of anti-vine weevil chemicals or, better still, anti-vine weevil biological control (best used in early to mid-spring or in early autumn) should prevent problems, but both need to be repeated on a regular basis. (*See also p.183.*)

LOOK FOR VINE WEEVIL GRUBS IN THE COMPOST

Poor drainage

If there are insufficient drainage holes, or the holes are blocked, compost soon becomes waterlogged and plant roots may start to die back. This will not be apparent at first, but once a certain proportion of root has died, top-growth suddenly suffers and the plant may appear to die "overnight".

Lack of nutrients

If a plant has been in a container for a long time and never fed, it could simply have used up all the nutrients in the compost and run out of steam. It is important to feed plants in pots regularly. The best time is from early or mid-spring until midsummer, but continue feeding bedding until late summer to help prolong its season. Trees and shrubs, however, should not be fed past midsummer, or the soft new growth that the fertilizer encourages may be hit by late frosts. To some extent, easily applied liquid feeds allow you to cater to particular needs – if, for instance, you are trying to encourage flowering, a high-potash fertilizer (tomato feed, for instance) is especially suitable.

Dangers of over-potting

When potting or repotting a plant, it is a false economy to try to save time by using a container several sizes bigger than the original. Even if you tease out the root ball slightly, the roots will take time to grow and make use of all the extra compost, which will remain wet and/or cold and may cause roots to rot. Use a container that is one or, at most, two sizes larger. If you have set your heart on using a particularly attractive but too-large container, put your plant in the correct size pot and stand it inside.

Exposure to cold

In winter, plant roots in containers are subject to far lower temperatures than if in open ground. It is common in particularly harsh weather for the root ball, or at least part of it, to get frozen. If this happens, large areas of root, or the entire root system, may be killed, although this will not be obvious until spring when the plant fails to shoot, or comes into growth but suddenly dies back. Protect vulnerable plants (*see opposite, top*).

⑩ Hole-ridden plant foliage

Growing a snail- or slug-prone plant such as a hosta in a container often reduces the amount of damage to leaves but it does not eliminate it. It does, however, make taking protective measures easier, although little can be done to deter caterpillars, which are best picked off.

> **WEEVIL VALUE**
> Because they prevent access to the compost, bands of Vaseline or non-setting glue should deter not only slugs and snails but also vine weevils from laying their eggs (*see above*).

Create a slug barrier

Slugs and snails can simply climb up the sides of a container, across the compost and onto the plant, and if leaves are touching the pot rim, their progress is made even smoother. To stop them, try spreading a continuous band of non-setting glue (available from pest-control specialists and some garden centres) or Vaseline around the outside of the pot. Make sure you cover the entire circumference and leave no gaps. Keep the band clear of debris or leaves which could act as "bridges" and renew it as necessary.

Self-adhesive copper strips provide a longer-term solution. Copper contains a natural electronic charge and even a thin strip around the circumference of the pot will make an effective barrier and makes handling the pot easier than glue or Vaseline.

Uncomfortable mulches

A mulch of sharp grit, crushed egg shells or cocoa shells seems to have some effect in deterring slugs. If any foliage is touching the rim, however, slugs or snails have easy access and the mulch will have little effect.

⓫ In need of winter protection

It is essential that plants grown in containers in exposed positions or which will be subjected to low temperatures are given some sort of protection in the coldest months.

Insulate roots

In most instances, it is a plant's roots that are the most prone to damage, although obviously in some cases the top-growth will need protecting, too (*see The Garden in Winter, p.00*). An unobtrusive way of insulating a root ball is to line the insides of the container with one or two layers of bubble-wrap plastic before planting. If a plant is already in its pot, tie bubble-wrap or other material such as hessian or even an old pair of curtains around the outside. Frost is more

PROTECTIVE BUBBLE-WRAP
Use a lining of plastic to insulate plant roots against cold weather, but make sure it does not block any drainage holes.

likely to harm roots where compost is very damp, so it is often best to keep containers on the dry side in winter.

Move to winter quarters

Sometimes, the container can simply be moved to a more sheltered corner of the garden or patio, or a collection of pots can be grouped around it to provide insulation. Better still, move the container into an unheated greenhouse, conservatory or porch. Another good solution is to plunge or bury the pot up to its rim in a spare patch of ground for the winter.

Wrap foliage

The top-growth of plants such as phormiums can be protected by a sheath of bubble-wrap polythene, but check that air can still circulate or fungal disease may develop. Temporary foliage protection will also help to prevent damage by cold wind.

⓬ Toppling containers

If young children use the garden, large pots that fall over could be dangerous, and at the very least it is disappointing if plants, or the pot itself, get broken.

The right size pot?

A tall plant, such as a mophead bay tree, in a small container may look attractive, but in gusty winds the pot is likely to fall over. Make sure that your pot is the right size for the plant, with the weight of the top-growth balanced by the weight of the container and compost. If you cannot or do not want to move the plant from its existing pot, try standing it inside a slightly larger, more stable planter.

Add weight

Composts based on soil or loam are considerably heavier than those based on bark, coir or peat. If a loam-based compost is unsuitable for the plant, or stays too heavy and damp, mix it 50:50 with peat-free compost. Adding grit improves drainage and also adds weight, as does a gravel or pebble moisture-conserving mulch.

⓭ Deterrents against theft

Expensive containers, just like statues, sundials and other garden ornaments, can be an easy target for garden thieves.

Bolts and spikes

Where a container stands on a hard surface you could fit a wall bolt through the container and into the paving. Both the paving and the base of the container would need to be drilled and then either end of the bolt fixed into position using a wall plug. Other garden ornaments could be secured in much the same way or even cemented into place at the base. Valuable items that are marked with your postcode are easier to trace and claim should they be recovered.

Weighty containers may deter opportunistic thieves, so putting a heavy layer of stones in the base at planting time may give some protection. A less permanent but highly effective deterrent is to plant up the container with a yucca or similarly spiky plant so that no burglar would want to handle it.

PLANTS WITH PRICKLES

Agave	*Ilex* (holly), good as
Chaenomeles	a standard
(flowering quince)	mophead
Crataegus	*Pyracantha*, small-
(hawthorn),	growing cultivars
clipped to shape	*Yucca*

TOO HARD TO HANDLE
Agaves have vicious spikes at the tips of the leaves that would deter all but the most determined garden burglar.

HANGING BASKETS AND WINDOWBOXES

SPARSE PLANTING
The planting looks inadequate and has never filled out. **15**

STRAGGLY PLANTS
Plants have become straggly and withered and stopped flowering. **15**

LOST COMPOST
Compost has a tendency to fall out through the basket liner. **14**

PRECARIOUS WINDOWBOX
Inadequate fixings fail to keep a windowbox securely in place on the sill. **16**

THE PROBLEMS

14 A hanging basket is shedding its compost.

15 The planting looks mean and sparse, and plants have become straggly and stopped flowering.

16 A windowbox needs to be made more secure.

17 How can watering a hanging basket be made less of a chore?

See also:

1–**13** Pots, tubs and planters, p.92.

Annuals and Bedding, p.40; Rooftops and Balconies, p.130; Choosing Fertilizers, p.158; Pests, Diseases and Disorders, p.178.

14 Compost is constantly being lost from a hanging basket

If a basket keeps shedding its compost, the liner is invariably at fault, especially if it is made of moss.

The right liner

When lining a basket with a material such as moss, pack it in really densely, making it at least 2.5cm (1in) thick. On the whole, the thicker the layer of moss the better. Placing an inner liner between the compost and moss will also help to prevent leakage. If you use polythene, perhaps from an old compost bag or a black bin liner, puncture it with plenty of holes so that drainage is not impeded. Old capillary matting can also be used to good effect. Choosing a purpose-designed liner such as one made from reconstituted paper, coir or recycled wool with a polythene backing will

also help. Or recycle an old, suitably coloured jumper. This will contain the compost well and, provided the basket is well planted, no one need know what lurks

beneath. Don't make the planting slits too large. If you are worried about damaging the plants as you poke them through when planting up, wrap a sleeve of plastic around the foliage to protect it (*see overleaf*).

Winter insulation

For winter plantings, choose a really thick liner which will both keep compost in and provide a good degree of insulation so that plant roots are less likely to be damaged by low temperatures. Coir matting liners are particularly suitable, as are a couple of layers of recycled woollen jumper.

RECYCLING OPPORTUNITY
An old woollen jumper makes an excellent hanging basket liner. Trim it to fit and use two layers if necessary.

⑮ Sparse-looking basket with straggly plants and few flowers

To look good, hanging baskets need to overflow with foliage and flowers, so it is essential to pack them with as many plants as you can. Provided the basket is kept well watered and fed, the plants will survive with only a small quantity of compost separating each root ball. Unfortunately, unless plants are tended regularly, they can easily dwindle to a few trailing stems with no sign of a flower bud.

Give plants a good start

Make sure that plants are well established before you hang the basket in place. Once planted up, leave it in a frost-free spot, protected from extremes of sunshine and wind, for at least a week, preferably two or three. This allows the compost to settle around roots, and the roots to start taking up moisture and nutrients before risk of being buffeted by wind. It will also give you a chance to see if there are any gaps in the planting or if thin areas develop in the liner. Don't skimp on the number of plants you use. Although plants will fill out to some degree, a meanly planted basket usually continues to look that way. (*See overleaf for some planting tips.*)

Pinch out tips

Many plants need to have their tips pinched out on a regular basis. Without this, growth is liable to

LOBELIA EXTRAVAGANZA
If you make use of their wide colour range, you could dedicate a basket to lobelias alone, especially if you mix bush and trailing types. It is essential to keep lobelias well watered.

become straggly. With some trailing plants, such as helichrysum and catmint (*Nepeta*), it is worth taking the scissors or shears to them once they have started to grow too long, as this will encourage stems to branch.

Ways with lobelias

Where planted around the sides of a hanging basket, trailing lobelias often start to look rather straggly by the middle of summer. To prevent this, alternate trailing and bush forms. As the bush lobelias develop, they help to hide the gaps created by the long, somewhat thin growth of the trailing plants. Although normally you might choose the same colour for both types of lobelia, you could instead make a feature of this method and use contrasting colours.

Feeding and light

Unless you have chosen suitable plants for a shady site, lack of sunlight encourages a straggly appearance, as does inadequate watering (*see p.103*). Some plants, particularly lobelias, will start to become straggly with the slightest stress from drought, but can usually be revitalized by trimming back, watering and feeding. Most proprietary composts contain

sufficient fertilizer for plants to grow well for a few weeks, but after that they will need supplementary feeding, especially if the basket is packed with plants. This could be in the form of controlled-release granules added at planting time or a high-potash fertilizer applied at least once a week while plants are being watered.

Keep on deadheading

Regular deadheading is even more important for plants in containers than for those in flower beds, because in containers they tend to be growing under more stressful conditions. Pinch out flowers as soon as they start to fade to prevent the plant wasting energy on seed formation and to encourage it to produce more flower buds.

CUT BACK LONG, STRAGGLING STEMS

DEADHEAD AS FREQUENTLY AS POSSIBLE

16 Precarious windowbox is insecurely fixed

If a windowbox is not to be a hazard, it must be securely fitted using a method that suits the style of window. If the window overlooks a pavement, provide a drip tray to catch any water that might otherwise fall onto passers-by below.

Fixing methods

If a box is to be fixed so that it hangs beneath a window (a casement-style window, for instance) you will need brackets fixed to the wall and the base of the box. Galvanized metal, L-shaped brackets, available from DIY stores, are ideal for this, unless you pefer something more decorative. You will also need wall plugs to hold the screws, and make sure that the brackets are screwed into brick rather than mortar, or they may work loose. Use at least two brackets each side of the windowbox. Always choose galvanized fixtures and fittings and/or brass screws which will not rust.

Small boxes that sit on the sill of a sash window could have slotted mirror plates attached to them which will fit over hooks screwed into the window-frame. For extra safety, screw metal eyelets into either side of the window recess and attach a length of fine chain or wire to the eyelets to hold the box in place. This is a useful method for terracotta troughs or

other materials that cannot be drilled. The plants' foliage should hide the chain or wire from view.

If the windowsill slopes, put wedges beneath the box so that it sits in a horizontal position. This will also help to ensure good drainage from the base of the box. If windowboxes are above a doorway or access route, fit a drip tray underneath.

Keeping in good repair

Wooden windowboxes, like wooden garden furniture, need maintenance, usually in the form of a coat of preservative every year or two. Boxes that have been painted will, from time to time, need rubbing down and repainting. At the same time, take the opportunity to check all fixtures and fittings and ensure that these are still in good condition, so that the box will stay firmly attached. The regular application of paint or wood preservatives may seem like an irritating chore, but remember that it gives you a chance to alter the colour of the windowbox as well as improving its appearance and helping to prolong its life.

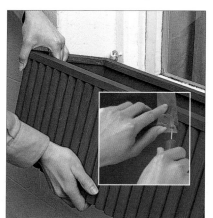

SIMPLE BUT SECURE
Slotted mirror plates, fixed to the back of a box (inset), can be slipped over hooks screwed into a wooden window-frame.

TIPS FOR PLANTING A SUCCESSFUL HANGING BASKET

- **AVOID MAKING** over-large planting slits in the liner, which increase the chance of it shedding both compost and water.
- **SIT THE BASKET** on a flowerpot while you plant it up. Put a layer of compost in the bottom, then start to add the first plants that will trail through the sides.
- **WRAP THE FOLIAGE** of each plant in a sleeve of polythene or paper to protect it as you push it through the basket liner from inside to out. After putting in the first layer of plants, add more compost to cover the root balls.
- **PACK IN** plenty of plants but make sure each root ball is surrounded by some compost. Finish by inserting the more upright plants in the top of the basket.
- **LEAVE A GAP** for watering of at least 2.5cm (1in) between the surface of the compost and the top of the basket liner. Water the plants in well.

PROTECT FOLIAGE WHEN PLANTING

⑰ How can watering be made less of a chore?

It is essential that compost is never allowed to dry out. Although it is possible to revive plants to some extent, if it happens regularly or is particularly severe, the plants will never fully recover.

Reduce moisture loss

A saucer or circle of polythene in the base of the basket helps to prevent water escaping before the compost has had a chance to absorb it. Thick liners such as those made from coir or polythene-backed wool help to insulate against high temperatures and so also cut down on moisture loss. When lining a basket, make sure that the liner protrudes at least 2.5cm (1in) above the compost surface, so that water does not run straight off the surface but has time to reach plant roots.

Adding water-retaining granules to the compost will certainly help. The granules absorb and hold onto moisture and then later release it into the surrounding compost. Follow the instructions on the pack as to whether the granules should be added dry or ready-moistened. Do not add more than the recommended amount. Some special container composts have these granules already incorporated. Moisture-retaining mulches can also be used to good effect. A lightweight material, such as cocoa shell, is often best but, if the bracket is secure and sturdy, you could use more ornamental small pebbles.

PULLEY MECHANISM
A pulley which allows you to lower and raise and lock the basket in position makes it easy to water and tend to plants.

HOSE ATTACHMENT
A purpose-designed lance which can be fitted to a garden hose simplifies watering.

Arrange easy access

Although a little unsightly, a pulley makes it easy to lower a basket that is awkward to reach and does away with the need for stepladders, a natural deterrent to watering.

Natural survivors

Choosing relatively drought-resistant plants such as those with silver foliage, like *Helichrysum petiolare*, *Cineraria maritima* and ornamental thymes and sages, plus of course pelargoniums, also increases the chances of the hanging basket staying in good condition even if the compost is allowed to dry out slightly.

Create a reservoir

You can buy specially designed reservoirs that channel water to the plants' roots. Insert them when planting. Alternatively, a small plastic flowerpot, stood the right way up, works in the same way, allowing water to dribble through the drainage holes close to the roots.

Revival method

If a basket has dried out completely but you think there is a good chance that the plants could be revived, remove it as soon as possible to a shady place. Water the surface gently using a watering can with the rose attached. Then, once the water has penetrated slightly (after about 10 minutes), try plunging the entire basket in a large tray or bucket of water. Lower the basket gently to avoid displacing plants and compost and leave it until the compost is thoroughly moistened and any bubbling has stopped. Support the basket on a large flowerpot in a cool, relatively shady, out-of-the-way spot, so that the plants have plenty of time to recover before being put back into stressful bright sunlight.

EXTREME HEAT
In very hot weather, it is worth moving a basket temporarily to a shadier, cooler area. Either have a bracket ready in place or simply support the basket on a large flowerpot.

DRAINAGE IN PLASTIC LININGS
An inner layer of plastic in a straw- or moss-lined manger or basket helps to prevent water loss but must be given drainage holes.

GARDEN FURNITURE

THE ENORMOUS RANGE of outdoor furniture now available – giving an ever-increasing selection of styles to choose from – makes buying garden chairs and tables something of a challenge. In turn, the different materials used in their manufacture all vary in their maintenance requirements. If your choice has already been made, you may now be finding that the furniture you acquired several years ago is starting to look the worse for wear and in need of renovation.

Q *Which is the best material for furniture that has to remain outside throughout the year?*

A Metal is a good choice, although rusting and flaking paint may pose a slight problem. You should be able to find either traditional or modern designs to suit your taste. If you want something lightweight go for aluminium, since it will not rust. If you can afford it, however, one of the hardwoods will last well and require only occasional maintenance.

Plastic or resin is generally cheaper than wood and metal furniture and has the bonus that it will be relatively unaffected by wet weather. Both materials are lightweight, and many plastic chairs are designed to stack neatly, useful in a garden where space is at a premium.

Whatever you choose, it will weather in some way but, on the whole, hardwoods and aluminium seem to age rather more gracefully than most other materials.

Q *Are there any guidelines when it comes to choosing an appropriate style?*

A Go for a look that will fit in with the surroundings (both house and garden) as well as suiting your purposes. Classic designs have the advantage of being less likely to look dated. Bright colours can be a distraction if your main purpose for being in the garden is to enjoy the plants and peaceful surroundings. You may also find you tire of flamboyant patterns on cushions or parasols. In the end, the most important thing is to make sure that furniture is well-built, designed to last, and that you really want it in your garden.

Q *Cast-iron nineteenth-century-style chairs and tables look wonderful in the garden but are extremely heavy and awkward to move around. Are there any lighter alternatives?*

A Powder-coated aluminium could be the answer as it is strong, looks very similar to its heavier cousins, but is only a fraction of the weight. It is becoming more readily available, often in interesting colours, and has the added advantage of not rusting when left outdoors.

Q *If a wooden bench is still in good condition, but some of the screws holding it together are badly rusted, what can you do?*

A Poor quality rust-prone fixings are often the downfall of garden furniture. Replace any rusting screws or bolts before the bench starts to fall apart using galvanized metal or brass screws that will not rust. In future, if you buy a similar piece of furniture, check that it has good quality fixings before you buy. This is particularly important if the furniture has to be regularly folded up. If areas of wood also start to deteriorate, it is possible on some styles of seat or bench to replace the occasional slat.

Q *If garden loungers are too bulky to bring inside, how can you protect them over winter?*

A You can buy zip-up or tie-on waterproof covers for garden furniture; these should help to keep the worst of the winter weather from damaging furniture that has to stay outdoors.

However, outdoor cushions or fabric covers are best removed if you are not using them for a while. Sun as well as winter wet can ruin them. Wrap them in polythene (first ensuring they are completely dry), then store in a dry place. Before you buy, check that covers and cushions can be removed for ease of storing and cleaning.

Q *Are there any advantages to choosing wooden garden furniture? And is buying hardwood furniture compatible with being environmentally friendly?*

A Wooden furniture has character, and the way it ages is attractive and unobtrusive in any garden setting. Even when rather old and decrepit, it has a certain charm. Most garden furniture needs to be of a medium weight – heavy enough to withstand the wind, but not too difficult to move around. In extremely hot or cold weather, a wooden seat is unlikely to be either uncomfortably hot or cold to sit on, a problem that often affects metal, plastic or resin furniture. As long as you choose something that has been reasonably sturdily constructed and maintain it properly, it should give you good service for many years.

Some hardwood furniture is still made from non-renewable sources. However, environmentally friendly companies now use timber produced from managed forests, where regular and suitable replanting takes place: their timber is clearly labelled as such. The best thing you can do is check the packaging of any potential purchase thoroughly. Bear in mind that hardwood furniture is definitely longer-lasting and easier to maintain than softwood.

Q *Is any special preparation needed before treating wooden furniture with a preservative and what is the best way to apply it?*

A It is essential that the furniture is completely dry when you treat it so, if necessary, move it into a shed or garage to allow it to dry off first. Remove any surface algal or other growth with a wire brush to create an absolutely clean surface. If the wood still appears very dirty, sand it down lightly. Follow the instructions on the packaging to the letter.

The feet of garden tables and chairs inevitably stand in water from time to time so these require extra-special attention. Clean them off thoroughly, then stand each leg in a saucer or small pot of preservative for several hours or overnight to ensure this rot-susceptible area is thoroughly protected against the weather.

Q *Wooden garden furniture sometimes turns a slight silvery colour. Does this mean there's a problem?*

A Some hardwoods, in particular teak, do take on a silvery sheen as they weather. There is no need to worry. This can look rather attractive but if you wish to preserve the original colour, and indeed further preserve the life of the timber, regularly rub in some teak oil, especially after furniture has stood outside during the winter.

Q *Some small disc-shaped fungi are growing out of a patch of rotting wood on an old table. How can they be controlled?*

A This is likely to be a fungus known as the many-zoned polypore, *Coriolus versicolor*, though there are many different fungi which you may find growing on rotting wood, both on garden furniture and on fallen branches or tree stumps. Their appearance indicates that furniture has been neglected and is in need of urgent attention.

Remove the fungal growth, together with any rotted wood, paring back the timber until it is completely sound. Fill small areas with plastic-wood or wood-filler. If large sections have become badly rotted they should be replaced if they make the furniture at all unsafe. Apply a timber treatment when you have finished patching up, to lessen the chances of these fungi reappearing.

Q *Is there a way of revamping sound but boring, faded wooden garden furniture?*

A Consider applying a coloured wood treatment. A wide range of tinted stains, containing wood

preservative, is currently available. You can also use these stains on fencing, trellis and other wooden garden features, making it easy to colour-coordinate your garden if you wish. Be sure you clean and prepare the surface thoroughly first.

Q *Is it okay to apply a fresh coat of paint to some metal furniture covered in old flaking paint? What is the best way of making sure that the new paint doesn't start flaking, too?*

A Yes, it can be repainted, but prepare the surface well first. Start by removing all paint flakes and rust with a wire brush. Choose paint that is specially formulated for use on metal; never use ordinary household paint. Follow the manufacturer's instructions for priming and application, allowing each coat to dry thoroughly before applying the next one. Carry out the work in a dry, well-ventilated, dust-free environment.

Q *What are the grey, pale green and yellow circular patches – some crusty, others almost leafy – that frequently appear on wooden surfaces?*

A Lichens of various types appear on many surfaces (including stones, walls and paving). Although they may look rather alarming, they are simply using the furniture as a surface on which to grow. They produce their own food materials and so will not rot the wood. There is no need to remove them and they give furniture a pleasantly weathered look. If you want to be rid of them, however, brush them away with a wire brush. Lichens rarely grow on freshly treated timber, so regular use of wood preservative helps to keep them away.

THE FAMILY GARDEN

IF YOU HAVE A FAMILY it is important that the garden should be a place that all its members can enjoy, whatever their age, and contain areas that are particularly appealing to all who use it. Most adults have no difficulty in supplying whatever is needed for their own recreation and pleasure, but making sure that the garden is a potentially idyllic yet relatively secure place for young children to run around in calls for other considerations. Taking a few basic precautions will help to make the garden a safe place for your own children and young visitors alike.

HAZARDOUS PLANTS
Some plants in the border are very spiky; others are toxic or may irritate skin. **5**

TRAMPLED PLANTS
Flowers frequently get battered and broken during play. **1**

CLUTTERED WITH TOYS
There is no storage space for toys, nor a place for toddlers to play. **3**

SCRUFFY LAWN
The grass receives a lot of hard wear and tear in some areas. **2**

OPEN WATER
A pool with a standing reservoir of water is a danger to children. **5**

❶ Broken and trampled plants

When your prized plants are hit by a football or eager pair of feet just once too often, it can be disheartening to say the least. If you get the children interested in playing a part in creating and looking after the garden they will be less inclined to do any intentional damage, but there will still be accidents.

Grow resilient plants

If you can, grow your most treasured and fragile plants as far away as possible from play areas. Nearby, try instead to grow those plants that are likely to survive the occasional battering. Some of the best are those that reshoot from the base fairly well. Resilient shrubs include viburnums, hypericums, *Kerria japonica*, euonymus, potentilla, philadelphus, dogwoods (*Cornus*), abelia, heaths and heathers (so bouncy they are almost like miniature trampolines), hardy fuchsias and periwinkles (*Vinca*). Some perennials are also tougher than others – try lamiums, bugles (*Ajuga*), hardy herbaceous geraniums, *Alchemilla mollis*, oriental poppies and rudbeckias.

Choose flowers that have child appeal

To encourage children to enjoy and want to look after a garden, try to get them involved by growing some of the plants they enjoy – plants that have faces in their flowers, for instance, or have silky or furry leaves that invite touch. Pansies, antirrhinums, poached egg flowers (*Limnanthes*), daisy-flowered plants such as anthemis and lamb's ears (*Stachys byzantina*) all have child appeal. It is worth growing a few easy annuals from seed (*see p.42*) such as candytuft, nasturtiums, nigella and cornflowers and letting the children help with their sowing and raising. Trying to grow the tallest sunflower in the neighbourhood keeps enthusiasm alive all through summer.

FUCHSIA

ANTHEMIS PUNCTATA

CORNFLOWERS

CANDYTUFT

SUNFLOWERS

STACHYS BYZANTINA

❷ The lawn has become scruffy and worn

It is much easier to make a lawn more hard-wearing if you know before it is laid that it will be used for children's play. Otherwise, try not to let it get too compacted and avoid mowing too short.

Select tough grasses

If you need to patch or renew the lawn (or if you know in advance that you need to create a durable surface) choose hard-wearing turf or grass-seed mixture. These are readily available from the usual suppliers and contain a particularly high proportion of relatively tough grasses, such as rye, which will withstand a fair battering.

Built-in bounce

In areas which receive a lot of hard wear, try pegging a rubber mesh into the soil before seeding or re-seeding. The grasses will grow through, hiding it, but the mesh will make the area less vulnerable. Make sure the pegs are well embedded and could not be a hazard. In some gardens that open to the public, chopped car tyres are incorporated into the base of the turf.

Good maintenance

Keeping the lawn fed, scarified and aerated (*see p.53*) will help to keep it growing well. Regular mowing is also essential, but avoid mowing too closely,

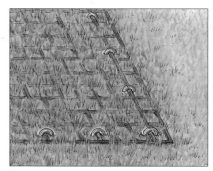
RUBBER MESH REDUCES WEAR AND TEAR

as this makes it more likely to succumb to wear and tear. Try to persuade all members of the household that it is not a good idea to play or even walk on it in frosty or very wet weather.

❸ Play spaces for toddlers

Play equipment can be great fun, but occasional tumbles are almost unavoidable. It is important that equipment is sound and strong and that the surface underneath will provide a safe landing.

Designed for play

Always choose equipment which is sturdily built. On the whole, metal-framed structures are cheaper than wood. If you opt for wood make sure that it has been treated with a non-toxic preservative. Its surface should also be sufficiently smooth for you to be confident that splinters will not be a problem.

Install play equipment in a spot visible from the house windows so that you can keep an eye on children. Keep it well away, too, from toxic or prickly plants. All equipment should carry the EC safety symbol (the letters CE). Systems are available which can be linked together, making them the perfect choice if you want to add to them year on year or change them as the children grow older and perhaps want something a little more adventurous.

SHIPSHAPE SAND PIT
A movable sand pit is useful, especially when it has a lid to keep out rain and pets, and toys can be stowed away inside.

A safe surface

It is essential to make the surface beneath play equipment as safe as possible while also ensuring that it is durable and can be used in all but the worst weather without becoming too muddy. Materials available include play-bark (like normal chipped bark but the pieces have rounded edges) and rubber matting, made from chunks of rubber held together to form a surface which looks a little like Tarmac but is slightly bouncy and much softer to land on. Both are good and although they may raise the cost of installing play equipment are well worth the investment. Play-bark is considerably cheaper and easier to obtain than rubber matting but has a shorter life expectancy and there is a chance that toadstools will grow on it. It is also possible to use tiles made from cork or rubber chippings, but these tend to be even more expensive.

Artificial turf is another option, providing a relatively soft landing and, although somewhat spiky, it is far longer lasting and more resilient than real turf and can tolerate a heavy pounding even in wet weather.

Sand pits

Installing a sand pit will encourage young children to enjoy being in the garden and also help to keep them away from other more fragile areas. Do not use builder's sand, which may be too sharp or caustic and may stain clothes, but instead invest in several bags of special "play sand". Make sure that when not in use the sand pit can be covered with a lid to keep both rain and cats out.

An area where young children can sit or play is essential: grass is perfect, but a plastic-backed mat is useful for days when the grass is damp early in the morning.

❹ A play area of their own

Older children often want to be outside in the garden but not necessarily under the constant gaze of nearby adults.

Screen them off

If you have sufficient space in the garden, the best solution is to create an area with some privacy where the children can go, perhaps by screening off a corner. Trellis planted up with climbers, a bamboo screen (made from canes or the plants themselves) or some palisade fencing will give a degree of privacy – a "den" where they can retreat and still enjoy the fresh air while escaping from adults and younger siblings.

It may be possible to plan such an area into your garden at the outset, while the children are still relatively young, and gradually change the play equipment as their interests and needs develop and change.

A CORNER DEVOTED TO PLAY

⑤ Water, toxic and spiky plants, and other hazards

Parents' anxieties about the dangers of plants may, in some cases, be unduly raised, although it makes obvious sense to train toddlers not to put things in their mouths unless you have told them they can. In a garden, there are also plenty of other features that could prove hazardous to inquisitive young children – especially water.

The dangers of ponds

Small children can drown in less than 5cm (2in) depth of water so it is essential that ponds and other water features with a standing reservoir of water are made safe by placing a galvanized metal grille over the water's surface. If this is fixed firmly around the pond's edge and set just beneath the surface, it should prevent the worst of accidents and yet not be too obtrusive. Alternatively, ponds can be filled in temporarily, perhaps converted into a bog garden or sand pit while children are young and then turned back into a pond once they are older. If a water feature is high on your list of priorities, opt for a bubble fountain or bubble millstone which has no depth to the water. Make sure that electrical fittings and pumps are safe. Preferably, have them installed by a professional. If you opt for a cobblestone fountain, check that there is no way the cobbles can be removed by children which would make the feature unsafe.

If you have a water butt, the lid must be secure. It is worth changing an old butt with a loose-fitting lid for one of the more modern designs with a safety device that prevents children from opening the lid.

Beware of some plants

Many potentially poisonous plants, such as lupins and foxgloves, are in reality unlikely to pose a serious threat because there is little about them that tempts children to eat them. But plants with brightly coloured poisonous berries or inviting dangling pods are a different matter and should be avoided.

Yew and laburnum are both poisonous, although a yew hedge is likely to be cut frequently enough to stop it producing berries. If you are desperate for a laburnum, choose *L. × watereri* 'Vossii' which flowers well but does not set seed. Similarly, be wary of any plants that may irritate skin. Widely grown examples include monkshood, which can have an irritant effect as well as being deadly poisonous, and rue and euphorbia, whose sap can produce an intensely irritant reaction in the presence of sunlight. Nowadays, the majority of plants posing a serious risk are clearly labelled, so check when buying.

SOME PLANTS TO AVOID

TOXIC OR IRRITANT PLANTS

Aconitum (monkshood)	*L. × watereri*
Digitalis (foxglove)	Lupins
Euphorbia	*Ruta graveolens* (rue)
Laburnum, except	*Taxus* (yew)

SPIKES AND PRICKLES

Berberis	*Pyracantha*
Prunus spinosa (blackthorn)	Roses
	Yucca

SAFE WATERS
Millstone fountains, which have no depth of water, are one of the safest options.

Plants covered with spikes, spines or thorns are worth avoiding. Where possible choose thornless roses such as 'Zéphirine Drouhin', 'Goldfinch' and 'Kathleen Harrop'.

If, having assessed the degree of danger, you decide not to eliminate every single problem plant from the garden, do ensure that children are warned of the dangers from the youngest possible age.

Other hazards

Steep slopes, loose steps or walling, and garden tools and machinery can all be hazards so make necessary repairs as soon as problems are noticed and don't leave secateurs and other sharp implements lying around or electrical machinery unattended. Ensure garden ornaments such as sundials, which make tempting objects to climb, are securely anchored in the ground.

Pet problems

If the garden is also used by the family's dog or cat, take great care to ensure that children never come into contact with the animals' faeces. As well as being unpleasant and unhygienic, these can be responsible for serious infections including toxocariasis and toxoplasmosis. Where possible, train your pet to use only certain restricted areas of the garden.

SAFETY GRILLE
Bricks set in mortar on the marginal shelf of a pond hold a wire-mesh barrier in place just below the water's surface.

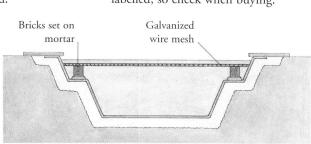

Bricks set on mortar   Galvanized wire mesh

ALLERGIES, ACHES & PAINS

THE GARDEN SHOULD BE a place of solace and relaxation, but today more and more people suffer from asthma, hayfever and allergies and, sadly, being among plants may make these worse.

Gardening can also aggravate difficulties with bad backs or joints affected by arthritis or RSI. Choosing the right plants, tools and techniques can help overcome problems to some degree.

Q *What is it that makes some flowers more likely to cause problems than others?*

A Broadly speaking, the flowers which are less likely to trigger an attack are those which are sterile (hydrangeas, for instance) or those which are pollinated by insects. In comparison with wind-pollinated flowers (such as grasses), insect-pollinated flowers tend to produce relatively small quantities of pollen, and this pollen is heavier and stickier because it is distributed by insects not air currents.

Q *Can you suggest a few plants which are suitable for growing in a low-allergen garden?*

A Among those which you could consider are campanulas, geums, Jacob's ladder (*Polemonium*), roses, weigela, hardy geraniums, hydrangeas, hostas, bergenia, phormiums, fuchsias, viburnums, smoke bush (*Cotinus*), clematis, passion flower (*Passiflora*), lamiums, peonies, periwinkle (*Vinca minor*), bugle (*Ajuga*) and creeping Jenny (*Lysimachia nummularia*).

Q *What are the main plants that should be avoided?*

A Try to avoid using grasses (particularly ornamental ones that are grown for their flowerheads), lilies and chrysanthemums and other plants with daisy flowers.

Q *Is it always the plant's pollen which is to blame?*

A It is often incorrectly assumed that pollen causes all the adverse reactions in sensitive people. However, there are other factors you should consider, particularly dust. The foliage of Leyland cypress tends to act like a dust trap – which is fine until the tree is heavily buffeted or disturbed, when the dust is released in large quantities. Similarly, furry foliage such as that on *Brachyglottis* 'Sunshine' (formerly *Senecio*) collects dust and so should be avoided. To make matters worse, this plant also has those troublesome daisy-like flowers.

Although grasses are often regarded as a major problem because of their pollen, it is worth asking yourself how many grasses are allowed to reach flowering size? In a typical lawn the grass is mown regularly and so flowering and seeding lawn grasses are a rare sight. Yet problems often arise when the lawn is mown. These are, in fact, largely due to the release of a chemical called coumarin from the surfaces of the blades of grass as they are cut.

Fungal spores may also cause problems, so it is wise to keep composting and the use of organic mulches to a minimum. Compost and mulch tend to be rich in the spores of fungi which are breaking these organic materials down. If you are trying to cut down on weeding by laying a mulch, you would be better advised to use ground-cover plants to smother the soil surface.

Q *If you are creating a low-allergen garden is there any reason why you should not include a water feature ?*

A Water features need not be avoided, but try to base your design around water which is slow-moving or static. Then the water will act like a dust trap. Water features such as fountains tend to do the opposite and, by stirring up the surface of the water, may be responsible for allowing even more spores and particles of dust to be released into the air.

Q *When building paths around the garden, what is the best material to use?*

A Paved paths, made from slabs, bricks and pavers, are the best option. Woodland-style paths composed of a thick layer of chipped bark are best avoided since these can often harbour large quantities of fungal spores.

Q *Can the type of material used for a garden's boundaries have an effect?*

A Many types of hedging, especially dense conifers, can act as traps for dust, spores and pollen, which are then readily released when the hedge is disturbed or cut back. A wooden fence or brick wall therefore makes a better choice.

Q **Which weather conditions make allergens more of a problem?**

A Damp, hot days are the ones to avoid being outside in the garden, when pollen and dust tend to hang in the air rather than being blown away. Relatively cool, dull days, when there is a slight breeze, tend to be less likely to cause problems.

Q **What tips do you have for gardeners who are getting stiff in the joints and quickly feel the effects of their labours?**

A If you suffer from a bad back or similar problems, it really is worthwhile doing a few limbering-up exercises to loosen up muscles before embarking on hard physical work. Tackle strenuous jobs, especially lifting, only if you feel sure you are up to them and don't be shy in calling on the help of friends, neighbours or relatives if necessary. Make sure you choose the right tools for the job, and that they are comfortable to use and in good working order. Afterwards, a relaxing warm bath really does help to make you feel better and will also help to relieve muscle tension but wrap up warmly afterwards.

Q **Gardening seems to involve a great deal of bending, which has become painful. How can it be kept to a minimum?**

A Try to reduce the amount of weeding you have to do and other work at ground level. If you can make a thorough job of clearing the ground first, laying landscape fabric on the soil surface and then planting through by cutting cross-shaped slits in the fabric should substantially help to suppress weeds. Either plant plenty of ground-cover shrubs and perennials that will soon hide the fabric, or cover the gaps between plants with a mulch of bark chips, cocoa shells or gravel.

Alternatively, bring the soil closer to you by creating raised beds. If you don't want to get involved in building brick walls, reconditioned railway sleepers or other kinds of timber block look attractive. Make sure old sleepers have been thoroughly cleaned. Even small patches of tar can cause a mess when they melt in hot weather. Drainage needs to be good – if the beds are built on paving, any hard surface at the base must be broken up. If the raised beds have solid walls of brick or stone, you need to build in a few small "weep-holes" towards their base to allow excess water to drain away. Also make sure you build the beds to a comfortable height. Since this will vary with individual requirements, experiment first to find what will be the right height for you so that you don't make problems worse. While you are building raised beds, it might be a good idea to incorporate the occasional seat or bench in the design so that you can take the opportunity to ease aching joints whenever you feel the need.

Q **Tools can be very expensive. What should you look for when buying to make sure they will help not hinder?**

A Spend plenty of time choosing gardening tools and check that they are comfortable to handle. This goes without saying for anyone suffering from arthritis or repetitive strain injury (RSI). Quality varies enormously and since, generally speaking, you get what you pay for, it is often worth going for the best you can afford. Check for the comfort of the grip on spades and forks and try to get a spade with a small ridge, or tread, along the top of the blade as this makes digging easier. Check, too, that the shaft length on larger garden tools is right for you. If you are fairly small, or not particularly strong, consider buying a border fork or spade, as these are lighter in weight than the full-sized versions. Once in regular use, it obviously helps to keep tools well-sharpened and to oil blades frequently.

Comfort with hand tools, such as secateurs, varies greatly from individual to individual. Much depends on the size of your hands and fingers. People who have difficulty gripping may find tools with large padded or spongy hand-grips the most satisfactory, and if you also need to exert pressure, for instance when pruning, a ratchet mechanism may help. When buying secateurs, make sure you can easily undo the safety catch. A few tools on the market have been specially designed for people with problems in gripping. Organisations for arthritis and RSI sufferers may be able to offer advice.

Q **How can you prevent gardening from giving you a bad back or making an existing back problem worse?**

A Avoid lifting heavy containers and bags of compost, grit and suchlike whenever possible by using a trolley or platform on castors. If you have to lift heavy objects, make sure you bend your knees and not your back, and position yourself straight in front of the object so that you avoid twisting your back as you lift. In the same way, if you use a rotary mower, push it back and forth directly in front of you, don't swing it from side to side because this can exacerbate problems for anyone with a weak lower back. Again, make sure tools for digging are the right height for you. It is possible to buy American-style long-handled spades which some tall people find more comfortable to use.

WATER FEATURES

IT IS OFTEN SAID that a garden is incomplete without some sort of water feature. Indeed, the range of ponds, pools, fountains, cascades and spouts is ever on the increase. How can you make sure that you keep yours working well and continuing to add that "touch of magic"? A water feature that has been seriously neglected can look (and sometimes smell) awful and could even be dangerous, yet one that has been carefully chosen, installed and maintained can be one of the delights of the garden, attracting wildlife and giving the garden a refreshing tranquillity.

PLANT AND ANIMAL PROBLEMS

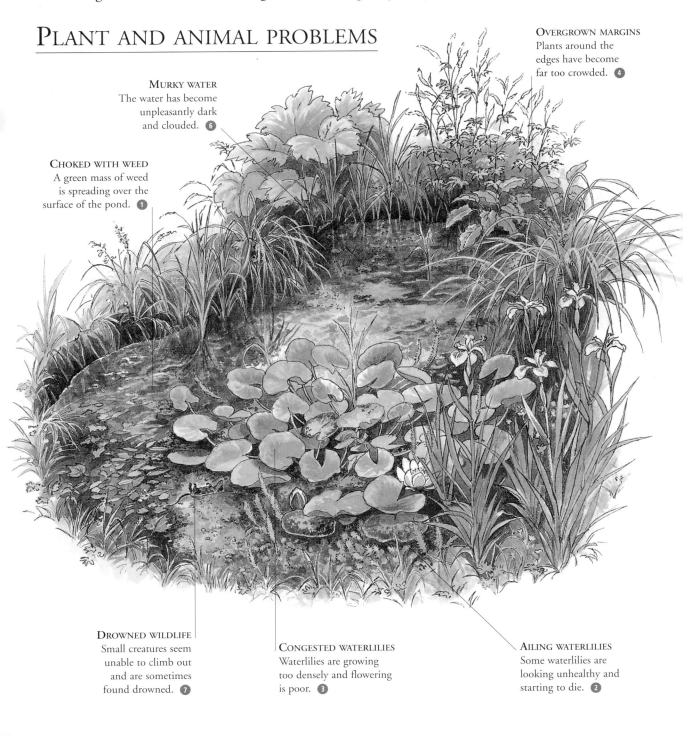

MURKY WATER
The water has become unpleasantly dark and clouded. ❻

OVERGROWN MARGINS
Plants around the edges have become far too crowded. ❹

CHOKED WITH WEED
A green mass of weed is spreading over the surface of the pond. ❶

DROWNED WILDLIFE
Small creatures seem unable to climb out and are sometimes found drowned. ❼

CONGESTED WATERLILIES
Waterlilies are growing too densely and flowering is poor. ❸

AILING WATERLILIES
Some waterlilies are looking unhealthy and starting to die. ❷

1 The pond is choked with weed

The two most common weeds are duckweed, which is made up of masses of tiny individual floating leaves, and blanketweed, which consists of numerous, often tangled strands of filamentous algae.

USE A STICK TO REMOVE BLANKETWEED

Remove the weed

Blanketweed can be removed by twirling a stick into a clump of it, like a fork into spaghetti. Duckweed is best removed using either a sieve or a long board with which you skim the surface, dragging the duckweed as you go. In large ponds you may have to attach the sieve to a pole. Although this works quite well, it is impossible to remove every single duckweed plant and in any case it would soon be reintroduced, often on the feet of birds and other wildlife. To ensure new pond plants are free of weeds, wash the roots and foliage before planting.

Safe disposal

Both weeds can be composted if you have an efficient composting system. As a precaution, let the weed dry out

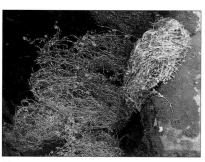

GIVE POND-DWELLERS TIME TO CRAWL OUT

before adding it to the heap. Or you can dig a hole and bury it. First, however, leave it at the pond's side for a day, so that newts and other pond inhabitants get a chance to crawl out.

2 Ailing waterlilies need attention

The most common reason for waterlilies failing to thrive or, worse still, dying is that they are not planted at the correct depth.

The right planting depth

This varies from species to species so always check the plant label carefully before you buy, just in case your pond does not have sufficient depth. Planting too deeply can be just as damaging as planting too shallowly. You can use bricks to build a plinth on which to place the pond basket so that it will be at the correct depth. Young plants often need to be planted nearer the surface than will be eventually required. If you use brick plinths, the bricks can gradually be removed as the plant grows and then, once it is mature, it will be at the

correct depth. If you are constructing a pond from scratch, design the sides so that they have plant "shelves" on several different levels. Pond baskets can then be rested on these.

Calm water needed

Another problem that may be responsible for unhealthy-looking waterlilies is that the water is not sufficiently calm for them. Waterlilies are most unlikely to thrive if planted

close to a fountain, spout or any other sort of feature that causes a lot of water movement.

Infected crowns

Occasionally waterlilies suffer from crown rots. Weak growth can result and eventually they may die off. There are no control measures available, but you should remove any infected plants to prevent the problem from spreading.

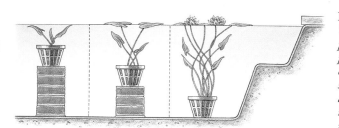

BRICK PLINTHS
To achieve the right planting depth, place a young plant on a stack of bricks so that its leaves are at surface level. As it grows, gradually remove the bricks.

❸ Some waterlilies have become congested

Once waterlilies get congested, the leaves tend to lift up out of the water and few flowers are produced.

Divide and rejuvenate

Waterlilies are best divided in mid- to late spring. There are two methods to choose from. Either carefully remove the waterlily from the pond and ease it from its pot. Cut away opened leaves, wash the soil from the roots and examine the base of the plant. Using a sharp knife, sever the rhizome about 15cm (6in) from the centre of the plant – the part with the most vigorous new shoots. Trim the roots

and replant this piece of rhizome in fresh aquatic compost and top with gravel. Discard the rest of the plant or make more rhizome sections from other vigorous areas to give to friends.

DIVIDING A WATERLILY
After washing the soil from the roots, cut away opened leaves and cut the rhizome in two. Retain only the part with the most vigorous new shoots and trim the roots. Replant, setting the crown just below soil level. Top with gravel.

Alternatively, lift the plants, wash the compost from the roots and remove the offsets which have developed. Replant the original and pot up the offsets if you have a home for them.

❹ Overcrowded margins

Before buying, check the ultimate height and spread of any marginal plant (the information should be on the label), especially if it is destined for a small pond. Where plants have already started to outgrow their position, regular cutting back or dividing is usually the answer.

Split herbaceous clumps

Most congested marginals can be divided in the same way as herbaceous perennials (*see p.33*). For smallish plants, either pull the root mass apart with your hands, or insert two hand forks, back to back, into the root system, then gently ease them apart to divide the plant into sections. Larger plants can be divided in the same way using full-size garden forks. Discard poorly growing or old sections (usually those at the centre of the clump) and replant the healthy sections as soon as possible. It may be necessary to use a knife or spade for particularly tough plants, such as large clumps of hosta, but take care not to slice through new growth buds.

Dividing irises and other rhizomatous plants

Plants that form rhizomes, like iris, may look more complicated to divide than clump-forming plants, but are in fact quite easy. The rhizomes are cut into portions and those with strong, healthy shoots are replanted.

1 LIFT THE PLANT and rinse the soil from the roots. Split the rhizomes apart with your hands or cut with a knife. Discard all portions without new shoots.

2 AFTER TRIMMING the sections of rhizome to be retained, trim the roots. Cut leaves back to 7–10cm (3–4in). Replant carefully without compressing the roots.

❺ Stolen fish

Herons and cats can be a real nuisance, spearing or hooking out fish from ponds. There is no easy solution to this problem.

Give fish a hiding place

Large, deep ponds with plenty of places for fish to hide are less likely to be troubled by these predators. In smaller ponds, planting up additional areas of marginal plants may help.

Physical barriers

Netting the surface should deter both herons and cats but may look rather unsightly and may also lessen the pond's appeal to the wildlife you want to attract.

Alternatively, herons (but not cats) can be kept from the pond by inserting short canes at 60–90cm (24–36in) intervals around the edge of the pond. Attach strong twine between them about 15cm (6in) above ground level. This acts as a trip wire and is extremely effective but does not harm the birds.

Dummy heron

Herons may be deterred by a plastic heron close to the edge of the pond. If realistic-looking, it can have a reasonably long-lasting effect.

❻ Murky water

If the water in your pond turns bright green or murky brown it is usually because of a build-up of algae, often those which float on the surface creating a "bloom".

Algal control

Various chemical treatments are available, but some may be unsuitable if the pond contains fish. An efficient yet relatively cheap control method is to plunge barley straw into the water. Contain it in some fine netting or mesh and anchor it under the water with a brick. You will need to replace it every six months. Proprietary blocks or pads of straw (sometimes combined with lavender) are also available.

Too much nitrogen

Ponds that are overstocked with fish are prone to developing algal bloom because the high nitrogen content in the fish excreta stimulates algal growth. Similarly, fertilizer which leaches into ponds from flower beds or lawns may also cause problems. Do not use fertilizers where there is a risk of their contaminating the water.

Pond plants should be potted into special aquatic compost, as fertilizer from standard composts is also likely to lead to increased algal levels. Even aquatic composts need to be kept within the confines of the planting basket, so lower plants carefully to avoid spilling any. Lining the basket with hessian helps to keep the compost in place, as does dressing the surface with gravel, which also reduces the risk of fish disturbing it.

Less sunshine, more oxygen

If a pond is in a very sunny position, algae are likely to build up. Although it is not a good idea to site ponds near trees because of the problems caused by fallen leaves, partial shade from nearby buildings, fences or walls is an advantage. In existing ponds, it helps to grow surface-floating plants such as waterlilies which will shade the water. If oxygen levels in the water are low, algal growth is also more likely to be excessive, so adding more oxygenating plants helps. These could include elodeas, microphyllums and ceratophyllums. They should be used at the rate of about one bunch per 20cm square (8in square) and then allowed to colonize nearly two-thirds of the pond. Topping up with tap water also tends to make algal problems worse (*see p.117*).

NET PONDS TO CATCH FALLEN LEAVES

Decaying vegetation

Rotting foliage releases nutrients that encourage algae to develop and toxic gases to build up beneath surface ice in winter. Cut back decaying foliage from pond and marginal plants before it flops into the water, and place a net over the surface in early autumn before leaves start to fall from trees. The net will need emptying at regular intervals. Having two nets – one fixed firmly over the pond and the second laid loosely on top of it – makes it easy to remove the top net, plus accumulated leaves, then replace it.

❼ Drowned wildlife

Since one of the delights of having a pond in the garden is the wildlife that it attracts, it needs to be safe for creatures to visit. Steep sides make it impossible for animals in difficulties to clamber out.

Create an escape route

Where you have an existing pond constructed with a flexible liner it may be possible to create a gentle incline for creatures to escape by carefully removing the liner around part of the pond edge and altering the slope of the soil beneath. If this is not possible, a duckboard or wooden ladder will be better than nothing but it is essential that it is placed at such an angle that animals can use it to climb out of the water.

Make a gentle beach

The best solution for an informal-style pond is to design the pond with at least one area around its perimeter that has a gently sloping side (*see next page*). If this is lined with pebbles and gravel, creatures have a much-reduced risk of falling in if they come to the water's edge to drink. If an animal falls in from another part of the pond's edge, provided it can swim, it will also have a decent chance of clambering out via the shallow slope.

❽ Dislodged plants

When pond plants have been carefully sited, it is reasonable to expect them to stay in place. But they sometimes mysteriously move.

Weigh them down

Wind or animals may cause pond baskets or newly planted pond or marginal plants to become dislodged. A layer of large pebbles on the surface of the compost will help to weigh the basket down. If the basket still moves, you may need to put a carefully placed brick on top. Where baskets are resting on a ledge or plinth, check that the area accommodates them comfortably and that it is level.

CONSTRUCTION FAULTS

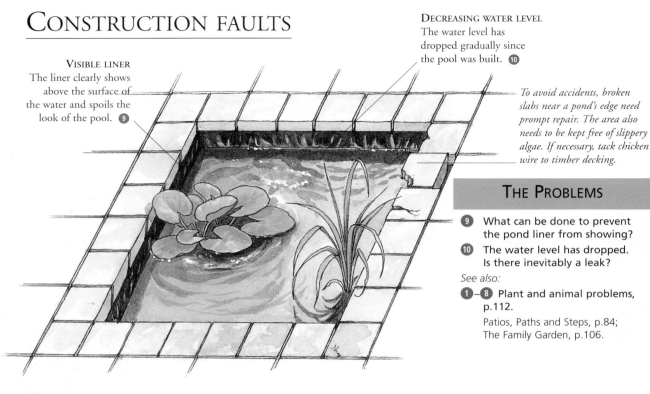

VISIBLE LINER
The liner clearly shows above the surface of the water and spoils the look of the pool. **9**

DECREASING WATER LEVEL
The water level has dropped gradually since the pool was built. **10**

To avoid accidents, broken slabs near a pond's edge need prompt repair. The area also needs to be kept free of slippery algae. If necessary, tack chicken wire to timber decking.

THE PROBLEMS

9 What can be done to prevent the pond liner from showing?

10 The water level has dropped. Is there inevitably a leak?

See also:

1–**8** Plant and animal problems, p.112.

Patios, Paths and Steps, p.84; The Family Garden, p.106.

9 A portion of pond liner is showing

This could be because of a fault in the initial siting. When making a new pond, check that the ground is level using a spirit level. Or, of course, it could be that the pond leaks.

Sloping site?

If the pond has been created on a slope, the liner on the higher edge will show however much you try to top up the water level. It may be possible to carefully remove the liner along this edge and add or remove soil so that the pond perimeter is at the same level all round. Check using a spirit level on a plank laid across the diameter of the pond. Once you have achieved the correct level you can tuck the liner out of sight again. If it is not possible to do this, try planting more marginal plants at the point where the liner shows. These should mask it for most of the year at least.

Create an overhang

With a formal-style pool, the edging slabs are best laid so that they overhang the edge of the pond by

MAKING A GENTLY SLOPING BEACH

approximately 2.5cm (1in) or more, so that the liner is hidden from view (*see left*). The greater the overhang, the larger the amount of liner that will be concealed.

Create a beach

If the problem occurs on an informal pond, where the edge has a gentle slope, use shingle, pebbles and stones of varying sizes to hide the liner and make the pond wildlife friendly (by giving easy access) and also enhance its naturalistic appearance.

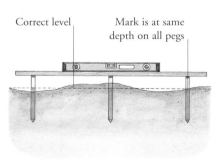

Correct level   Mark is at same depth on all pegs

CHECK THAT THE GROUND IS LEVEL
Tap in one peg with a mark at the required soil level. Tap in others, check and adjust levels. Smooth the soil surface to the peg marks.

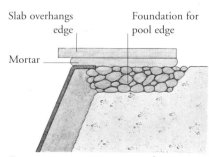

Slab overhangs edge   Foundation for pool edge

Mortar

SLABS OVERHANG THE POOL'S EDGE
Lay a foundation to create a safe, firm edge, then bed the edging slabs on mortar so that they jut over the lip and hide the liner.

⑩ Decreasing water level

Water levels may drop due to evaporation in hot weather, but if topping up doesn't solve the problem, there may be a leak. When building a new pond, use plenty of cushioning material, as well as removing stones or other sharp objects, before laying a flexible liner.

Topping up

When topping up, try to avoid using tap water, which tends to increase algal problems, and instead use pond water or stream water if at all possible, as this may contain water fleas and other organisms which will help to keep the algae down. If you can buy a few freshwater mussels from a water feature specialist, these will help to eat vast quantities of algae and so keep the water clear.

Bailing out

If the leak is close to the top of the pond it may be relatively easy to repair, and you can wait until the level has dropped to just below the damaged area. If there is a slow or concealed leak, however, you will most probably have to bail the water out and allow the sides or base to dry off before it can be mended. Try to keep as much of the original water as possible, storing it temporarily in large buckets, old dustbins or other suitable watertight containers. You could make a temporary pond by digging a hole, lining it with plastic and filling it with water to house wildlife and fish. Take particular care to avoid injuring wildlife as you do this and try to save as many creatures as possible. Large volumes of water will have to be removed using an electric pump or by siphoning, but these methods are more likely to harm or kill wildlife so bail out as much water as possible by hand.

How to repair a puncture in a flexible pond liner

Repair kits for butyl or plastic liners are generally available from pond-liner suppliers and usually consist of some double-sided adhesive tape with which to patch the damaged area. If not contained in the kit, you will also need a patch of liner fabric. The liner needs to be thoroughly clean and dry before you attempt to repair it. Once repaired, make sure that the adhesive is dry before refilling the pond. If the tear is at all large, it is best to renew the entire liner.

1 WIPE THE DAMAGED area of the liner dry and clean it with a cloth and a little alcohol.

2 PLACE A PIECE OF double-sided adhesive repair tape over the hole and peel off the backing.

3 PRESS A PATCH, cut from a spare piece of liner, onto the tape, sealing it carefully at the edges.

How to repair a crack in a concrete-lined pool

Ponds that have been built with a concrete shell are much harder to repair successfully than flexible liners, and where damage is severe it is generally better to replace the whole thing. If the leak is caused by a tiny, hairline crack, it may be possible to solve the problem by painting the area with pond sealant. To repair a slightly larger crack, let the concrete lining dry completely after draining. Chisel out the crack along its entire length, making it deeper, wider and a little longer. The channel created should be wider at the base than the top, to help keep the repair cement in place for longer. Fill with mastic cement and leave to dry.

1 USE A CLUB HAMMER and chisel to make the crack slightly wider and deeper, with the base wider than the top.

2 CLEAN AWAY ANY ALGAE and debris from around and inside the crack using a wire brush.

3 CAREFULLY FILL the entire crack with a waterproof mastic cement and allow it to dry thoroughly.

4 FINISH BY PAINTING the area with a pond sealant as a further check against leaks and to prevent toxins leaching.

INSTANT IMPROVEMENTS

TIME IS SHORT and you are not ready, or able, to completely revamp the mess which sits outside your door. What can you do quickly and relatively cheaply to make the garden look more cared for? Here are some ideas for jobs that will act as a "quick fix", turn the garden into something that looks reasonably presentable to family and friends, and give you a breathing space before you get down to tackling expensive, more ambitious, longer-term projects.

1 Start by having a thorough tidy up.

Before you do anything else take a long hard look at the whole garden and decide what can be thrown away. A determined tidy up can be quite satisfying and, if a garden has been neglected, will begin to make it look cared for. In a newly acquired plot, you may unearth some useful items or plants in the process. If there is a lot of rubbish or debris, consider hiring a skip. (*See Site Clearance, p.82.*)

2 Mow the lawn and neaten up the edges.

It is amazing how much better the whole garden will look when given a kempt, neat lawn. This is not a job for winter but it should be near the top of the list in spring, summer and autumn. Use a half-moon edging tool or, if the lawn is small, you can often get away with using a spade held vertically, though this requires extra care. If the grass has been allowed to grow really long, do not make the first cut as short as you normally might and be prepared for the lawn to look rather sorry for itself initially. Once you start to cut it regularly it will soon pick up. (*See Lawns, p.52.*)

3 Take out the secateurs and deadhead faded flowers.

A few minutes armed with a pair of secateurs, or even a sharp pair of scissors, will work wonders. Deadhead all spent flowers (which will also help to ensure plentiful blooms the following year) and at the same time, remove any diseased, dead or deteriorating stems and leaves. Also remove as many weeds as possible.

4 Fill dull corners with colourful pots, tubs and hanging baskets.

Plant up as many containers as you can. Once positioned in some key places around the garden, they will transform it. You can use seasonal bedding for immediate results, or more permanent plants such as small shrubs and grasses. Underplant them with bulbs wherever possible to prolong the season of interest. If you prefer to concentrate on the most visible area of the garden, the patio perhaps, a few eye-catching containers will have huge impact.

Introducing some pots into a dreary front garden helps create a welcoming impression; use them to line a set of steps up to the front door. Make sure that access routes are kept clear and that any dangerous areas (such as loose paving) are not made more treacherous by being concealed.

Hanging baskets, whether planted for a spring, summer, autumn or winter display, are another way to brighten drab areas or help to detract the gaze from an ugly wall or shed. Remember they can be hung in many more places than by the front door. Attaching them to a shed, pergola, or arch, or supporting them on stands on the patio is equally effective. (*See Containers, p.92.*)

5 Mend and brighten up fences and attend to hedges.

Broken fence panels can make the garden look a wreck and may encourage intruders, both human and animal. Replace the whole panel if badly damaged. Carefully detach any climbing plants and lay them on the ground or create a temporary support for them. It is usually possible to re-use existing fixtures and fittings but, if in doubt, replace them and remember to use galvanized metal so that there will be no problems with rusting. Before replacing a panel, check that the adjacent fence posts are still well anchored and in good condition; if not, these may need to be replaced (*see p.81*). A new fence panel will no doubt look very different from the remainder of the fence, often sticking out like a sore thumb, so why not take the opportunity to change the colour of the entire fence?

There is now a host of colours in outdoor wood treatments. Choose one which will look good with the main colour theme of the house, hard surfaces and nearby plants. Remember that light or bright shades can help to cheer up a gloomy garden but do choose a colour you will be happy to live with month after month. Newly planted climbers or wall shrubs usually take a while to grow. For those first few years, while they are still small, use annual climbers to decorate empty expanses of fence.

Overgrown hedges can dominate a garden and if left untended will only become more of a problem. The best time of year to cut them back, and the extent to which you can safely do so, varies from plant to plant so check in a reliable reference book. As a rule it is better to err on the side of caution and carry out extensive renovation over several seasons. Most conifers, such as the common hedging cypresses, cannot be cut back far as this will reveal inner layers of dry, brown foliage and, unlike deciduous hedging, conifers are not able to produce the necessary replacement growth to mask these ugly areas. (*See Hedges and Screens, p.16.*)

6 Introduce instant pick-me-ups to beds and borders.

Completely revamping or, indeed, creating borders from scratch can be time-consuming and expensive. If you have recently acquired a new garden, it pays to wait and see what bulbs and herbaceous perennials are hiding beneath the soil's surface. But, in the meantime, sparse-looking borders or bare patches of soil can look pretty depressing. For the first year or two why not fill gaps with seasonal bedding plants, perhaps combined with a fast-growing shrub or two, such as lavatera. This type of planting may only be temporary (or something you regard as such), but it will provide just the sort of instant pick-me-up needed to give you time to draw up long-term planting plans.

You cannot expect every part of your garden to look good every day of the year but you can cheat. An off-season area can be transformed by the addition of a few pot-grown plants that are at the peak of their flowering performance, bought straight off the shelf at your local garden centre or nursery. These can be popped in among existing plants whose leaves should be able to mask the containers. Pots of lilies are ideal for the purpose. Remember to water these plants in pots. When concealed in a border

they are easy to forget. As soon as the flowers have faded, and the weather conditions are suitable, you can plant them into their permanent positions.

If you have alkaline soil but a passion for lime-hating plants such as rhododendrons, azaleas and camellias, concealed pots allow you to have your favourite shrubs in the chalkiest of gardens.

7 Spruce up dingy sitting-out areas.

A patio or terrace can look a real mess if slabs are unevenly laid or have become broken and discoloured. A stiff yard broom and some proprietary patio cleaner, plus a bit of muscle-power, will soon clean the slabs and make them less likely to get slippery during wet weather. If you remove broken slabs and either replace them or use the gaps as planting holes, the patio will look even better. If you decide to put some plants in the gaps, you will first need to clear away any subsoil, cement or other material on which the slabs were bedded. The gap can then be filled with good-quality topsoil, with some added organic matter and fertilizer to get the plants off to a good start. (*See Patios, Paths and Steps, p.84.*)

8 Smarten up the garden shed, inside and out.

A scruffy shed may not only make a poor job of protecting its contents, it can also be a real eyesore. Replacing the roofing felt will improve its appearance and ensure that the roof is watertight. The timber beneath the felt must be allowed to dry out completely before you replace the felt. You may be able to use the old covering as a template for the new and remember that when felt is overlapped, this must be done so that rain is directed away from the wood. Painting exposed timber surfaces with

a suitable wood treatment will also make the shed look smarter; perhaps you could even coordinate its colour with your fence. It is worth introducing some kind of order inside if you always have to hunt among piles of clutter to find the right tool. Put up suitable hooks on the walls and install some shelves.

9 Turn your attention to neglected or overgrown trees.

You are lucky if you inherit an atractive old mature tree with a new garden provided, of course, it does not completely dominate the garden or cast it into deep shade. However, the tree's appearance may be spoiled by broken or hanging branches or bits of dead wood in the crown. These may even be dangerous, especially if you wish to create a seating area close by or if the garden is used by children. If the tree is small, you may be able to tackle the problem yourself, but if in any doubt employ a reputable tree surgeon. Once the work is done, treat yourself to a garden seat to put under the tree's leafy boughs, or perhaps hang a swing from a suitably sturdy branch. (*See Garden Trees, p.8.*)

10 Splash out on something big.

If a new garden suffers from being rather empty it may take several seasons for your efforts to show returns. If the budget allows, why not splash out and buy at least one really large plant. It may seem extravagant but it will help to bring a sense of maturity to the garden, even if the majority of it has only just been planted up. Plan carefully where to put the plant before buying and make sure that you dig a large planting hole, with room to spread out the roots, and prepare it particularly well so that the plant establishes properly.

FILL GAPS IN BARE BORDERS • SPRUCE UP THE PATIO • SPLASH OUT ON A BIG PLANT

SHADY SITES

MOST GARDENS HAVE SHADE at some stage of the day. Where it is created by trees, its density will be directly related to the density of their canopy and, if they are deciduous, to the time of year. In this sort of site, you can have colourful flowers for much of spring but, during the rest of the year, use the shade to advantage to grow plants that need a place away from direct sun. More permanent shade cast by buildings also calls for an appropriate choice of plants, but an imaginative use of colour and building materials can also help to transform the area.

SHADE FROM TREES

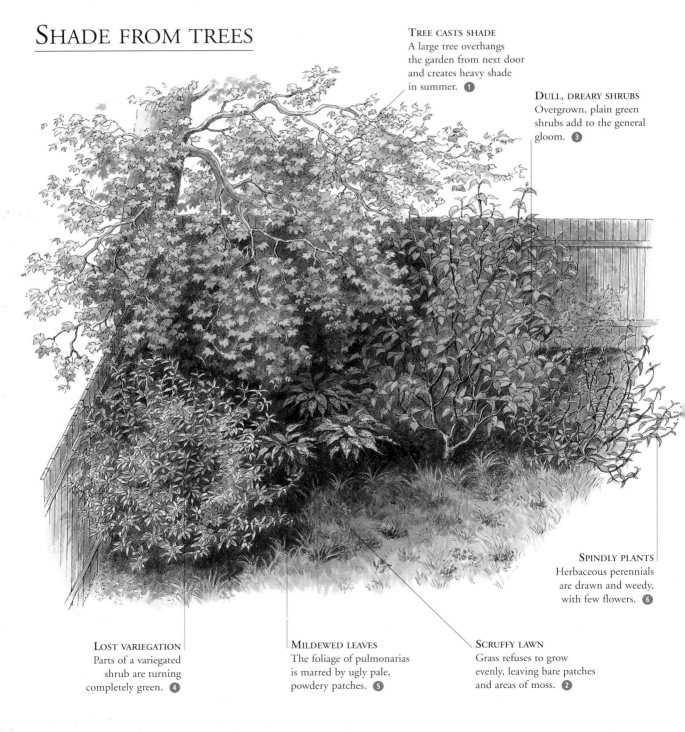

TREE CASTS SHADE
A large tree overhangs the garden from next door and creates heavy shade in summer. ❶

DULL, DREARY SHRUBS
Overgrown, plain green shrubs add to the general gloom. ❸

SPINDLY PLANTS
Herbaceous perennials are drawn and weedy, with few flowers. ❻

LOST VARIEGATION
Parts of a variegated shrub are turning completely green. ❹

MILDEWED LEAVES
The foliage of pulmonarias is marred by ugly pale, powdery patches. ❺

SCRUFFY LAWN
Grass refuses to grow evenly, leaving bare patches and areas of moss. ❷

1 Large tree creates heavy shade

Few plants will manage to grow beneath a tree with a large canopy unless the size or density of the crown is reduced in some way.

Let in more light

It should be possible to lessen the shade, even if the tree is quite large, by either lifting its crown (removing some of the lower branches, *see p.10*) or reducing the size of its crown (both height and spread). You could also thin the crown, so that the extent of the canopy is untouched but the density of the branches and foliage is reduced. Bear in mind that this sort of work will probably need to be done regularly, so costs may mount. Although legally you may be entitled to remove overhanging branches from a neighbour's tree, it's obviously best to discuss the matter first, and you should certainly not have any further work carried out

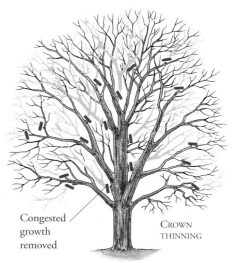

Congested growth removed

CROWN THINNING

without permission. You are also legally obliged to offer to return any prunings. Whether the tree is your own or someone else's, check it is not covered by a Tree Preservation Order, growing in a Conservation Area or protected by other legislation.

2 Scruffy lawn needs drastic action

There are few remedies for a failed lawn in constant shade from trees. Reducing the amount of shade should help, as will improved lawn care. Ultimately, however, it may be better to get rid of the grass in favour of a more appropriate surface.

Shade-tolerant grasses

If creating a lawn from scratch in a shady garden, choose a shade-tolerant grass seed mixture or shade-tolerant turf. These are composed of grasses that perform quite well in shade and considerably better than grasses in normal seed mixes or turf. Unless the shade is particularly dense, these mixtures make it possible to achieve a fairly good-looking lawn.

Is a lawn really necessary?

A completely different surface may look better and be easier to manage than grass, for example pea shingle, pavers, or pavers mixed with gravel.

You could also retain lawn in some areas but use a different surface where the shade is densest. Bark chippings are a sympathetic material near trees and shrubs, although they gradually rot down and will need replenishing from time to time. They are easily used in combination with bulbs and shade-tolerant perennials, perhaps planted as ground cover.

CARPET WITH GROUND COVER
In light shade, use ground-cover plants such as this bugle, Ajuga reptans *'Multicolor'; it needs some light to keep its foliage colours.*

ASSESSING SHADE LEVELS

• **LIGHT AND PARTIAL SHADE** Light or dappled shade is found at the edge of trees' canopies or by walls or fences. Since plenty of plants prefer such conditions, it presents the least problem. Many plants also enjoy a spot in partial shade, created as the sun moves across the sky and casts a shadow over different areas for a portion of the day.

• **DEEP SHADE** This occurs in areas that are permanently shaded, for instance by tall buildings or quite often your own house. It presents much more of a challenge, especially where walls create a rainshadow. Wherever possible, increase light levels by making use of reflected light (*see p.125*). Evergreen trees also create deep shade.

• **DRY SHADE** The most difficult to cope with, this is found under trees, especially evergreens, and in the shadow of high hedges. As well as casting shade, trees draw nutrients and copious amounts of water from the soil. If herbaceous plants are to succeed, the dry soil needs to be improved with large amounts of organic matter.

③ Dull, overgrown shrubs add to the gloom

Shade from dense growth can be alleviated by thinning, and a climber can add interest to a shrub such as lilac that offers little after flowering. An irredeemably dull shrub, however, may be best replaced.

Thin out the branches

Where stems grow thickly from the ground, prune out a proportion at the base – not more than one in three or four stems in any one year. You may need to use loppers or a pruning saw. A shrub with branching stems is usually best thinned by cutting some of the main stems back to a new,

THIN OUT A THICKET OF STEMS AT THE BASE

A COPPICED HAZEL WILL QUICKLY RESHOOOT

upright sideshoot rather than simply trimming back the side-branches.

Add a climber

After thinning, try planting a pale-flowered climber, such as clematis, to grow through the shrub, or plant some interesting perennials and spring and autumn bulbs beneath. Pale-coloured flowers will help to brighten the area. When planting close to a large shrub, enrich the ground by working plenty of well-rotted organic matter into the hole and position the climber outside the shrub's rainshadow. Train its stems in to the lower branches and keep well watered until it is fully established.

CLEMATIS 'BEES' JUBILEE'

Could it be coppiced?

A few shrubs, such as hazel (*Corylus*), elder (*Sambucus*) and some willows (*Salix*) and dogwoods (*Cornus*), can have all their stems cut back to the base every few years. Perennials and bulbs soon start to flower well in the extra sunlight they receive. Coppicing also enlivens an area thickly planted with shrubs by changing its appearance and the way it affects the growth of other plants from year to year.

Better alternatives

Consider replacing a dull shrub with something more interesting, perhaps with gold or variegated foliage or strikingly coloured stems. Or choose a shrub with a strong architectural outline, such as a mahonia. This does well in shade as well as having beautifully scented yellow flowers.

SHRUBS FOR LIGHT SHADE

ARCHITECTURAL SHAPES

Acer, including *A. palmatum* (Japanese maple)	*Buxus sempervirens* (box), clipped
Bamboos, many	*Fatsia japonica*
	Mahonia

VARIEGATED OR STRIKING FOLIAGE

Aucuba japonica 'Variegata'	*Elaeagnus*, some
Cornus alba (dogwood), some	*Euonymus*, some
	Ilex (holly), some
	Photinia

FLOWERS AND FRUIT

Camellia	*Magnolia stellata*
Daphne mezereum	*Rhododendron*
Halesia	*Skimmia*
Hydrangea	

④ Variegated shrubs produce all-green shoots

It is not uncommon for variegated trees and shrubs to start producing all-green foliage, but it needs to be dealt with quickly.

Prune out the shoots

There are many reasons for reversion, but it is particularly common in shady sites, because all-green leaves are more efficient at harnessing the limited amount of natural light needed by plants to grow. Whenever the problem occurs, prune out all reverted shoots promptly, since they are almost always more vigorous than variegated growth and will take over.

Improve light levels

To minimize the tendency for plants to produce reverted growth, try to improve the amount of light reaching them, perhaps by reducing tree shade. Bear in mind, too, that some shrubs are more prone to reverting than others, in particular variegated forms of elaeagnus and some of the variegated maples, for instance *Acer negundo* 'Flamingo'.

REVERTED SHOOTS NEED TO BE PRUNED OUT

❺ Plants under shrubs suffer from powdery mildew

As well as casting shade, shrubs or trees draw moisture and food from the soil so that it tends to get dry and rather starved, particularly in sites where the shrubs and trees have been growing for many years. In these conditions, plants are prone to powdery mildew attack.

Dealing with mildew

Powdery mildew (*see p.185*) not only disfigures plants, it can also cause extensive damage. Do all you can to keep the area as moist as possible by regular watering and also by laying a deep mulch while the ground is damp.

USE A STRIMMER FOR LARGE AREAS OF FOLIAGE

Once herbaceous plants such as pulmonarias, which are particularly prone, have finished flowering, cut back leaves quite hard to remove the source of infection. Tough plants like this should bounce back and produce masses of fresh new foliage despite such seemingly harsh treatment. With a large planting, using shears or a strimmer makes the job a lot quicker, but you will need to remove the chopped-off leaves and destroy them.

SLUGS AND SNAILS
These can be a real problem in shade, especially if damp. Control them regularly, experimenting to see which method works best for you (*see p.183*).

❻ Spindly herbaceous plants produce few flowers

Tempting though it is to plant colourful sun-loving perennials or annuals, trying to grow them in a shady position usually results in few, if any, flowers and weak, leggy plants.

Choose appropriate plants

The only real solution is to make sure, before buying, that plants suit the situation you have to offer.

Shade-tolerant plants may lack brightly coloured flowers, but interesting leaf textures and shapes, of ferns and alchemilla for instance, can be just as rewarding. Flowers are usually at their best under deciduous trees in spring, when bare branches let through plenty of light. The choice of what to grow is much greater where the ground is reasonably moist, although symphytums will usually manage to flower even in dry shade.

A few perennials which prefer sun will nevertheless grow fairly well in light shade, or areas that receive sunshine for a portion of the day, but do expect a bit of legginess and not only a shorter flowering period but fewer, smaller flowers as well. Try busy Lizzies if you need instant colour.

USEFUL PERENNIALS

GROUND COVER AND FOLIAGE PLANTS

Ajuga reptans (bugle)	Ferns
Alchemilla mollis	Hosta
Bergenia	Lamium maculatum
Epimedium	Pulmonaria (lungwort)
Euphorbia, some	Vinca (periwinkle)

SPRING AND SUMMER FLOWERS

Cimicifuga simplex	Geranium, especially G. phaeum
Corydalis	Heuchera (coral flower)
Dicentra	
Digitalis (foxglove)	Hyacinthoides non-scripta (bluebell)
Doronicum	
Eranthis hyemalis (winter aconite)	Primula
Erythronium (dog's tooth violet)	Symphytum (comfrey)
Filipendula (meadow sweet)	Tellima grandiflora
	Tiarella cordifolia
Galanthus (snowdrop)	Trillium
	Waldsteinia ternata

POLYSTICHUM SETIFERUM

LAMIUM MACULATUM 'BEACON SILVER'

ALCHEMILLA MOLLIS

HOSTA 'HADSPEN BLUE'

BERGENIA 'SUNNINGDALE'

WALDSTEINIA TERNATA

TIARELLA CORDIFOLIA

EPIMEDIUM X PERRALCHICUM

SHADE FROM BUILDINGS

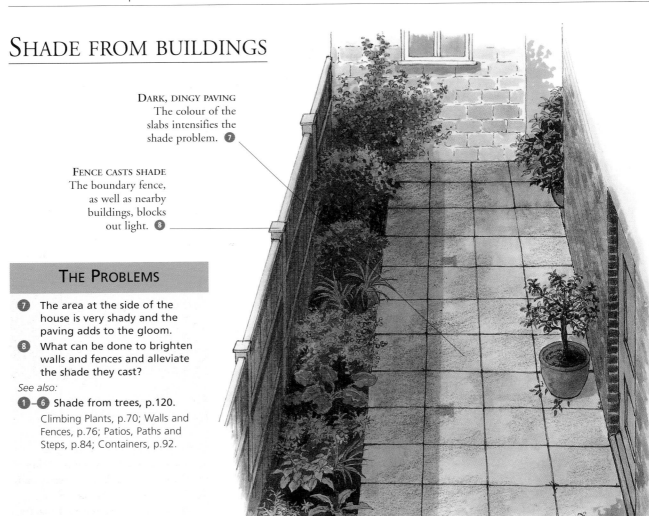

DARK, DINGY PAVING
The colour of the slabs intensifies the shade problem. **7**

FENCE CASTS SHADE
The boundary fence, as well as nearby buildings, blocks out light. **8**

THE PROBLEMS

7 The area at the side of the house is very shady and the paving adds to the gloom.

8 What can be done to brighten walls and fences and alleviate the shade they cast?

See also:

1–**6** Shade from trees, p.120.
Climbing Plants, p.70; Walls and Fences, p.76; Patios, Paths and Steps, p.84; Containers, p.92.

7 Dark, dingy paving

In areas that receive little natural light, dark-coloured paving accentuates problems of shade.

Use a pale colour

Pale-coloured paving slabs, pavers or decking will help to lighten up an area shaded by buildings. In some situations, pale pea shingle will have the same effect but, since it is easily trodden into the house, avoid laying it right up to a door. With the range of outdoor timber preservatives now available, it is easy to give decking an unusual coat of colour, or you could use yacht paint with a granular, non-slip finish. This is particularly useful where decking has a tendency to get damp and slippery.

Add a decorative element

Introducing a pattern into paving can enliven a gloomy area, for instance, a simple combination of pale and dark pavers or bricks. Textural detail will also help, such as introducing a small area of cobbles or the occasional decorative tile.

HAND-MADE PAVING TILE

EFFECTIVE PAVING PATTERN FOR A SHADY AREA

8 Walls and fences cast heavy shade

Lightening the colour of walls and fences will help to make the whole area seem brighter and will actually increase the amount of light by reflection. A carefully placed mirror can have the same effect. Any extra light will in turn improve the health and vigour of plants.

Brighter walls

Streaked grey concrete or building blocks, or a dilapidated brick wall or brown fence will all contribute to making a shaded garden even darker and gloomier. Brick and concrete surfaces often respond well to cleaning and once clean will usually seem a lot brighter. A coat of special masonry paint can transform them into something really attractive. This is a good solution for town gardens and alleys. Masonry paint is usually available in both smooth and textured forms and in a wide range of colours, including pale shades which help to lighten a dark area.

Wooden surfaces such as fences, trellis or the side of a shed (or decking on the floor) can be treated with tinted wood stains and preservatives. Again there are ample colours to choose from but make sure you buy an exterior formulation.

MIRROR IMAGE
An artfully designed and placed mirror increases light levels by reflection and makes a small space appear much larger.

ALLEYS AND COURTYARDS
In shady town gardens, white-painted walls reflect light, while strong-shaped evergreens do not need much sun to grow well and make an elegant yet dramatic impact.

Tricks with mirrors

A carefully positioned and regularly cleaned mirror on a wall can serve many purposes, making the garden seem larger as well as brighter as it reflects plants, views and light. Position it so that it has maximum opportunity to reflect light and carefully train a climber or nearby shrub to mask its edges.

Shade all year?

Shade levels may vary a great deal during the course of the year and it is important to take this into account. In most cases, the shade is less extreme during summer when the sun is brighter, out for longer and higher in the sky. If shade is cast by a nearby deciduous tree, however, you should find that the garden is less shaded in early spring before the leaf canopy develops and again in autumn once the leaves have fallen.

Colourful mulches

Mulches are another way of adding colour to borders at the foot of a wall or fence and also to containers. Use pale shingle, add some sparkle with glass nuggets or introduce texture with an assortment of shells.

Flowers and foliage

Choosing plants with pale foliage or flowers will make the whole area seem brighter. Provided the plants are suited to shady conditions, they should perform well. Evergreens such as *Choisya ternata* 'Sundance' and variegated ivies are particularly useful as they retain their bright leaves throughout the year. You need not rely entirely on colour. Any plant with an architectural shape, such as a mahonia, or a delicate texture, such as hardy ferns and epimediums, can be used to great effect. This is a good place, too, for using clipped yew and box to great effect.

Containers planted up with flowers which are not particularly shade tolerant can also be introduced on a short-term basis. As long as they are rotated around the garden so that they spend plenty of time in adequate light, they should perform perfectly well for a limited period in fairly dense shade.

Using climbers which will thrive in shade will help to brighten a wall or fence and again choosing those with pale-coloured flowers or variegated foliage will help to make the area seem lighter.

SEASIDE & WINDY GARDENS

VERY FEW GARDENS are set in an ideal location, but perhaps the two hardest situations to cope with are sites that are buffeted by strong winds or, worse still, seaside gardens where the plants are subjected to the effects of both wind and salt. Each type of site requires a certain tenacity on the part of the gardener, but if the necessary measures are taken to protect against wind, and suitable plants are chosen, there is no reason why a beautiful garden cannot be created. And many such sites have the bonus of a splendid view beyond.

THE PROBLEMS

1. Shrubs and trees develop a stunted or lopsided shape.
2. Leaves get shredded and scorched by wind.
3. Plants in containers on the patio dry out and become shrivelled looking.
4. Newly planted plants refuse to grow or are difficult to get established.

See also:

Hedges and Screens, p.16; Improving the Soil, p.148.

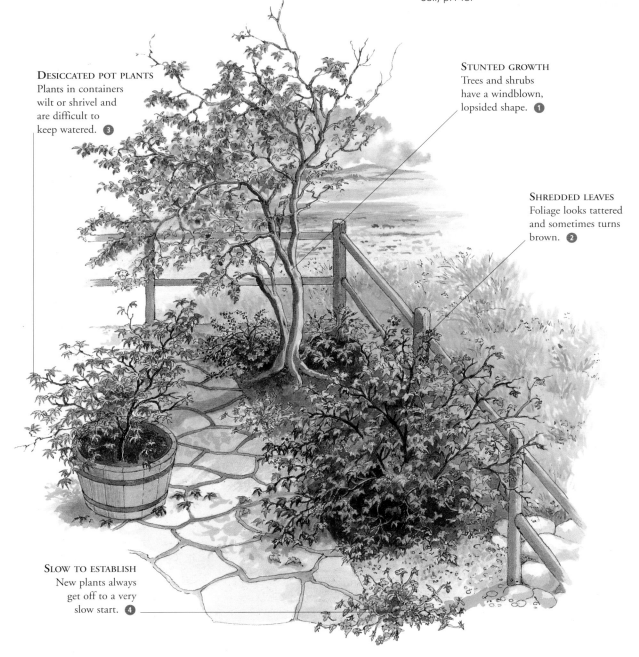

DESICCATED POT PLANTS
Plants in containers wilt or shrivel and are difficult to keep watered. ❸

STUNTED GROWTH
Trees and shrubs have a windblown, lopsided shape. ❶

SHREDDED LEAVES
Foliage looks tattered and sometimes turns brown. ❷

SLOW TO ESTABLISH
New plants always get off to a very slow start. ❹

❶ Stunted, lopsided plants

*When exposed to strong winds, trees
and shrubs develop a battered,
uneven shape, stems and branches
break and, if winds are laden with
salt, growth is even further reduced.*

Filter the wind

Creating a windbreak, or a shelter belt
of trees if you have the space, should
reduce this kind of damage. In many
gardens, a hedge of suitably wind-
and, if necessary, salt-resistant shrubs
or trees will give sufficient protection.
Alternatively, some form of fencing
will do the job. A variety of materials
can be used. Windbreaks should not
be solid, since wind still needs to be
able to pass through but at a much-
reduced speed. If forced up over a
solid barrier, it creates a down-
draught and eddying on the other
side. Depending on the size of the
plants needing protection within a
garden, the windbreak should be
anything up to 4m (12ft) high. The
average windbreak will reduce wind at
ground level on the other side for a
distance of 7–10 times its height.

Planting a windbreak

Since smaller plants cost much less
and generally establish better than
larger ones, it makes sense to buy
young bare-root hedging plants rather
than container-grown shrubs or trees.
It is essential to choose plants that
can withstand wind and, in maritime

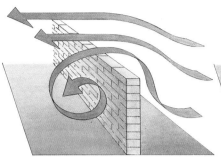

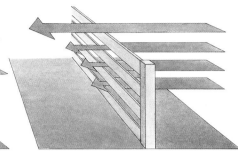

INEFFECTIVE WINDBREAK
*A solid wall or fence makes a poor
windbreak. Wind that cannot pass through
is forced up and over and then pulled down
on the other side creating turbulence.*

EFFICIENT WINDBREAK
*Ideally, a windbreak should have about 50
per cent permeability. Wind can still pass
through but at a much reduced speed that
has less chance of damaging plants.*

sites, salt as well. In most cases, plants
can be spaced 45cm (18in) apart,
preferably in a double row.

Aids to establishment

To help a hedge or shelter belt get
established, give the plants temporary
protection – a semi-permeable fence,
for example. Improve the soil before
planting, especially if it is thin and
sandy, by digging in plenty of well-
rotted organic matter, and keep it well
weeded; vigorous weeds can easily
smother small, young shrubs. In
constant wind, plants may need initial
staking or tying in to a support of
wire and stakes. Position the wire on
the side of the prevailing wind so that
the plants do not blow onto it and tie
loosely with a figure-of-eight knot to
stop the stems from chafing.

PLANTS TO PROVIDE SHELTER

TREES FOR SHELTER BELTS

Acer pseudoplatanus
  (sycamore)
Alnus glutinosa
  (alder)
Crataegus monogyna
  (hawthorn),
  C. persimilis
*Cupressus
  macrocarpa*

Eucalyptus gunnii
Fraxinus excelsior
  (ash)
Pinus nigra
Populus alba
  (white poplar)
Quercus ilex (holm
  oak)
Thuja plicata

SHRUBS FOR SEASIDE HEDGES

Aucuba japonica
Elaeagnus pungens
  'Maculata'
Escallonia
Euonymus
Griselinia littoralis
*Hippophae
  rhamnoides*

Ilex x *altaclarensis,
  I. aquifolium*
  (holly)
Olearia
Prunus spinosa
  (blackthorn)
Pyracantha
Rosa rugosa

Fences and other types of windbreak

The best windbreaks have a
permeability of about 50 per cent.
Wooden fences with gaps between
the laths the same width as the laths
themselves are ideal and reasonably
durable as long as the timber is
pressure-treated. Posts obviously need
to be strong and very secure. Stout
trellis offers some protection, as do
willow or hazel hurdles, though these
are not long-lasting. Purpose-made
plastic mesh will not enhance the
garden but works and gives useful
protection to a newly planted hedge.

HURDLES ARE HANDSOME IF NOT VERY DURABLE

WINDBREAK MATERIALS

• **STURDY TRELLIS,** formed from stout
timber laths, with a 15cm (6in) grid.

• **RANCH-STYLE** (baffle) fencing made
from horizontal timbers, 15cm (6in)
wide, with 15cm (6in) gaps between.

• **FENCING PANELS** formed from
2.5cm (1in) vertical or diagonal timber
laths with 2.5cm (1in) gaps between.

• **POLYPROPYLENE MESH** purpose-
made and available in various colours
and thicknesses.

2 Shredded and scorched leaves

In any exposed position avoid plants with large leaves (unless they form a tight rosette at ground level) since they are easily battered and shredded by wind. Salt scorches shoot tips and leaves and can cause serious damage, sometimes killing plants, so in coastal gardens choose salt-tolerant plants. A windbreak helps to minimize damage.

Signs of salt damage

Salt damage is not always easy to recognize since it can look similar to extreme wind scorch. Typically, younger, softer and less protected growth is the first to suffer and shows discolouration, followed by rapid scorching and drying of the foliage. Occasionally salt deposits may be seen on leaves or stems, although this generally only occurs very close to the sea, or after extremely bad weather when winds carry a particularly high level of salt. Salt damage may also cause internal staining of stems. To check for this, carefully peel back the bark close to the affected leaves and you may see a brownish stain running the length of the stem from the point where it joins the leaf stalk. The distance wind can carry salt inland varies greatly with topography and prevailing weather but, in extreme conditions, it may be for several miles.

Small leaves stay beautiful

On the whole, plants indigenous to windswept places, such as thrift (*Armeria*), have small leaves, capable of withstanding a regular battering. Because small-leaved plants have less surface area through which moisture can be lost, they are also good at coping with drought, whether caused by drying wind or fast-draining soil.

THIN TOPSOIL

IN COASTAL GARDENS ground is liable to be rocky with a meagre covering of sandy soil that gives plants a poor foothold and little in the way of food and water. It really is important to try to improve the soil's ability to retain moisture and nutrients if plants are to grow well. Regularly dig in plenty of well-rotted organic matter – eg garden or mushroom compost, manure, leaf-mould or spent hops – preferably at least once a year. Mulch to prevent moisture loss through evaporation and endeavour to choose suitable plants.

Choosing shrubs for windy and salt-blown sites

Plants that grow naturally by the coast are generally the easiest to establish. Native seasiders such as tamarisk and broom (*Cytisus*) can look attractive even when they develop a windblown shape. It is also worth taking a look at nearby gardens to see which plants are thriving and which are scorched or showing other signs of wind or salt damage. Coastal gardens do, however, often offer the chance to grow some shrubs of borderline hardiness, such as cistus, since they are not affected by frost and very low winter temperatures.

TAMARIX RAMOSISSIMA
'PINK CASCADE'

ROSA RUGOSA

HYDRANGEA PANICULATA 'PRAECOX'

ELAEAGNUS 'QUICKSILVER'

CYTISUS X *PRAECOX* 'ALLGOLD'

SEASIDE SHRUBS

HIGH SALT TOLERANCE

Choiysa
Cistus laurifolius
Cordyline
Hebe
Lonicera pileata
Phlomis
Rosa pimpinellifolia, R. rugosa
Spiraea, most
Viburnum, evergreen types

SOME SALT TOLERANCE

Berberis, many
Buddleja davidii
Caryopteris x *clandonensis*
Ceanothus, many
Cistus, many
Cotoneaster, many
Hydrangea macrophylla
Hypericum calycinum
Laurus nobilis (bay)
Lavenders, many
Lavatera arborea
Mahonia, most
Santolina

Perennials that can cope with salt-spray and wind

Although easier to protect from wind and salt, herbaceous plants can suffer just like shrubs and trees, so it is important to choose those that grow well in unpropitious sites. Be guided by what grows naturally on exposed hills and by the sea, and characteristics they have in common, such as small or quill-like leaves and glaucous or succulent foliage.

KNIPHOFIA 'GREEN JADE'

ZAUSCHNERIA CALIFORNICA 'DUBLIN'

ERYGNIUM X TRIPARTITUM

CROCOSMIA X CROCOSMIIFLORA 'JACKANAPES'

OSTEOSPERMUM 'BUTTERMILK'

ARMERIA MARITIMA 'VINDICTIVE'

SEASIDE FLOWERS

HERBACEOUS PERENNIALS

Achillea
Agapanthus
Anemone x *hybrida*
Centranthus ruber
Crambe cordifolia
Cynara scolymus (globe artichoke)
Crocosmia
Dierama pulcherrimum
Echinops (globe thistle)
Eryngium (sea holly)
Euphorbia, several
Hemerocallis (daylily)
Iris germanica, *I. unguicularis*
Kniphofia (red hot poker)
Limonium playphyllum (sea lavender)
Lychnis, several
Nerine bowdenii
Osteospermum
Phormium tenax
Sedum, many
Senecio cineraria
Veronica, many

❸ Desiccated container plants

Whether affected simply by exposure to wind or also to the salt it carries, plants in containers are prone to drying out, since their roots have only a limited amount of soil or compost to tap into.

MARITIME MULCH
A layer of shells, pebbles and sparkling glass nuggets helps to conserve moisture. Any mulch must be applied to moist compost.

Containers and mulches

Because of their lower porosity, plastic or glazed ceramic containers will lose less moisture from their surface than terracotta. It is also possible to help retain moisture and protect plants from wind by moving containers into sheltered areas. Grouping them offers plants an extra degree of protection and helps to minimize the amount of moisture lost from foliage. Ensure that plants are kept watered, perhaps by using a trickle irrigation system, and mulch the surface of the compost while moist. You could use a material with a seaside theme, such as pebbles or seashells. It is essential to choose a good moisture-retaining compost. Loam-based composts usually dry out slower than soilless types, and incorporating moisture-retaining granules will also help (*see p.94*). Using a 50:50 mixture by volume of loam-based and loam-free compost often provides good moisture retention with adequate drainage.

❹ Slow to establish

Shrubs and trees can often withstand wind and salt when fully grown, but are vulnerable in the early stages.

Temporary protection

Make a windbreak to protect plants while they are getting established, especially during the first two winters, by attaching polypropylene mesh or lengths of split bamboo or reed to well-driven-in stakes, or putting up a hurdle on the plant's windward side.

Polypropylene mesh protects a newly planted shrub

TEMPORARY SHELTER AIDS ESTABLISHMENT

ROOFTOPS & BALCONIES

ANYONE WHO LOVES PLANTS will want to have a garden of some sort, even if it is not at ground level. Provided a rooftop or balcony is structurally suitable – or can be made so – either area has great potential. Sites such as these generally bring a few difficulties that will need to be overcome – wind and watering often being the greatest obstacles to success. However, a surprising range of plants can be grown and will bring satisfying, even edible, rewards.

Q *Can a roof garden be created on any kind of flat roof?*

A Before starting work or even planning a roof garden, it is essential to get it thoroughly checked out by a structural surveyor. Creating a garden on an unsuitable roof could have disastrous and very expensive consequences. Even if you have just moved in to a house or flat with an existing roof garden, it is often still worth having it checked over, just in case this was not done in the first place or it has since deteriorated. This is one job you really cannot afford to economize on.

Be sure to make any necessary structural improvements before you start bringing in heavy compost, containers or other materials. In addition, try to find out exactly how much weight the balcony or roof can safely support and if any parts are more capable than others of bearing substantial loads. Likewise, check if there are any areas that should be avoided. Remember that even loam-free compost is a great deal heavier wet than dry.

Q *What sort of roof surface is suitable for a garden?*

A If you need to put down a new surface on a roof – or balcony – it is essential that any material is weather resistant and as lightweight as possible. Good quality, properly installed, pressure-treated timber decking is popular. Existing concrete surfaces can be painted using special concrete paint, often sold for treating garage floors. Incorporating sand into this sort of paint, or buying a formulation that has already been given a rough texture, will ensure that there are less likely to be problems with the surface becoming slippery when damp.

Q *How can a scruffy balcony be be given an instant facelift? There are plans to improve it properly in the long term, but something bright and cheerful is needed in the meantime.*

A Start by adorning the walls and any other vertical surfaces with hanging baskets, windowboxes and mangers. These can either be planted up each year with varying seasonal bedding, such as petunias or *Bidens ferulifolia*, or with longer-term plants including small evergreen shrubs to provide year-round interest. Perennial climbers such as clematis will cover quite large areas fairly rapidly and fast-growing annual climbers such as *Eccremocarpus scaber*, black-eyed Susan (*Thunbergia*), morning glory (*Ipomoea*) or sweet peas (Lathyrus odoratus) provide quick colour. Grow them up railings or against a support system of wires or trellis attached to walls or windbreaks. If possible, choose some scented plants (especially sweet peas) which will waft their perfume through open windows.

Q *How can the time-consuming and difficult task of watering lots of plants in containers be made easier?*

A It is essential to include a convenient and adequate access point to the roof for you to carry watering cans up if there is not already a source of water. If possible, extend the domestic pipework to take water up to the roof and have a hose connection or install a trickle irrigation system with a drip-feed linked to every container. Make sure any outside pipes are well lagged, since roof gardens can be particularly exposed and the pipes may freeze in winter. Or you may be able to arrange a system where the water to those pipes can be turned off and drained before cold weather sets in.

Q *What are the best ways to ensure that weight on a balcony or roof garden is kept to a minimum?*

A Start by using lightweight composts. These are usually loam-free but remember they do have a tendency to dry out fairly quickly. If necessary use a mixture of a loam-based and a loam-free compost. Instead of using stones or traditional crocks at the base of containers for drainage, use crumbled-up chunks of expanded-polystyrene plant trays or packaging; these will provide perfectly good drainage channels, but at only a fraction of the weight. The type of pot you choose will also hugely influence the total weight. Attractive as it may be, terracotta is relatively heavy and there are now some fairly good-looking and convincing fake terracotta materials available. Similarly, plastic containers, although perhaps not necessarily the most pleasing to the eye, if carefully planted can be well concealed and do not weigh very much. They can often be made to look more interesting by a coat of paint or some other form of decoration – some mosaic perhaps. Unattractive but lightweight containers can also be used towards the centre of a group of containers, so that the container itself will be hidden by more attractive ones around the outside.

Q *What is the best way of counteracting problems of wind on roofs and balconies?*

A If possible, erect a good quality windbreak. It can be made from an attractive screening material or trellis. By increasing the amount of shelter, you will find that you can grow a much wider range of plants. You will also be more inclined to enjoy sitting out on the balcony or roof garden.

There are many different screening materials now available. These include bamboo and heather screens, both of which look ornamental as well as providing shelter. They will, however, need to be supported on a well-constructed, rigid framework.

It may also be possible to grow relatively tall plants around the outside of a roof garden that will also filter the wind. Clipped box, for example, could be used to good effect. Make sure that whatever plants you choose are fully hardy and that any needing a degree of protection are grown towards the centre of the area.

Q *How can time spent feeding lots of plants in containers be reduced?*

A Incorporating controlled-release fertilizer granules into the compost at planting time will certainly help to reduce the need to feed. These granules have a resin coating which ensures that fertilizer is leached out into the compost when it is moist and warm and that this ceases when the compost is either very cold or dry so that plants receive food only when actively growing. These granules should keep plants adequately fed for about six months. The exception is summer bedding which will also benefit from additional feeding with a high-potash liquid fertilizer.

Q *Windbreaks may be essential but they look rather dull. What can be done to brighten them up?*

A Most non-living windbreaks can be fitted with a support system of wires which you can use to train lightweight climbers, in particular flowering annuals such as morning glory (*Ipomoea*), cup-and-saucer vine (*Cobaea scandens*), climbing nasturtiums or sweet peas. Most clematis will also provide an attractive addition to vertical surfaces.

As long as they are sufficiently sturdy, you may also be able to fit mangers to windbreaks and fill them with a colourful assortment of trailing plants.

Q *Is it possible to grow shrubs or trees in containers?*

A All sorts of plants will grow surprisingly well in containers, including shrubs and trees, provided they are kept well supplied with water and food and the container is

sufficiently large. Make sure that pots are stable and that you do not allow plants to become top-heavy. You will probably need to keep any tree or shrub's size and shape under control by trimming or pruning it on a regular basis. Japanese maples (as long as they are well protected from wind), bamboos, box and camellias, to name but a few, grow well in large containers and should prove reasonably long-lived.

Trees and shrubs can also be underplanted with seasonal bedding or bulbs to ensure that every possible scrap of space is used to advantage to provide colour and interest for as much of the year as possible.

Q *Is it possible to grow vegetables on a balcony or roof garden?*

A There are quite a few vegetables which can successfully be grown in containers including peppers, tomatoes, beans, potatoes, courgettes, lettuce, chard, cucumbers, melons and even carrots. If you want to grow beans, unless the area is adequately sheltered, it may be best to stick to dwarf French beans rather than trying to grow runner beans. They are less likely to be affected by wind and, because they are self-pollinated, the plants should still form plenty of pods even if there are few visiting insects. Check seed catalogues for varieties which are described as being particularly good for growing in containers, such as the cucumber 'Patio Pik' or the tomatoes 'Tumbler' and 'Tiny Tim', which bear cherry-sized fruits. Herbs, too, will grow well in a sunny, sheltered spot provided that they are given good drainage.

Wherever you grow vegetables in containers, you will need to make sure that you keep them adequately watered and fed, since the majority are fairly hungry crops.

HOT, DRY SITES

MANY OF US HAVE GARDENS which have several quite distinct areas in them, and this means they often include a part that is hot and prone to becoming dry during the summer months. Water shortages can make areas like this particularly difficult to maintain, so what can you do if you want to be certain that such an area looks good even when conditions are at their most extreme? With the right choice of plants, careful use of water and a suitable planting and maintenance regime, a hot, dry site can be an interesting and rewarding part of the garden.

RUN-OFF AND EROSION
Water runs straight off a slope, and plants are difficult to establish. **5**

HIGH WATER CONSUMPTION
The garden depends on using mains water, which is wasteful and sometimes subject to supply restrictions. **3**

CAUSE FOR CONCERN
Plants in pots, which need frequent watering, cause problems at holiday time. **1**

SCORCHED LEAVES
The foliage of some plants quickly burns in the sun. **4**

WILTING FOLIAGE
Leaves droop as soon as weather turns dry, but hand-watering is time-consuming. **1**

PARCHED LAWN
A dry, brown lawn is far from the refreshing sward it should be. **2**

THE PROBLEMS

1 How can plants be prevented from wilting so quickly and watering made less time-consuming? And what steps can be taken at holiday time?

2 The lawn soon turns brown and parched. Is there a remedy?

3 What are the best ways to reduce mains water consumption, and are there any rules for using recycled water?

4 Why do some plants scorch and shrivel so readily?

5 Water runs straight off a slope, often taking the soil with it.

See also:
Lawns, p.52; Containers, p.92; Improving the Soil; p148.

① Plants wilt and watering is never ending

The only way to reduce time spent watering and avoid borders full of wilting foliage is to improve the soil's capacity to retain moisture and choose drought-tolerant plants.

Improve the soil

You can save both water and time spent watering if, before planting, you do all you can to make the soil more moisture retentive. On a light sandy or chalk soil or fairly heavy clay, it will help to dig in plenty of bulky organic matter. On a heavy soil, incorporate grit to reduce the risk of cracking during dry weather, since deep fissures allow moisture to escape from the soil. When planting among other plants in an established bed or border, it is important to improve the soil texture over the largest possible area.

In addition, all plants whether new or established should be regularly mulched. A 5–8cm (2–3in) layer of bark chippings, cocoa shells, well-rotted manure, garden compost or leaf-mould should be applied to moist soil. When mulching, take care not to mulch right up to the plant stems since this may make them rot. Moisture loss is also encouraged by windy conditions, and in an exposed garden it is well worth creating some sort of shelter to reduce loss of water by evaporation (*see p.127*).

Watering priorities

To avoid wasting water, concentrate on those plants or parts of the garden that need it most.

• Newly planted plants and transplants need watering until their roots have had time to grow out into the soil and become capable of tapping into all available moisture.

• When sowing seed outside, ensure that the bottoms of the drills are moist and that the seeds themselves are covered in a layer of moist soil. If the moist soil is then capped with a little dry soil, it helps to maintain a damp environment for germination.

• Most fruit and vegetables need water when in flower or forming fruit (including pods and cobs) and tubers, or there is likely to be a decrease in yield or cracking or splitting which can lead to total wastage.

• Vegetables grown for their leaves, such as lettuces, tend to run to seed without watering and will certainly have a rather tough texture. Other thirsty crops include beans, celery, courgettes, cauliflowers, cabbages, cucumbers, tomatoes, leeks and peas. Remember that vegetable crops can be mulched as well as ornamentals.

• Containers usually require a lot more water than plants in open ground (*for ways of conserving moisture, see p.94*).

Choose natural heat and drought survivors

In dry sunny sites, try to concentrate on plants that require relatively small amounts of moisture. As a rule, avoid anything with big floppy leaves which quickly lose moisture through their large surface area. Plants with small, waxy, shiny or hairy leaves are generally best able to cope with dry conditions and high temperatures. Fleshy succulents have the ability to retain water, quill-like leaves tend to lose little moisture and grey or silver foliage is good at reflecting glare. A plant's origins can often be a good indicator of drought tolerance. For instance, a Mediterranean native such as rosemary will easily be able to withstand long, dry periods. Check labels when choosing plants as you can save a lot of time watering by concentrating on plants described as needing a well-drained soil and sun.

PLANTS FOR DRY PLACES

Acanthus mollis
Allium, most
Aquilegia
Arbutus unedo (strawberry tree)
Aubrieta
Brachyglottis (formerly *Senecio*)
Cedars
Cistus
Convolvulus cneorum
Cordyline
Cotoneaster, most
Epimedium
Euphorbia, many
Foxgloves, some such as *Digitalis ferruginea*
Geraniums
Hebe
Helianthemum
Irises, bearded
Junipers, many
Lavender
Papaver orientale (oriental poppy)
Pelargoniums
Phlomis
Phormium (New Zealand flax)
Pines, including the dwarf pine *Pinus mugo*
Pyracantha
Rosemary
Sage, and many other salvias
Saxifraga
Sedum
Stachys byzantina (lamb's ears)
Thymes
Vinca (periwinkle)
Yucca

SEMPERVIVUM CILIOSUM

IRIS 'GOLDEN MUFFIN'

GERANIUM SANGUINEUM

BRACHYGLOTTIS 'SUNSHINE'

Effective watering

In order to reduce the amount of moisture lost by evaporation, water in the early evening or at dusk or, if this is not possible, very early in the morning. This allows time for the water to penetrate and be taken up by plant roots. It also reduces the risk of scorching leaves. On very dry soil, first lightly dampen the surface to help the water penetrate the soil and then water thoroughly a few minutes later. The initial dampening will reduce the risk of the water running straight off and being wasted.

Wherever possible, use recycled, or grey, water. Generally speaking, less water is wasted if you use a watering can rather than a hose. Using a seep hose (a hose with a porous surface, usually made from recycled car tyres) is an efficient way of watering. Because the water comes out so slowly, the plants can take it up without any risk of run-off. A seep hose is particularly useful in a newly planted area where it can be arranged around the bases of plants and hidden by a mulch, which will also help to reduce evaporation.

Useful planting techniques

There are several ways of ensuring that the water you do apply goes directly to where the plant needs it – at its roots – and is not wasted by run-off or evaporation. A pipe, such as a short length of hose, inserted at planting time will channel water straight to the roots. Let one end

protrude 2–3cm (1in) above soil level and put a little gravel or grit in the end near the roots to prevent it becoming clogged with soil.

Creating a slight hollow in the soil around the base of a plant when planting will give water from irrigation and natural rainfall time to penetrate the soil and reach the roots rather than running straight off the surface. Both methods are useful on sloping ground where watering in and getting new plants to establish can be particularly difficult.

WATER COLLECTS IN A PLANTING HOLLOW

SEEP HOSES
A gravel garden is a good place to lay a seep hose. The gravel will prevent it from getting clogged with soil, and the hose will steadily supply water to a small, newly planted plant.

HOLIDAY CONTINGENCIES

• A NEIGHBOUR who can pop in at regular intervals to water plants, especially those in pots, is the greatest help. They can check, too, that there is no build-up of pests or diseases that needs to be dealt with. If this is not possible, consider linking a small, not necessarily expensive, trickle- or drip-irrigation system to your most precious containers. It can be linked to a timing device so that water is supplied regularly at a suitable time of day.

• GROUPING POTS helps to reduce the amount of water lost by evaporation, both from the surface of the compost and simply because the plants at the centre of the group are shaded and insulated. It may also be worth moving containers temporarily to a shaded spot. Lining porous pots with plastic before planting, adding water-retaining granules to compost and mulching all reduce the amount of watering needed. Also be sure to leave a sufficient gap between pot rim and compost for water to collect and penetrate.

② Parched lawn

Although the lawn may be one of the first areas to show the effects of drought, it is often also one of the first to recover as soon as rain returns.

Realistic expectations

Despite the fact that the lawn may look really dry and parched, it is surprising just how quickly it will green up again once it has received

rain. During hot, dry weather do not mow it short since this increases water loss through evaporation. Provided it is cut regularly and the clippings are not too long, it is also quite acceptable to leave the clippings on the surface since they will act like a thin mulch and should not create a build-up of thatch or any other significant problems. Fine lawn mixtures, which are not drought-

tolerant, should be avoided unless you want to spend time watering and water supply is not a problem. A typical family or utility lawn is, however, really quite tough.

AVOID SPRINKLERS
These are wasteful and, if left in place for too long on beds and borders, may cause surface capping which is detrimental to soil structure and to plants.

③ High water consumption

It makes sense to store surplus rainwater or recycle domestic waste water whether it is to provide a secondary supply, reduce water bills or, perhaps more importantly, help to conserve natural resources.

Install a water butt
A garden cannot have too many water butts and you should try to install one wherever possible. They can be linked to downpipes from the roof of the house, greenhouse, conservatory, shed or garage. You can also use a special diverter to fit a butt to a downpipe from your bathroom to allow you to recycle "grey water" – water that has come from the bath, hand-basin or shower. The fairly small quantities of soap, shampoo or bubble bath it contains will not harm plants.

A water butt must be installed on a firm, level surface that can take its weight when full of water, so that there is no risk of it toppling over. The tap must be at a convenient height to fit a watering can underneath. The butt should have a close-fitting lid, preferably with a safety catch in a garden used by children. A lid will also prevent leaves and other debris or wildlife from falling in.

USING GREY WATER

- **DISHWASHER** and washing machine water should not be used unless the water from a washing machine is taken from the final rinse only.
- **DO NOT USE** water if softener has been added either to the water supply or to a specific appliance.
- **POTATO PEELINGS** or other vegetable particles in the water will not cause a problem and will soon compost down.
- **USE AS FRESH** as possible, to decrease the likelihood of grey water developing an unpleasant odour.

Using water from a butt
In order to keep the water fairly fresh and prevent it from becoming smelly, empty the butt completely on a regular basis, preferably every autumn. In a large garden, where a sizeable supply is needed, butts can be linked to one another by inserting a pipe into the overflow socket, and you can attach a hose that allows you to transport water across the garden. If you connect a small submersible pump to a hose, it will boost delivery to far corners. Similarly, seep hoses can be connected directly to water butts.

④ Scorched leaves

Leaf scorching due to lack of water or hot, bright direct sun can be a problem in a very sunny parts of a garden or in particularly hot, dry weather. Some types of foliage are more vulnerable than others.

Beware pale foliage
On the whole, avoid plants with golden or variegated leaves, as pale leaves or parts of leaves tend to scorch much more readily than tougher all-green foliage. A golden-leaved mock orange (*Philadelphus coronarius* 'Aureus') will soon become speckled and spotted with unsightly brown marks. Even the leaves of golden forms of sun-loving plants such as marjoram (*Origanum*) can turn crisp at the edges. If you want to include variegated plants, place them where they can enjoy a little dappled shade.

It is also important not to wet foliage just before or during a period of bright sunlight, since droplets of moisture on a leaf's surface tend to act like tiny lenses, magnifying the sun's rays and causing scorching of the tissue beneath. As a rule, it is obviously best to avoid plants whose label suggests they need to be grown in full or part shade.

⑤ Water runs straight off a slope

Where soil is very dry, water will run off a slope before it has had a chance to penetrate the ground. It can also take some of the soil with it, causing erosion.

Surface treatments
Plants towards the top of a slope suffer from drought more readily than those at the bottom. Indeed, if soil is fairly moisture-retentive, damp areas can build up at the base of a slope while the top remains very dry. If all or part of the garden is on a slope, you could create terraces to reduce erosion and water run-off. Where a slope is extreme, or on smaller slopes,

PLANT THROUGH LANDSCAPE FABRIC ON SLOPES

attaching mesh over the whole surface and planting through is a good way of combating both problems. Woven landscape fabric can be used in the same way. In addition, planting with ground-cover plants which hug the surface and have wide-spreading root systems will help, as the roots themselves keep the soil in place. *Geranium macrorrhizum* is ideal.

Careful watering
Never use a strong jet of water on a slope, as this exacerbates the problem. When planting, creating a slight depression helps (*see Useful planting techniques, opposite*). Although a mulch may tend to slip off the slope, it is still worth applying as it makes it easier to establish new plants.

THE GARDEN IN WINTER

ALL TOO OFTEN a garden is almost abandoned in winter, partly because cold, sometimes wet weather prevents you from getting outside to enjoy it, but also because the garden itself has lost its appeal. Winter weather does bring its own problems, damaging certain plants and affecting ponds and lawns, but the garden need not be bereft of colour and interest. Some plants come into their own at this time of year and there are bound to be some fine days when you will want to venture outside or at the very least appreciate them from the windows of the house.

SNOW DAMAGE
The weight of snow on branches has pushed a conifer permanently out of shape. ❶

FROZEN POND
The pond has iced over, trapping the fish beneath. ❷

BROWNED FLOWERS
The blooms on early-flowering shrubs have turned brown. ❹

DREARY SCENE
The garden looks extremely dull without a trace of colour. ❺

UPROOTED PLANTS
Some plants have been lifted out of the soil by a heavy frost. ❽

MUDDY TRACKS
Footprints and wheelbarrow tracks scar the lawn. ❼

1 Snow has damaged trees and shrubs

Snow can have an insulating effect, but its weight will also ruin the shape of hedges and conifers.

Tie up conifers

Conifers are more prone to damage than deciduous trees or shrubs, largely because snow adheres to their foliage. Although the initial weight may not be too great, if snow refreezes it becomes much denser and, if it is then covered by a second layer, branches may be pushed outwards and downwards. This is particularly damaging if the conifer has a conical or columnar shape. In areas where snow damage is prevalent, it is worth tying in some of the outer branches with wire to keep them upright and prevent snow from accumulating.

After damage has occurred, it is still worth wiring in the remainder of the tree. Remove the affected branches, making sure you achieve a clean cut. Unfortunately, a conifer may never regain its shape since little regrowth is likely to occur from the centre of the tree.

DAMAGE LIMITATION
Wiring prevents a large volume of snow from collecting on a conifer's branches. Tapering the sides of a hedge limits the weight of snow that can press down from the top.

Protecting smaller plants

On the whole, the insulating effect of a blanket of snow is beneficial to small plants. Temperatures beneath may be low, but they are unlikely to fluctuate as much as those above. It is usually not advisable to knock snow off, but if plants are prone to snow damage, you could give them some sort of shelter. For instance, cover them with an upturned flowerpot held in place by a heavy stone or with a specially constructed small wooden shelter.

Well-shaped hedges

If a hedge is trimmed so that it is slightly narrower at the top than the base, it will be less likely to accumulate snow or be torn apart by strong winds. Where heavy snowfall is a regular occurrence, clip the top to a point.

FROST POCKETS

IF PART OR ALL of your garden is in a valley or hollow, or if it is on the side of a slope, it could be in a frost pocket. Frost pockets occur where dense, very cold air moves downwards and the frost collects in the valley floor or becomes trapped behind any sort of barrier, such as a hedge running across a slope. Unfortunately, as the cold air accumulates, the area at risk gets larger as the cold air backs up the slope. A hedge, fence, wall or planting of trees may help to prevent cold air moving down into your garden but could also be contributing to your problems.

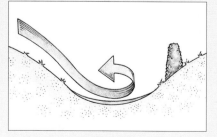

MAKINGS OF A FROST POCKET
Without any kind of barrier to prevent dense, cold air from rolling down a slope, the valley floor or hollow at the bottom will form a potential frost pocket.

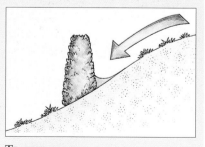

TRAPPED FROST
A hedge will help to stop frost moving down a slope, but it may also trap the frost within your garden. Removing a few plants from the hedge will allow some of the cold air to flow through.

② How can a pond be prevented from freezing over?

How much ice forms clearly depends on the severity of the weather, but if a pond freezes over completely the creatures living in it may be harmed and the pond lining damaged.

Dangers of freezing

If a pond freezes over, potentially toxic gases tend to build up beneath the ice and may kill fish or wildlife. In addition, if the pond has rigid plastic or concrete sides the pressure of the ice layer expanding and pushing against them may make them crack or split. Floating a log or ball on the surface tends to decrease the rate at which freezing

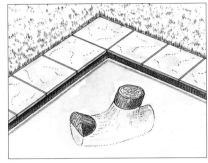

A LOG PREVENTS A POND FROM FREEZING OVER

occurs and, more importantly, also relieves some of the pressure and so decreases the risk of cracking.

Melt a hole

Do not smash ice on a frozen pond because the resulting vibrations may be fatal to wildlife or fish. Instead, melt a hole to allow toxic gases to escape by holding a pan of boiling or very hot water on the surface. You may need to repeat this regularly.

CHILD SAFETY Take precautions if children visit the garden and put up barriers or warning tapes around a frozen pond. Young children will not realize how thin ice can be nor how dangerous.

TAPS AND HOSEPIPES

• **OUTSIDE TAPS** should be drained and isolated, if possible, before cold weather sets in so that should they freeze up you do not run the risk of having a burst pipe inside the house or greenhouse. If you wish to continue using a tap, some sort of insulation is essential. Lagging the water pipe and the tap itself with old carpet, bubble-wrap polythene, old curtains or anything else which will provide a degree of insulation is well worth while.

• **HOSEPIPES** should not be left outside over winter as their fabric may be damaged by cold weather, especially if they remain out for several years in succession. Drain all the water from the hose before storing it. If you wish to leave the hose in the garden because you still need to use it, be sure to drain it each time after use. Leaving water inside greatly increases the risk of the hosepipe rupturing.

③ Cracked or split tree trunks

This sort of damage tends to occur in climates where very cold nights are followed by bright sunny mornings. In such areas, where there are lots of trees, you can sometimes even hear the sound of the bark cracking.

Natural healing

Occasionally this kind of damage occurs to trees or shrubs which have particularly thin bark. It is most likely when tree trunks are frosted or frozen and then touched by early morning sun which causes a rapid thaw. Unfortunately there is little you can do to prevent it other than planting shrubs nearby which will provide protection from both frost and the sun's rays. If such damage occurs, leave the cracked or split areas alone as the tree is more likely to heal well if left to its own devices.

TYPES OF FROST

THE VERY WORD FROST may fill a gardener's heart with fear, but there are several types. The most apparent are not necessarily the most damaging.

• **BLACK FROST** is more likely to occur when the air is relatively dry and it will cause the softer stems and foliage of plants to turn black.

• **GROUND FROST** occurs when the soil temperature falls below freezing point.

The depth to which the frost penetrates the ground, and the amount of damage it causes to plants, will depend on how long the freezing temperatures last and just how low they fall.

• **HOAR FROST** makes plants look as if dressed to appear on a Christmas card. Large sharp crystals of ice form on stems and foliage as a result of water condensing from a humid atmosphere.

④ Browned flowers

The flowers on some shrubs that bloom early in the year are often marred by the effects of frost.

Avoiding damage

The flowers on plants such as camellias and magnolias are prone to damage by frost. To some extent you can avoid this by planting in a suitable position, for instance a well-sheltered area of the garden or against a wall or fence that receives sun from late morning on, not early in the day. The sun causes rapid thawing of frozen areas and it is as a result of this that petals turn brown. If particularly harsh weather is forecast, it may also be worth covering frost-prone flowering plants overnight with some netting or fleece. On the whole, pale-coloured flowers tend to look worst if touched by frost so you could perhaps opt for darker shades in places where frost damage is likely, perhaps red camellias instead of white.

❹ The garden is dull and depressing and needs brightening up

Trees and shrubs with eye-catching bark, bright foliage or berries can have great impact in winter. A few plants bloom at this time of year, and if you do not cut back some perennials, their seedheads can look spectacular. Added to this, evergreen shrubs, such as rosemary, and plants with a dramatic outline, such as yucca, look striking under a dusting of snow or frost.

Magnificient seedheads

Although many plants are cut back at the end of their main season of interest, there are some which, if left, not only help to protect the crown of the plant but also look stunning when covered with a hoar frost. This is especially so with many grasses. Some seedheads, such as spherical alliums, add architectural form; others even bring colour. One of the most flamboyant herbaceous perennials for brightening up a winter garden is *Iris foetidissima*, whose seedheads split open to reveal orange-red seeds within.

COAT OF CRYSTALS
Frost lends a magical touch to a skimmia laden with berries and to the remains of summer-flowering perennials (inset).

Winter flowers

Winter-flowering heathers have double value since their flowers are combined with attractively tinted foliage. Many forms of the double pompon daisy (*Bellis perennis*) put on a good show of pink, red or white flowers in late winter and early spring, as does dainty *Cyclamen coum*. Winter pansies flower well given sufficient sun and yellow winter aconite (*Eranthis hyemalis*) and snowdrops can carpet small areas. In early spring the roll call gets longer, with crocus, *Iris reticulata*, spring snowflake (*Leucojum vernum*), *Anemone blanda*, early daffodils and narcissi, and wallflowers. Hellebores such as *H. niger* and *H. orientalis* are invaluable, while some shrub flowers bring fragrance too (*see list below*).

Colourful stems, leaves and berries for seasonal interest

Shrubs brighten the winter garden in all sorts of ways. *Berberis temolaica* and pyracantha have brilliant berries while some dogwoods (*Cornus*) and willows (*Salix*) have vivid stems. For good colour, cut stems to the ground in late spring. There are golden conifers and variegated varieties of elaeagnus, euonymus, holly, ivy and periwinkle. Even herbaceous plants such as bergenias, euphorbias and lamiums have handsome winter foliage.

ILEX X MESERVEAE
'BLUE PRINCESS'

PICEA GLAUCA
'COERULEA'

OPHIOPOGON PLANISCAPUS
'NIGRESCENS'

HAMAMELIS X INTERMEDIA
'ARNOLD PROMISE'

CORNUS ALBA
'SIBIRICA'

ELAEAGNUS X EBBINGEI
'GILT EDGE'

COLOUR AND SCENT

STRIKING FOLIAGE AND STEMS

Arum italicum 'Marmoratum'	*E. amygdaloides* 'Purpurea'
Bergenia 'Ballawley'	*Helleborus argutifolius*
Cornus stolonifera 'Flaviramea'	*Lamium maculatum*, especially 'White Nancy' and 'Beacon Silver'
Elaeagnus, variegated types	
Euonymus, variegated types	*Salix alba* 'Britzensis'
Euphorbia, many such as	*Tiarella polyphyllya*

SHRUBS FOR FRAGRANCE

Chimonanthus	*L. fragrantissima*
Hamamelis (witch hazel)	*Mahonia*, many
	Sarcococca
Lonicera x *purpusii*,	*Viburnum*, many

6 Protecting plants against winter weather

Any tender plants will need moving into a greenhouse or some place where they are sheltered from frost, but it is also worth protecting plants of borderline hardiness. In some cases a combination of cold and wet can be lethal.

Dry mulches

Once established, hardy perennials should not need protection but if they have been recently planted, or for perennials that are not assuredly hardy, it is worth trying to provide the crowns with some form of insulation. It may be possible to wedge a free-draining dry mulch of bark chippings, crushed bracken, dry leaves or straw among the remains of the stems. Alternatively, the mulch can be held in place by a cage of chicken wire. This will help to prevent the mulching material from being scattered over the garden by cats, birds or mice which might be searching through it for food. Mulches like this can also make a haven for slugs, so clear the area thoroughly of slugs and snails before covering the plant and check well when the mulch is removed in spring.

MOUND CHIPPED BARK OVER PLANT CROWNS

HOLD STRAW IN PLACE WITH CHICKEN WIRE

HESSIAN CAN BE USED TO PROTECT CLIMBERS

Move it or wrap it

Half-hardy or tender perennials generally need to be brought into a protected area for winter. A porch or cool greenhouse is often sufficient, but does need to be kept frost-free. Some plants, such as dahlias, are best lifted in late autumn and their tubers stored in trays of dry compost in a frost-free shed or greenhouse.

It may be possible to protect larger, slightly tender plants that cannot be moved inside with a jacket of fleece or other protective material. Use a thick-grade fleece or several layers. Fleece is better than bubble-wrap plastic since it allows reasonable air circulation and so is less likely to encourage the growth of premature new shoots beneath the protective covering or the development of moulds and other fungal problems.

Where susceptible shrubs are grown against a wall, you can attach a cage of galvanized wire to the wall and fill it with a bulky dry mulch material. Providing the material is not packed too tightly and is removed promptly in spring, there should be no significant problem with moisture accumulation and rot. A covering of hessian or thick woven netting will also give a small amount of protection against frost and is fairly easy to put in place against a wall. It is particularly useful for keeping frost from spoiling early flowers.

Soggy soil can kill

Many plants, particularly those of Mediterranean origin or with silver foliage, such as *Convolvulus cneorum*, suffer in the winter, not as a result of the cold but because of winter wet, so anything that will improve drainage during winter is well worthwhile. This may mean incorporating grit, gravel or bulky organic material into the soil in the whole area before planting and working some extra grit into the bottom of the planting hole. If adding a new plant to an already established border, try to improve drainage in the largest possible area.

It is also worth checking that no excess soil, mulch or plant debris has accumulated around the base of the plant which could help to harbour moisture and cause rot. Always check advice on labels before buying. Any plant described as needing a free-draining soil is unlikely to succeed if the ground is heavy or has a tendency to lie wet in winter.

Protection for pots

Plants in containers are particularly prone to winter damage because their root balls are exposed to very low temperatures. Plunge pots in spare ground, wrap them with insulating material or at least move them to a more sheltered position before cold weather sets in (*see p.99*).

Try tying up leaves

Some plants, including phormiums, tree ferns and some of the hardier palms, will be more likely to survive the winter undamaged if their foliage is tied up to protect the crown or growing point before the worst of the weather sets in. The foliage must be completely dry when you do this and, once tied, needs to be able to deflect rainwater from the main body of the plant. If moisture accumulates in the central areas of the plant it may cause it to rot.

❼ Muddy tracks

Winter is often the only season you can find time for carrying out repairs and new projects. You may, though, not only churn up a lot of mud in the process, but also damage the soil or lawn.

Protect soil

Walking on wet soil, particularly if it has a heavy structure, should be avoided at all costs. Ideally, any major jobs should be postponed until the soil has dried out. Even digging can damage soil structure if air spaces are squeezed out from between particles and compaction results. Keep cultivation to a minimum and use a fork rather than a spade. It is far better to delay a job until spring than risk damaging the soil. For essential work such as fence repairs, lay a temporary walkway of boards or stepping stones on the soil to allow access. If you know in advance that work is needed, cover the area with polythene sheeting in order to prevent rain from making the ground wetter.

Look after lawns

Try to avoid walking on the lawn when it is covered in frost or snow, as the grasses are particularly susceptible to damage then. Even though it may look unharmed at the time, it will be more prone to a range of diseases once it moves into growth again.

❽ Frost heave

A heavy frost may lift up the soil around a plant, perhaps exposing areas of vulnerable root.

Press back in place

Roots of trees, shrubs or sometimes herbaceous perennials which have been recently planted may sometimes be lifted out of the ground by a heavy frost. Any sign of frost heave should be dealt with immediately. Usually it is a simple matter of gently but firmly pushing the plant's root ball back into the ground with your foot. Remember that just because you have pressed it down once does not mean it will stay there; further heavy frosts may lift it again.

❾ When to tidy up?

To some extent, whether you leave tidying dead foliage until spring or "put the garden to bed" in autumn depends on personal preferences but it can also affect plant survival rates.

Autumn or spring?

Some people prefer to tidy up spent leaves and flowers once plants fade in autumn. However, it is well worth leaving any foliage that will enhance the garden in winter. In addition, if plants are at all tender, have been newly planted or are in an exposed site, the dead foliage (as long as it is not diseased) and old stems may provide useful protection to the plant's crown beneath. Penstemons, for instance, are more likely to survive if not trimmed back until spring.

Put in markers

If plants die back leaving no sign of their whereabouts, mark their positions with small canes or labels to avoid damaging them while working on the bed. Remove the marker in spring once the plant has grown sufficiently to be seen. Alternatively, draw a simple plan to remind yourself where dormant plants lay hidden. If areas are planted up with bulbs, make a simple barrier of canes and twine to prevent people walking on the area.

Trim away tatty foliage

If tattered leaves early in the year hide a plant's flowers or mar its appearance, it is worth trimming them away, taking care not to damage unfurling shoots. *Helleborus orientalis* (but not *H. niger*) and epimediums benefit from this, as do pulmonarias. Hardy ferns often keep their foliage through the winter, but cutting it away in spring allows you to see the attractive new fronds much better.

CLEARING AND MARKING
Cut off foliage that spoils the garden's appearance in early winter and mark the position of plants that die right back (inset).

HOW FROST DAMAGE OCCURS

FROST ITSELF can do a great deal of damage. However, it is the thawing and refreezing of plant tissues which have been frosted that is often even more damaging. As the sap in a cell freezes, it increases in volume and may damage the cell walls (in just the same way as a frozen water will rupture a pipe) possibly killing a large area of leaf or stem or, in extreme cases, the whole plant. Symptoms of frost damage, such as blackening and general deterioration of tissue, are likely on tender or half-hardy plants, those which have been recently planted, and on softer tissue such as flowers, buds and new leaf-growth. Even hardy plants can be damaged by frost, particularly if it occurs in late spring and the plant has already put on plenty of growth. Plant roots, particularly in containers, can also be damaged or killed by frost, and it is not unusual to see symptoms such as bark splitting on woody stems.

IN THE GREENHOUSE

IF YOU ARE LUCKY ENOUGH to own a greenhouse, you should find that it greatly increases the range of plants you can grow and extends the growing season quite substantially. That is the theory at least, but all too often it seems that greenhouses become more of a breeding ground for pests and problems than they do for plants. If your greenhouse falls into this category (or if you want to make sure that it never does), try to get to grips with the problems, if possible in the early stages, so that you can really use the greenhouse to best advantage.

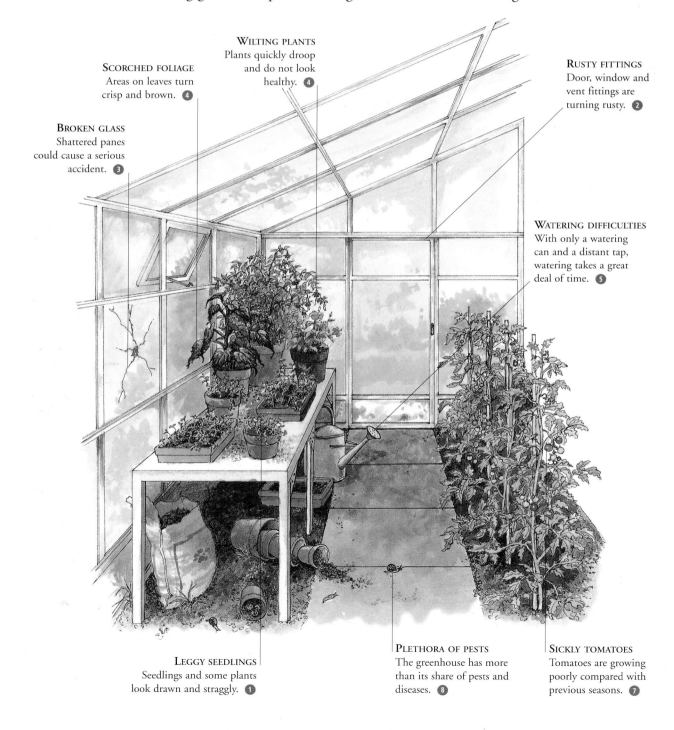

WILTING PLANTS
Plants quickly droop and do not look healthy. **4**

SCORCHED FOLIAGE
Areas on leaves turn crisp and brown. **4**

BROKEN GLASS
Shattered panes could cause a serious accident. **3**

RUSTY FITTINGS
Door, window and vent fittings are turning rusty. **2**

WATERING DIFFICULTIES
With only a watering can and a distant tap, watering takes a great deal of time. **5**

LEGGY SEEDLINGS
Seedlings and some plants look drawn and straggly. **1**

PLETHORA OF PESTS
The greenhouse has more than its share of pests and diseases. **8**

SICKLY TOMATOES
Tomatoes are growing poorly compared with previous seasons. **7**

THE PROBLEMS

1. Plants, especially seedlings, get tall and straggly, and tomatoes are slow to ripen.
2. How can a wooden greenhouse frame be prevented from rotting and greenhouse fittings from turning rusty?
3. Panes of glass are sometimes hit by the children's football, and the prospect of a serious accident is worrying.
4. Cuttings collapse, plants wilt and leaf edges get scorched.
5. The greenhouse is a long way from a tap. How can the time spent carrying heavy watering cans be reduced?
6. What sort of heating, that doesn't cost too much to run, would ensure that a wider range of plants survive the winter?
7. The tomato plants in the greenhouse border are growing poorly for no obvious reason.
8. The greenhouse seems to be a haven for pests and diseases. What are the best ways of dealing with them?

See also:

Propagating Plants, p.28;
Seed Sowing and Collecting, p.38; Pests, Diseases and Disorders, p.178.

Reduce shade from trees

Although a greenhouse needs a fairly sheltered site, it is essential that it is not in too shady a spot. It may be possible to prune trees back or reduce the size of their crowns in some way (*see p.10 and p.121*). Although extensive pruning may increase the need for artificial shading in summer, it will help to improve plant growth at the beginning and end of the year and reduce the risk of glass being broken by falling branches.

❶ Leggy plants, seedlings and cuttings

Spindly plants, tall straggly seedlings and slow-ripening tomatoes generally indicate poor light levels.

Let in the light

Dirty glazing or an accumulation of leaves on the glass will severely reduce the amount of light reaching plants. Clean glazing regularly (but particularly at the beginning and end of the year when natural light levels are low) using a stiff brush and soapy water or a proprietary cleaner. You may need a broom for the roof, or a broom tied onto a pole. Quite often debris, especially algae and sometimes moss, gathers where the panes overlap. The easiest way to remove it is to wiggle a plastic plant label or strip from a margarine or yoghurt tub up and down between the two panes. Once the grime is loosened, it can be washed away. When using any sort of cleaning agent, cover plants or, better still, remove them to avoid risk of

SCRAPE GRIME FROM GLAZING
A plant label or strip of plastic from an old yoghurt pot makes a good tool for removing algae from between panes of glass.

scorching them. Cleaning the glass inside as well as out may also help to decrease problems from overwintering pests such as red spider mite.

Occasionally excessive quantities of greenhouse shading may have been used or the shading may not have been washed off early enough. It is generally best to remove it as soon as sunshine levels start to drop, usually in early autumn.

Orientation has an effect on light levels

If a greenhouse is not orientated to receive the right amount of light at certain times of year, plants may suffer. It is rarely feasible to move a greenhouse that is already in position but if you are planning to put up a new greenhouse, choose the most appropriate orientation for your purposes. Siting it north to south on its longer axis will make best use of light in summer. However, for raising lots of plants in late winter or early spring or overwintering tender plants, it is best orientated with the longer axis running east to west, as this will ensure good light levels for a high proportion of the day while the sun is low in the sky.

Artificial lighting makes short days longer

Installing artificial lighting that mimics daylight or using mercury or sodium lights will help if legginess is largely restricted to small plants or seedlings. Using artificial lighting could also encourage plants to flower earlier in the season and plants such as basil to crop for longer when natural light levels decrease. But it will, of course, increase running costs.

USE A GROWING LAMP
The light from a lamp suspended above plants will improve growth. Special electrical fittings are needed in the moist atmosphere.

❷ Preventing rot on a wooden frame

Wooden-framed greenhouses need regular maintenance, but if rot has already set in, prompt action is required to stop it spreading.

Initial selection

If you can, choose western red cedar as this resists rot well, does not warp and needs relatively little maintenance. Cheaper timbers such as redwood may lower the cost initially, but will need to be pressure treated before the framework is erected and will also need to be painted regularly with a timber treatment.

Check for water leaks

If guttering or downpipes are blocked, water may accumulate on the framework and cause rot. Check regularly and if necessary fit chicken wire or purpose-made protection wires to prevent leaves from clogging the guttering. You can also fit a crown of chicken wire over the mouth of the downpipe. First use a rod to clean out any leaves that have already collected in the pipe and flush them through with water from a hosepipe. Replace broken guttering or downpipes promptly, since leaking water will encourage rot.

Fitting a water butt to the downpipe is certainly a good idea, but ensure that the butt has an overflow pipe or that the water diverter automatically ceases to fill it once full. Water spilling out from a butt is often the cause of wood rotting.

Repairing rotten timber

Slight darkening or discolouration are the first signs of rot before the wood starts to develop a soft texture. Where rot has already started, scrape away the whole of the rotted area until you reach sound wood. Fill with a proprietary wood filler and smooth it over. Make sure that the cause has been remedied first. If large areas have rotted, it is usually necessary to replace the whole section to avoid structural problems, resulting in panes of glass loosening and falling.

RUSTY FITTINGS

UNLESS FITTINGS are made from brass, or their galvanized coating remains intact, they may turn rusty. Deal with the problem quickly, because if key bolts and screws are affected, structures may be damaged or become unsafe. Clean off rust using a wire brush, then coat metal surfaces with oil or an anti-rust paint as appropriate. Regularly rubbing an oily rag over potential problem areas will help to prevent rust from developing in the first place.

IN NEED OF RENOVATION?

• INSPECT THE FRAMEWORK of a neglected greenhouse to see if part needs replacing or whether it can be repaired. When renewing glazing be sure to fit horticultural glass. Sometimes glazing may fall out simply because glazing pins have deteriorated or putty has worked loose. It should be relatively simple to replace pins and scrape out and replace old putty. A properly working and fitting door is essential, so any repairs to its frame are a must. Check that hinges or runners are kept well-oiled, so that they run smoothly, and that glazing in the door is also secure. Check, too, that any automatic vents are working properly and replace these if necessary.

• TEST STAGING to see if it is strong enough to carry the weight of large numbers of pots and trays if you plan to do much propagating. If made from wood slats, you may be able to replace only those that have deteriorated. Treat the wood with a suitable preservative.

• CHANGE THE SOIL in borders; nutrients are likely to be depleted and the soil may be harbouring diseases.

❸ Broken glass

In a garden used by children, the greenhouse often seems to act like a magnet for balls and other missiles, and there is always the worry that breaking glass will cause injury.

Safety glazing

When buying a new greenhouse, it is worth considering using either toughened or laminated glazing, at least for the lower panes. This slightly increases the initial cost, but has a huge safety advantage. Toughened glass is harder to break than normal horticultural glass and, if it does get broken, it forms numerous cubes which are less likely to cause serious injury. Laminated glazing is made up of three parts and is extremely difficult to break.

Installing toughened or laminated glass at the top of the greenhouse is difficult, since both are considerably heavier than standard horticultural glass but accidents are much less likely to occur on the roof.

Cheaper alternatives

If the greenhouse is already glazed, or if cost is a major factor, you can fix special sticky transparent plastic sheets onto all or part of the glass. These will not stop it from breaking but will hold the broken pieces together and greatly reduce the risk of injury. Another option is temporarily or permanently to replace some of the glazing with polycarbonate sheeting. Although this is opaque, it still allows a high percentage of light through, has insulating properties and is, of course, almost harmless when broken.

Barrier planting

If it is not feasible to replace glass or use sticky plastic sheeting, try some strategic planting, by positioning fast-growing, possibly prickly, plants such as roses to shield the greenhouse from children and vice versa. Keep trees nearby well maintained, removing dead or hanging branches which might fall and break panes of glass.

❹ Wilting plants and scorched leaf margins

In strong sunlight or too much heat, leaf edges may scorch, cuttings collapse and plants generally suffer. Some sort of shading and adequate ventilation are essential.

Paint or blinds?

Shading is needed as soon as weather turns hotter and brighter in late spring, both to reduce the sun's glare and to help keep temperatures down. The cheapest way of providing it is to use white shading paint which can be applied once a year, topped up if necessary, and removed as soon as it is no longer needed. It is, though, not the most attractive method and if the greenhouse is in a prominent position you may prefer to install blinds. These vary in price considerably and may be made from a variety of materials including wood, fabric, metal and plastic.

Wooden blinds are usually fitted on the exterior and can be rolled up or down as necessary. They are often made from slatted hardwood and, although expensive, weather well. Fabric roller blinds, fitted inside the greenhouse, are also readily available.

Whatever sort of blind you choose, it is essential to measure up accurately and follow installation instructions carefully, particularly where the blinds need openings over roof vents. Exterior blinds will not damage plants, such as vines, growing close to the greenhouse roof but weathering may shorten their lifespan. In some cases, shading may be needed only on the part of the roof that faces the sun. The blind manufacturer may be able to advise or your own observations will help you decide.

If additional temporary shading is needed for small plants, seedlings or cuttings, arrange them so that they are shaded by a ring of larger pots and plants, or rig up temporary shading, perhaps using a few sheets of newspaper. Plants such as ferns that require extra shade in summer can be placed beneath the staging.

BLINDS MUST ALLOW ROOF VENTS TO OPEN

Leaf scorch

Sunlight itself can scorch foliage, but the problem will be intensified by careless watering. Droplets of water which land on leaves tend to act like magnifying glasses and intensify the sun's rays. Shading will certainly help to alleviate the problem but, generally, try to avoid wetting foliage just before or during periods of bright light and also before temperatures suddenly drop in the evening, since this increases the likelihood of disease developing. Any chemicals should be applied with great care, particularly to leaves, and should never be applied just before a period of bright light. Condensation drip can also cause similar problems, and plants which are particularly prone to scorching should be kept well away from areas where this is likely.

Ventilation

If a greenhouse is not adequately ventilated, temperatures will build up rapidly on a hot sunny day and extreme damage can soon occur. Most good greenhouses are supplied with both roof vents and windows, but roof ventilation is often inadequate on cheap models.

If you find that the greenhouse is regularly getting too hot, consider replacing some of the existing roof lights or glazing on the sides with roof vents or windows.

Vents which open automatically at a given temperature are a boon if you cannot check the greenhouse during the day. Set them to open at just below the optimum temperature for the plants so that fresh air enters before it gets impossibly hot. You could also install side louvre ventilators which allow good air circulation without having to leave windows ajar, useful if you are concerned about animals such as cats getting in. Windows and vents can always be fitted with fine mesh which will keep out smaller creatures, including pests such as aphids. However, this will also reduce air circulation and you may well need to introduce some additional vents.

LOUVRE VENTILATORS INTRODUCE FRESH AIR

> **HOW MUCH VENTILATION?**
> As a general guide, try to ensure that the total area for ventilation – vents, windows and louvres – is equivalent to one-sixth of the floor space.

GOOD AIR CIRCULATION

UNLESS YOU MAINTAIN a buoyant atmosphere, plants grow poorly while pests and diseases thrive. In summer, shading and ventilation are essential and installing a fan will also help to keep air moving. In really hot weather, damp down hard surfaces using a hose to reduce the temperature and increase humidity. Even in winter good air movement is essential, since stagnant air encourages disease, in particular grey mould. If you use electricity for heating, include at least one fan heater.

❺ A lot of time is spent carrying heavy watering cans

Watering is one of the most important jobs in a greenhouse, and it pays to use time-saving devices.

Install a water butt

If a water butt is connected so that it receives rainwater from the greenhouse roof, it will provide a readily accessible supply (*see p.135*). Do not use its water, however, on seedlings or cuttings, since it may contain disease-causing fungi.

Watering aids

Standing seed trays and pots on capillary matting allows them to take up moisture whenever it is needed. The matting needs to be laid on heavy-duty polythene on top of the

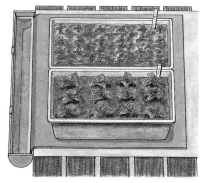

Capillary matting
A length of gutter makes a good reservoir. The matting draws water from it and the moisture in turn is absorbed by the compost.

staging or preferably in a shallow tray with one end of the matting linked to a deeper tray that is kept full of water.

Upside-down plastic drinks bottles with the bases removed make useful funnels for channelling water direct to the roots of plants in growing bags.

Good practice

Try to water in the evening to reduce wastage by evaporation. Watering in bright sunshine increases the risk of scorching if foliage or petals get splashed. Using a watering can rather than a hose makes it easier to direct the water accurately. It is essential that all plants receive the correct amount of water; the majority need to have their compost kept moist at all times. Erratic watering can cause damage on some plants, for instance blossom end rot on tomatoes and peppers.

❻ Some method of heating is needed

Heating enables you to grow a wider range of plants and give your own home-raised plants an early start. However, since it can be expensive, consider how much heat you really need for the plants you plan to grow.

Insulate it

It makes sense to install insulation in late autumn as soon as temperatures start to fall. One of the easiest ways is to fix bubble-wrap polythene to the frame using pins on wooden-framed greenhouses or special fixings on aluminium. The disadvantages are

LINE GLASS WITH BUBBLE-WRAP FOR INSULATION

that it will decrease light levels inside and, if fixed over the roof and sides, will make ventilation rather difficult.

To lower costs, you could consider heating just part of the greenhouse or heating it to a higher temperature. A cheap way of doing this is, after insulating it, to partition off the end furthest from the door with a curtain of bubble-wrap polythene.

Heating options

Electric heaters require a safe electricity supply. Sockets should be of a type approved for greenhouse use so that there is no risk of water seeping in. The heaters are easy to use, present no problems with fumes or water vapour and usually contain thermostats so that you can achieve a precise temperature. Running them, though, is often rather expensive, especially if they incorporate a fan. But, where possible, a heater with a fan is preferable because it will also move the air around. Tubular heaters are much cheaper to run, but you would probably also need to use a small fan heater or fan to improve air circulation. Tubular heaters are also

considerably more expensive to buy and may be difficult to relocate should you need to move them.

Paraffin heaters are the cheapest option but do not have thermostats and unless well maintained may give off fumes which are toxic to plants. In addition, as paraffin burns it produces water vapour which can create a damp atmosphere and may in turn encourage disease. This makes adequate ventilation essential, which in turn means losing some heat.

If your greenhouse is close to the house, it may be possible to extend the oil or gas central heating. Installation is likely to be expensive, but it should be fairly cheap to run. However, keeping a system like this at the desired temperature is not always easy and you may need to heat the greenhouse at times when you are not heating the house.

INSTALL A THERMOMETER
To check that the heating is doing its job, have at least one independent maximum and minimum thermometer to record lowest and highest temperatures.

❼ Tomatoes in a border are growing poorly

The most likely reason for a poor crop of tomatoes is attack by fungal disease. The fungi responsible build up in the soil if you grow tomatoes, cucumbers or related crops for several years in succession without changing it.

Soil carries an infection

The fungi that cause fungal wilt or foot- and root-rotting diseases are not visible to the naked eye, so the only way that you can tell they are present is when plants grow poorly or even die. The only solution is to change the soil in the borders or grow future crops in growing bags, containers or sterilized compost. To change the soil, dig it out completely, taking it right down to the base of the trench, and replace it with fresh soil or a mixture of compost, manure and grit (*see Benefits of borders, right*). If you change to using containers, make sure that their bases are not in contact with the infected soil or pave it over.

Signs of virus

If the border soil is new, the problem may be caused by a virus infection. Symptoms include stunting, general poor growth and yellow flecks, ring spots or streaks on the leaves. Remove virus-infected plants promptly.

Cultivation problems

Another possibility is that nutrient levels are seriously depleted (due perhaps to an exceptionally large tomato crop being produced in the border the previous year). If this could be the case, feed regularly with a high-potash liquid feed.

Sometimes problems are attributed to tomatoes and cucumbers being grown together. The difficulty lies in cucumbers needing more heat and humidity than tomatoes so you may have to compromise the environments of each plant to some extent. One solution is to partition off one area in some way so that you can increase heat and humidity for the cucumbers.

BENEFITS OF BORDERS

- **PLANTS IN BORDERS** tend to crop better than those in pots and growing bags and are easier to maintain. If space is limited, put temporary staging over the border for raising plants early in the season. Once removed, use the border for growing tomatoes, melons, aubergines and cucumbers.
- **MAKE BORDERS** at least 90cm (3ft) wide and fill with good garden soil enriched with manure. Where soil is heavy, dig out the border to a depth of 60–90cm (2–3ft) and fill the bottom 13–15cm (5–6in) with grit to improve drainage. Substitute poor soil with a mixture of loam-based compost such as John Innes No. 3, manure and grit. Border soil needs replacing every few years or soil-borne diseases tend to build up, resulting in crop failure.
- **VINES** usually perform better if their roots are in soil outside the greenhouse and their stems trained through to the inside. Failing this, grow them in a sizeable greenhouse border. If outside, you will need to make an opening at the base of the greenhouse and probably enlarge it as the vine grows.

❽ What are the best ways to deal with pests and diseases?

The protected environment in any greenhouse is unfortunately likely to prove a happy breeding ground for a wide range of pests and diseases (see pp.178–85).

Hygiene and prevention

Many pests and diseases such as grey mould can be kept at bay if you take strict hygiene measures, including promptly removing dead, dying or sickly plants. At least once a year, have a thorough clean-out, scrubbing down staging, glazing and framework. This will help to eliminate pests such as red spider mite, which tends to overwinter in cracks. Choose a time when the greenhouse is fairly empty or you can find a temporary home for the plants. Also scrub pots and trays after use with plain or soapy water or diluted proprietary greenhouse disinfectant; check them before re-use.

Fine mesh fitted to vents, windows and over the door will help to reduce the number of pests that can enter. Examine plants for pests before buying and consider putting them in "quarantine" in a suitable place for a few days before bringing them into the greenhouse.

You can do a lot to reduce the damage done by pests and diseases by ensuring that plants are kept in good condition by careful watering, feeding and temperature control. Then, even if attacked, they are better able to produce replacement growth.

Biological controls

The greenhouse is the most suitable place to use biological controls. A predatory mite, *Phytoseilus persimilis*, can be used against glasshouse red spider mite, and a parasitic wasp, *Encarsia formosa*, against glasshouse

whitefly. For aphids, use a parasitic wasp, *Aphidius*, or the larvae of a midge, *Aphidoletes*. Certain caterpillars can be killed by the bacterium *Bacillus thuringiensis*. Purchase the right quantities for the size of your greenhouse and level of infestation. The producers will give instructions as to the best way of distributing the predators and parasites within the greenhouse. These vary from product to product.

Using chemicals

If you decide to resort to chemicals, follow the instructions carefully because although often very efficient, not every product is suitable for use on every type of plant. Also take care that you are not endangering yourself if spraying in a confined space. Open the door and as many vents and windows as you can to reduce risk.

IMPROVING THE SOIL

IT IS A RARE TREAT to find a "perfect" soil. In reality, most of us take on something which is in need of improvement. True, you should try to work with the soil rather than against it, and you can generally create a garden of some sort on very heavy soil or poor, thin sandy soil. But if you want to get the most from your plants you will need to keep your soil "in good heart" and do what you can to improve it. Looking after the soil is fundamental to most good gardening.

Q *How can you tell what sort of texture a soil has – whether it is clay or sandy?*

A Take a small quantity (about three teaspoonfuls) of moist soil and gently rub and squeeze it between your fingers. A heavy clay will feel sticky and can be readily rolled or made into a shape; a clay loam will hold together quite well but will not feel as smooth and the surface won't remain intact if pressed into a shape; a sandy loam will feel slightly gritty and will hold together only partially when compressed; and a sandy soil will feel gritty and cannot be rolled into a ball or pressed into a shape.

It is important that your sample is typical of the majority of soil in the garden, and does not contain mulch or other materials that have been added to a planting hole. Loam, which has the ideal balance of mineral particle size and so gives good drainage yet retains moisture, is easier to work with than heavy clay or sandy soil. But do not be disheartened whatever you have – very few gardens start off with a perfect soil.

Q *Are there any advantages to having a heavy soil?*

A Heavy soils are generally more fertile and have a higher nutrient content than sandy soils. These are less able to hold on to nutrients but are much lighter to dig – a real advantage for anyone with a bad back.

Q *What is the best way to deal with a very heavy soil?*

A It is definitely worth digging in materials that will improve the soil's texture and increase aeration. Forking in large quantities of horticultural grit helps. Unless you have only a limited area to improve, it works out a lot cheaper to buy the grit in bulk – by the cubic metre – rather than in lots of small bags from a garden centre. Bulky organic matter is effective, too – for example, well-rotted manure, garden compost, composted shredded bark or leaf-mould. Some manures are perhaps better than others for heavy soil; pig manure is often inclined to make a clay soil even stickier. It is also worth incorporating old potting compost or the contents of used growing bags.

In the first instance, try to double dig the area (to two spits deep – each spit the depth of the spade's blade), incorporating plenty of organic matter as you go. Take care not to bring any subsoil to the surface or mix it with the topsoil. Thereafter, it is generally better to avoid working the soil too much as this may itself cause compaction and deterioration of structure. Instead, organic matter can be added to the surface as a mulch in autumn. It will gradually find its way down to the deeper levels, aided by earthworms.

Lime may also be used on heavy soils. This encourages clay particles to bind together into clusters. Air spaces are created between these clusters, improving aeration and drainage. Using lime, however, will obviously make soil more alkaline.

If the garden is waterlogged, you may be best off installing a drainage system, although this may prove costly even if you put it in yourself.

Q *What can be done to improve a light, sandy soil?*

A Soil additives such as well-rotted manure, leaf-mould, garden compost and composted shredded bark are really important to help improve texture. All these materials will increase the soil's ability to retain moisture and therefore hold on to nutrients, while manure and garden compost actually contain nutrients.

Q *What is wrong with using fresh manure in the garden?*

A As manure rots down, it produces ammonia, which may cause scorching and other damage to plants, so never use it fresh as a mulch or a soil improver. Stack fresh manure for at least 18 months before using it.

Q *What is wrong with using sawdust or wood chippings to open up a heavy soil?*

A Wood chippings, sawdust and straw should be avoided because, as they are broken down, they tend to rob the soil of nitrogen, which is vital for healthy plant growth. Either compost down these materials before using them or, if this is not possible, apply them at the same time as a high-nitrogen fertilizer or plenty of well-rotted manure, either of which will help to compensate for the nitrogen depletion.

Q *Digging with a spade on heavy clay soil is hard work. How can it be made easier?*

A The answer is simple, don't do it! It is far better and easier to work a clay soil using a fork. A spade tends to smear or compact the soil slightly as the blade moves through it, often making problems of poor aeration, waterlogging and compaction worse.

Q *Mulches are often recommended for light soils. Do they also benefit heavy clay? And what are the best mulching materials to use?*

A Mulches are good for any soil. Organic materials will gradually be incorporated into the soil by earthworms, improving the soil structure in the process and, in some cases, also releasing valuable nutrients. While laying on the soil surface, a mulch will also help to reduce water loss by evaporation. Although clay soils are better able to retain moisture, some have a tendency to crack during dry periods which may damage plant roots and also allow evaporation from lower down in the soil. A mulch should help to prevent or at least reduce cracking. To be effective, a layer of mulch needs to be 5–8cm (2–3in) deep, and must be laid on moist soil.

Most mulching materials can be used regardless of the soil pH but mushroom compost is generally very alkaline in reaction and so will tend to make soil more alkaline. If you use chipped bark, make sure you buy bark and not chipped wood.

Q *Many newly planted shrubs have failed on a heavy soil, even though the planting holes were well prepared. What has gone wrong?*

A You have probably inadvertently created a sump effect. If a soil is heavy and wet and you then dig a planting hole in the normal way, adding plenty of organic matter, you will make a sump and water will be drawn in from the surrounding heavy, wet soil. When planting in heavy soil, it is essential to create a much larger hole than usual and also to improve the soil all around the planting hole. If there is no sudden change in soil texture, your plants are less likely to end up becoming waterlogged.

Q *What is the pH of a soil, and how can it be determined?*

A The pH is the term used to quantify the soil's acidity or alkalinity. It may be described on a scale of 1 to 14, with a neutral soil having a pH of 7; soils with readings higher than 7 are alkaline, and those below 7 are acid. Various chemical or electronic probe-type testing kits are available. You will probably need to test the soil in several areas of the garden since it may vary.

Q *What sort of problems are caused by a very acid soil? If necessary can it be made less acid?*

A Unless your soil has been contaminated by something that has made it excessively acid, there are plenty of plants that will grow perfectly happily in it. However, many vegetables prefer an alkaline soil and, if growing these, it would be worthwhile trying to lower the pH slightly. This is fairly easily done by applying lime in the form of calcium carbonate, which is easy and safe to use and readily available from garden centres. Although lime in this form is unlikely to scorch plants, it is still best to apply it well in advance of planting, spreading it evenly over the soil and then digging it in. The amount needed depends on the soil type, its present pH and the pH you wish to achieve. Work this out carefully because it can vary from 110g (4oz) to 450g (1lb) per square metre (square yard). Instructions should be supplied with the lime.

If a relatively small increase in pH is needed, you could dress the soil with lime around growing plants, but do not let the lime touch the foliage. Adding alkaline materials such as mushroom compost to the soil will also raise the pH slightly.

Q *What are the main problems on very alkaline soils, and how can alkalinity be reduced?*

A Generally speaking, alkaline soils are more restricting in the range of plants you can grow, but it is still best to choose suitable plants rather than try to alter the pH dramatically. However, you could apply sulphur, either to the soil prior to planting or around existing plants and, provided it is done with care, there should be no risk to the plants themselves.

The pH can be lowered slightly by digging in or mulching with acidic materials such as chopped bracken or cocoa shells. The quantity needed depends on existing pH, soil type and the pH you are trying to achieve. Do not dig in mushroom compost, which is itself alkaline. Making a soil more acid or less alkaline is harder than making it more alkaline.

THE VEGETABLE PLOT

NOTHING BEATS THE TASTE of home-grown vegetables. Picked fresh, they will have a wonderful flavour, a supreme texture and be packed full of nutrients and, if you garden organically, have no trace of chemical residue. Sadly, people often shy away from vegetable growing, believing it to be strictly for experienced gardeners. Nothing could be further from the truth. There are bound to be problems and some are not easy to avoid or overcome without effort. But, with vegetable growing in particular, the answer often lies in improving the soil.

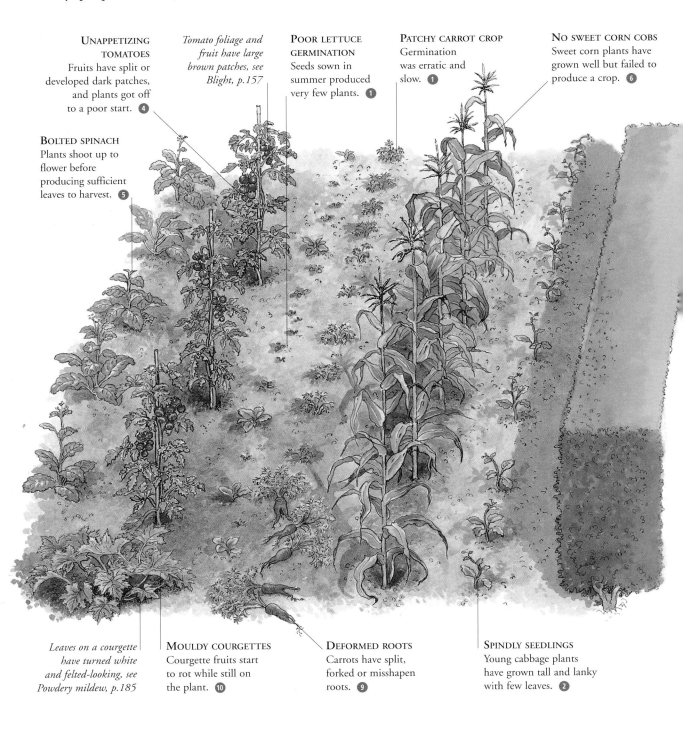

UNAPPETIZING TOMATOES
Fruits have split or developed dark patches, and plants got off to a poor start. **4**

Tomato foliage and fruit have large brown patches, see Blight, p.157

POOR LETTUCE GERMINATION
Seeds sown in summer produced very few plants. **1**

PATCHY CARROT CROP
Germination was erratic and slow. **1**

NO SWEET CORN COBS
Sweet corn plants have grown well but failed to produce a crop. **6**

BOLTED SPINACH
Plants shoot up to flower before producing sufficient leaves to harvest. **5**

Leaves on a courgette have turned white and felted-looking, see Powdery mildew, p.185

MOULDY COURGETTES
Courgette fruits start to rot while still on the plant. **10**

DEFORMED ROOTS
Carrots have split, forked or misshapen roots. **9**

SPINDLY SEEDLINGS
Young cabbage plants have grown tall and lanky with few leaves. **2**

1 Germination is very poor or gappy

There are several possible causes of poor germination. The seed itself may not have been viable, or poor conditions may have inhibited germination. Or the seed might have made a meal for a hungry creature.

Adverse temperatures

With crops that are sown early in the season, especially parsnips and carrots, a soil that is too cold and damp may be to blame. If possible, delay sowing by a week or two until conditions have improved; the crop will usually have caught up by harvest time. If you are determined to sow early, cover the soil with plastic or horticultural fleece a week or two before sowing. Fleece helps to warm the soil but allows rain through, making it the more suitable of the two for light, free-draining soils where cold is the problem. If you leave the fleece in place until the seeds have germinated, this will also help to bring the crop on a little earlier, but if you are using polythene, remove it promptly or arrange a support so that it is not in contact with the seedlings. Fleece or polythene mini-tunnels can be kept in place until the crop is a fair size. In particularly hot weather, a few crops, notably lettuce, may fail to germinate because temperatures are too high.

A NET TUNNEL PROTECTS PEA SEEDS FROM BIRDS

Stolen seed

Quite often the seedbed may be perfectly well prepared and the seed viable but either it is stolen by birds or mice or the seedbed is disturbed by cats. Protect the seeds by driving in some twiggy sticks around the seedbed or making a "cage" of chicken wire (*see p.43*). Once germinated, seedlings are less likely to be damaged by birds, but keep the barrier in place as long as possible to deter cats. If you string cotton between the sticks or canes, keep it taut so that it cannot become tangled around birds' feet.

If seeds are stolen by mice, the only answer is to use traps. Humane traps are available and, provided they are checked regularly, any mice caught can be released elsewhere.

Stale seed

Since there are generally far more seeds in a packet than are needed, it is tempting to keep them from one year to the next, or maybe longer. If you do this, store the seeds carefully or germination may be poor.

Washed away?

In dry weather, seeds will need to be watered in although this itself can cause problems. If you use a hose or sprinkler (or if rainfall is very heavy), seeds may be washed away or into clumps. Instead, use a watering can with the rose attached or, if you really need to use a hose, attach a head that produces very fine droplets.

Prepare a seed drill to the correct depth

If seeds are not sown at the correct depth, germination may be haphazard. Check the recommended sowing depth on the seed packet and stick to it. If the soil has been worked so that it has a fine tilth (structure) it is easier to take out a seed drill of an even depth all along the row.

1 RAKE THE SOIL several times, varying the direction, to produce a fine tilth and remove stones.

2 SOW IN A DRILL of the correct depth. Press the seed lightly so that it is in contact with moist soil.

3 DRAW BACK THE SOIL so that the seed is evenly covered and is not displaced. Water gently.

❷ Spindly seedlings and plants lack vigour

There are various reasons why a crop may not grow as well as it should, and it is important to try to determine what is causing the problem as soon as it becomes evident.

Tired soil?

Many vegetables are "hungry" and need good nutrition. Where soil is poor and perhaps has had crops grown on it intensively for a number of years, pathetic-looking plants are almost inevitable. It is essential to prepare the soil really well by incorporating plenty of well-rotted manure or garden compost, and perhaps applying a general fertilizer. Soil improvement is best carried out in autumn but, if necessary, you can do it shortly before planting in most cases. Exceptions to this include potatoes and carrots, where newly manured soil is likely to encourage scab disease on potato tubers and fanging or forking of carrot roots.

DRY, LIGHT SOIL This can affect plants' growth because they cannot take up nutrients. Improve soil by incorporating organic matter, and mulch to conserve moisture once crops are large enough.

Lack of light

Shade from trees, hedges or fences will cause rather drawn, leggy growth. Reduce the shade if you can, perhaps by pruning trees and

ADD MANURE TO TIRED, POOR OR LIGHT SOIL

shrubs or cutting back hedges or, where possible, move the vegetable plot to a sunnier spot. Where the shade is cast by a wall, painting it white will help to increase the light levels slightly because of the reflected light created.

Nearby trees, shrubs and hedges may also cause problems because they take a considerable amount of moisture and food from the soil. If this is the case, soil improvement is again the answer and you will probably need to combine this with regular feeding and, of course, watering and mulching.

Look to the roots

Sometimes diseases are responsible for poor growth of young plants, for instance clubroot on brassicas (*see p.157*) and fungal foot and root rots on many other plants. Pests such as wireworm, eelworm, chafer grubs and leatherjackets (*see p.55*) may also injure root systems so that plants fail to thrive or possibly die. It is essential to try to find the cause of the problem in order to remedy it, even though this may mean sacrificing a plant so that you can examine all parts carefully.

Avoid root disturbance

Any root damage while transplanting from seed trays or pots into the open ground will cause a setback. Plants may pick up after a week or two but it is important to try to avoid injuring root systems. Wherever possible, grow plants in cells or small pots so that root balls can remain intact. In hot weather, transplant towards the end of the day to reduce stress on the plant, or shade transplants with netting until they have recovered and settled in. Watering while roots become established also helps to ensure plants get off to a good start.

CELL-RAISED BRASSICA SEEDLING

❸ Yield was much lower than expected

If you try to fit too many plants into a small space you may reduce yield rather than increase it. Choosing an appropriate fertilizer may also play an important role in producing a plentiful crop.

Room for development

Check that the final spacing between plants is correct and that they have been thinned out at an early enough stage. Undue competition is likely to result in none of the plants cropping particularly well and the overall yield being reduced. With some vegetables, such as onions, close planting may not reduce the total yield but will instead give you a large number of smaller-sized onions.

Poor cultivation

Lack of feeding and inadequate watering are also a common cause of poor cropping. Soil improvement and feeding throughout the season will go a long way towards improving cropping, plus of course ensuring that plants are adequately watered and, if necessary, mulched. Some fruiting crops, such as tomatoes and peppers, do best if given a high-potash fertilizer. Those grown for their leaves, such as cabbages, generally need a fertilizer that is high in nitrogen. It is important to choose the correct feed for individual crops.

4 Poor tomato plants produce few or unappetizing fruits

Weather plays a major part in the success or otherwise of outdoor tomatoes, but some problems are also due to poor cultivation.

SPLIT SKIN

BLOSSOM END ROT

Uneven watering
In extreme circumstances, an erratic supply of water will result in blossom end rot, where the tomato fruits develop a black, leathery patch at the base and fail to develop normally. But in less adverse conditions, tomatoes tend to form a rather tough skin when water is in short supply. When they start to receive it once more, they start to swell again, which splits the skins. Regular watering, improving the soil before planting and mulching will all help to reduce the problem. In the greenhouse, providing extra shade also seems to help. Whether growing tomatoes in open ground, a greenhouse border or large containers, try to ensure plant roots receive an adequate and even supply of moisture.

Starved of food
Plants such as tomatoes are very hungry feeders. Initial soil improvement is important, but plants also need regular feeding with a high-potash liquid fertilizer, usually sold specifically as a tomato food. This should be applied at the intervals stated on the pack. Begin feeding once you see the first tiny fruitlets.

Inspect the roots
Where plants themselves are in generally poor condition, they may be suffering from some form of foot or root rot. Lift at least one plant and carefully examine the roots. If these are brown or otherwise discoloured and rotting, this suggests foot and root rot and usually indicates that tomatoes have either been grown on the same site for more than one season, or perhaps that the conditions under which the plants were raised were unhygienic.

Unacclimatized
Moving plants from the protected environment of a greenhouse or cold frame into open ground too quickly, without allowing sufficient time for them to get hardened off or acclimatized to outdoor conditions, can set plants back considerably. This often causes poor growth, a slight purpling of the foliage and a tendency for leaves to scorch easily. When the weather improves, the plants usually pick up, but the ultimate crop may still be affected. Similarly, even when plants have been adequately hardened off, they are likely to suffer if the weather suddenly turns colder after planting out.

Outdoors or in?
Ensure that the varieties you choose to grow outside are suitable for the purpose. They need to be considerably tougher than greenhouse varieties. Both seed packets and catalogues should state this clearly. Avoid varieties about which you are at all unsure and, in any case, try to grow tomatoes in the warmest and most sheltered position possible.

5 Crops bolt before they can be harvested

When vegetables produce flowers or seeds prematurely, before they have produced a crop worth picking, this is called bolting. It is very common with spinach, onions, lettuces, Chinese leaves and bulb fennel.

Insufficient water
Dryness at a plant's roots encourages bolting, particularly on crops such as lettuce and spinach, so improve the soil's capacity to retain moisture (*see p.148*) before sowing or planting, mulch and, if necessary, water crops.

Variety counts
Choice of variety can also affect the likelihood of bolting. Avoid growing particularly early varieties of those crops which you know are susceptible to bolting. It is also worth checking seed catalogues to find varieties which are noted for showing resistance to bolting. When growing onions, raising the crop from sets as opposed to seed will help, particularly if you obtain heat-treated sets.

Chilled out
Exposure to low temperatures at a certain stage of growth is often responsible and is particularly common if there is a late or cold start to the spring. This can be avoided by not sowing or planting too early, while weather is still variable, or by giving protection when temperatures are likely to drop. Horticultural fleece or fleece mini-tunnels often provide sufficient cover, or a foldaway mini-polytunnel is easy to put over when very cold nights are forecast.

A MINI-POLYTUNNEL PROTECTS AGAINST COLD

6 Poor sweet corn crop and misshapen cobs

Lack of sweet corn cobs, or cobs with malformed, shrivelled or sparse kernels, is usually due to a pollination problem.

Arrange in a grid
When kernels on sweet corn cobs do not develop as they should, or few cobs form at all on the plants, it is generally because they have not been properly pollinated.

This may happen where the crop is in too windy or exposed a site, or if weather conditions are very poor. However, the most common reason is that pollination is not occurring because plants are being grown in a row. Sweet corn is pollinated by the wind and this is much more efficient where plants are arranged in a grid

SWEET CORN SHOULD BE PLANTED IN A BLOCK

formation. Even if you are only growing say six plants, you should still grow them in two rows of three.

7 Artichokes galore

Delicious as they are, Jerusalem artichokes can become almost like a weed since any tiny fragment of tuber which gets left below ground is likely to form a new plant the following year.

Cradle planting
Obviously you need to dig and fork the area thoroughly to search for stray tubers after harvesting, although you will almost certainly leave at least one piece behind. In future seasons, one of the best ways of minimizing the problem is to make a "cradle" of chicken wire and plant the tubers in this. It will contain them as they multiply and then, at harvesting time, you can simply lift the cradle and all the artichokes with it.

8 Always a glut or a famine

The problem of all your lettuces being ready for the table at the same moment, followed by a dearth for the next two months, is a familiar one. The solution to having a smooth supply of vegetables lies largely in being sufficiently self-disciplined to sow little and often and to plan the space in your plot well.

Successional sowing
Making successive sowings is the key to ensuring that you can enjoy vegetable crops over a long period and avoid having one huge glut. With some crops, such as courgettes, this is easier said than done but with many, such as carrots, lettuces and French beans, successive sowing really does make a difference. Always check the seed packet for advice as to the period of time over which the seed can be sown. If you can provide some form of protection at either end of the season, perhaps in the form of cloches or mini-polytunnels, this will also help to extend cropping and mean that it should be able to start earlier in the year and carry on for longer.

Grow a range of varieties
Sometimes choosing a range of varieties will help solve this problem. With carrots and peas, for instance, there are varieties best suited to early, mainstream and late cropping. Seed catalogues show the various options, so try to select a range and sow only a few of each. Although F1 varieties crop very well and reliably, they do have a tendency to produce their crop all at the same time.

Be disciplined
It is also important not to get carried away (and this is certainly easier said than done) and sow too many of any one vegetable, especially if space is limited. Having a small number of a wide range of crops is much better than having lots of plants of the same thing, particularly something like a courgette which, once it gets going, will produce a phenomenal number of fruits. It is worth making a note of approximate cropping levels of some of your favourite vegetables and bearing this in mind when choosing and sowing seed the following year.

MAKING THE MOST OF A SMALL SPACE

- **INTERPLANTING** Individual plants of some crops take up relatively little room on the ground yet require fairly wide spacing. Interplant the bare soil between sweet corn plants, for example, with fast-maturing vegetables such as lettuce, spinach or chard. Yields will not be lowered significantly, if at all.

- **INTERSOWING** Some seeds, such as parsnips, are very slow to germinate, so it makes sense to sow seeds of a fast-growing vegetable such as radish or lettuce between the parsnip seeds. The seedlings of these crops will mark the row, making weeding easier, and the radishes or lettuces can be harvested before they start to compete with the main, parsnip, crop.

- **GOOD TIMING** It pays to make use of every square metre of soil for as much of the year as you can. As soon as one crop is harvested, aim to have something waiting in the wings to fill the gap. After lifting early potatoes in early summer, fertilize the ground and plant seed potatoes to produce another crop of new potatoes for harvest from mid-autumn onwards. Or, sow oriental vegetables, chard, spinach or lettuce for harvesting later in the year.

❾ Why do root crops, such as carrots, fork or crack?

Cracking or forking (fanging) in root crops is usually caused by unsuitable growing conditions. It may not be possible to cure the problem once it has developed but it can often be avoided.

Poor watering

Uneven or erratic watering often causes root crops to split, so it is important to improve the soil's capacity to retain moisture and to ensure that plants are not subject to fits and starts of watering. A mulch over the area should help to keep soil moisture levels relatively even.

Recent manuring

Forking, or fanging, may be the result of growing root crops in a soil which has been manured too close to sowing time. Wherever possible, dig in manure in the autumn, well before the crop is sown. Excessive manuring may also encourage forking.

Inadequate thinning

If roots are a good shape but very small it may be because the seedlings were not thinned adequately. Try to sow carrot seed evenly but sparsely along the row so that you can achieve the correct spacing without having to thin seedlings too much. Excessive thinning should be avoided, simply because the smell of even lightly crushed foliage may attract carrot fly.

Stony soil

Large stones can cause distorted roots so remove them before preparing the seed drill, and where the topsoil is rather shallow or very stony choose varieties described as stump-rooted. Since these are shorter, they are better able to develop normally. You could also grow root crops in a raised bed which would allow you to create a useful depth of soil. A short-term alternative is to dig out a wide trench that is slightly deeper than the ultimate length of the carrot roots and fill this with sieved soil, so that nothing will distort the roots as they grow.

STUMP-ROOTED CARROTS SUIT STONY SOILS

❿ Mouldy courgettes

Sometime fruits form in the normal way but then start to rot at the end with the flower.

Cause and prevention

If the flower rots, the rot soon spreads into the developing fruit and it becomes inedible. If the rotting fruit is left on the plant, the deterioration may even spread back into the plant itself. Wet weather or watering from above increases this problem and encourages the rot to spread. In most cases the fungus grey mould (*Botrytis cinerea*) is involved and the spores are readily splashed onto other areas of the plant or nearby flowers.

Remove infected fruits promptly and try not to wet the flowers or developing fruits. Clearly this cannot be avoided if it rains, but when watering yourself, direct the water to the base of the plant, beneath the leaves. This will also reduce problems with powdery mildew. In wet weather, carefully removing the flower from the fruit once it starts to fade helps to prevent rot from developing.

⓫ Onions turn soft while in store

Wide-necked bulbs do not store well, and the better onions are ripened, the longer they are likely to keep.

Good harvesting

If wet weather conditions encourage onions to form wide (bull) necks, the bulbs are best used immediately. However, good cultivation will help to stop bull necks from developing, and giving bulbs the chance to ripen thoroughly will also help to prevent rotting. Bending or tying the foliage is not now regarded as good practice because it may hinder ripening. Instead, wait until the foliage is starting to turn yellow before lifting. If you need to hasten the process, lift the bulbs very slightly using a garden fork. Allow bulbs to dry off naturally but also fairly rapidly. It often helps to spread them on a wire rack. If damp weather is forecast, move the onions to a cool part of the greenhouse or a cold frame or other protected, well-ventilated area.

Fungal infection

Sometimes rotting in store is due to onion neck rot (*Botrytis allii*). This generally infects growing plants but symptoms may not show until bulbs are in store. Promptly remove any that are starting to rot to prevent spores from spreading. The problem is more likely on inadequately ripened bulbs but is also exacerbated by poor storage conditions. Onions need a cool, well-ventilated, frost-free place. They can be stacked in trays or tied into ropes, but freedom from damp and good air movement are essential.

LEAVE ONIONS TO DRY AFTER HARVESTING

⑫ Runner beans fail to form pods

The most likely reason for poor pod set on runner beans is that the plants are not receiving enough water, but choice of variety can play its part, too.

More moisture needed

Runner beans require a huge amount of water, so it is important to prepare the soil carefully. The best material for increasing soil's capacity to retain moisture is well-rotted manure dug deeply into the soil, but garden compost and leaf-mould also work well. Alternatively, some people add shredded, moistened newspaper.

The amount of watering needed depends a lot on weather conditions and soil type, but thorough watering is essential for a good crop, usually many litres at a time for a wigwam of five or six plants, so that the moisture penetrates to the roots. Mulching the soil surface around the supports is also a good idea.

Try a different variety

The choice of variety may also affect pod set. On the whole, it seems that white-flowered varieties such as 'White Lady' often do better because they seem less likely to be attacked by nectar-robbing bees. Instead of entering the flower in the normal way, through the front, and pollinating the flower as it goes in search of nectar, this type of bee has taken to cutting into the back of the flower to steal the nectar. It does not, therefore, pollinate the flower at the same time. Similarly, climbing French beans such as 'Blue Lake' seem to be better able to set a good number of pods if moisture is slightly erratic. If pollination is poor due to windy conditions or other factors affecting the number of pollinating insects on the wing, growing a variety such as 'Red Rum' which is self-pollinating, should help to improve pod set slightly.

Bird damage

Birds may also be responsible for a poor crop of beans as some of them damage the flowers in such a way that they cannot produce pods. If this is the case, you will see shredded bean flowers on the plant and the ground beneath. If birds are a problem then the only solution is to net the beans with pea and bean netting or something similar.

KEEPING CHEMICALS TO A MINIMUM

• **CONTROL AND COMMONSENSE** However carefully you tend your crops there are still likely to be some problems. Chemical controls may be available for most of them but, on the whole, even non-organic gardeners prefer to avoid using too many chemicals on edible plants. Organic or commonsense methods are often readily available as alternatives to a battery of chemicals.

• **WHEN TO ACT** Prompt action, whether in the form of chemical or non-chemical controls is always best and should enable you to prevent most problems from getting out of hand. However, not all problems necessarily demand control. Diseases such as powdery mildew and rust often attack fairly late in the season and may have little effect on the overall yield of crops such as courgettes and garlic.

• **BARRIERS AND TRAPS** In some instances it may be possible to prevent a problem by using a barrier to stop the pest or pathogen from gaining access to the plant. Barriers such as horticultural fleece or very fine mesh may, for example, prevent attacks by caterpillars, aphids, carrot fly and cabbage root fly. It may be possible to trap other pests such as slugs. A small plastic drinks bottle, sunk about 2.5cm (1in) into the soil, with beer or milk in the bottom and holes cut into it 2.5cm (1in) above soil level, will trap slugs but not harm beneficial beetles.

• **PICK OFF PESTS** Wherever possible pick off or collect up pests or the infected parts of plants to prevent problems from spreading. Any severely infested or infected plants are best removed completely as they are unlikely to crop well and will only increase the likelihood of the problem spreading.

• **CHEMICALS AND THE ENVIRONMENT** If you do decide to use fungicides or insecticides, make sure that you only do so when absolutely necessary and that you choose the right product for the job and apply it at the correct rate and frequency. This way you should achieve the desired effect with minimal impact on the environment. Wherever possible, use products that are specific in action and so less likely to harm beneficial insects. Insecticides should always be applied with great care and at dusk so that damage to pollinating insects is kept to a minimum.

• **GOOD PRACTICES** Good garden hygiene and cultivation are essential if you are to keep problems to a minimum. Plants that are grown well, under suitable conditions, and cared for properly, will be

FLEECE MAKES AN EFFECTIVE BARRIER

less likely to succumb to pests or diseases in the first place and, if they do, they can generally recover or make up for any losses more easily. Good spacing, removal of debris and regular feeding and watering are particularly important. Crop rotation will also help to reduce the risk of problems building up to damaging levels and so should be practised in even the smallest vegetable plot. Similarly, many problems can be avoided if resistant varieties are grown. These will not necessarily be resistant to more than one or two common problems, but can still be used to great effect. Check seed catalogues to see which varieties are currently available.

VEGETABLE PESTS, DISEASES AND DISORDERS

LIKE ANY OTHER AREA of the garden, your vegetable plot may play host to a variety of pests and diseases. Some are specific to individual crops or to several which are closely related. Others, such as grey mould or powdery mildew, may be found on plants throughout the garden (*see pp.178–85*). Many pests and diseases can be avoided or the damage kept to a minimum by following the suggestions opposite, but some are harder to control and may require chemical or organic remedies.

Carrot fly

Carrots, parsnips and parsley and celery roots may be tunnelled by creamy-yellow maggots and brown marks may appear on the outside. Damaged roots are prone to rotting in store. Reduce the risk of damage by sowing carrots after late spring or by harvesting before late summer. Plants raised beneath fleece or fine mesh should not be attacked because the low-flying adults cannot gain access to lay eggs. Treatment with pirimiphos-methyl may be worthwhile. The varieties 'Sytan' and 'Flyaway' are less susceptible.

Cabbage root fly

Cabbage, broccoli, calabrese, Brussels sprouts, swedes, turnips and radishes may be attacked by white maggots which eat their roots and cause plants to wilt and die or crop poorly. Young plants are particularly prone. Effective non-chemical methods of preventing damage include fitting "collars" of carpet underlay, about 10cm (4in) in diameter, around the base of each plant or covering the entire crop with well-anchored fleece so that the female fly cannot lay her eggs around the base of the plants. Pirimiphos-methyl can also be used to treat plants.

Clubroot

Affected brassicas and related plants develop a massively swollen root system which does not function properly, resulting in plants which wilt readily and a poor or non-existent crop. Improving drainage and raising the soil pH (*see p.149*) helps to reduce damage. Infected plants must be removed promptly and burned or placed in the dustbin. Raising plants in individual 5–8cm (2–3in) diameter pots so that they develop well-established root systems will reduce the effect of the disease. Check catalogues for resistant varieties such as calabrese 'Trixie', kale 'Tall Green Curled' and swede 'Marian'.

Onion fly

Onions, leeks, shallots and garlic may all be attacked and young plants collapse when the roots are eaten by white maggots. Later in the year, maggots may tunnel into the bulbs making them prone to rotting and very unappetizing. Remove infested crops promptly before the maggots move into the soil to pupate. Onion fly is less of a problem on onions grown from sets than on seed-raised crops. The soil may also be treated with pirimiphos-methyl.

Potato and tomato blight

This fungus is most troublesome in moist, muggy weather. Affected foliage develops brown patches and dies off; the whole top-growth may be killed. Tomato fruits develop a brown discolouration and potato tubers discolour internally, often making crops inedible. Spraying plants before they become infected with a copper-based or mancozeb fungicide may help. Remove infected foliage promptly and burn it or put it in the dustbin. Do not compost. Potato varieties showing some resistance include 'Cara', 'Estima' and 'Romano'.

Flea beetle

These tiny beetles cause the foliage of many crops, in particular brassicas, to look as if peppered with shot. Sometimes the holes do not pierce the leaf and brown spots result. Seedlings are most likely to be damaged significantly so try to sow or plant out at a time when growth should be rapid. Protecting plants with fleece will minimize damage. Chemical treatment is rarely necessary but derris, bifenthrin or pirimiphos-methyl can be used.

Wireworm

These are small orange-brown larvae that tunnel into potatoes and carrots and may damage the bases of seedlings. They are particularly troublesome on newly cultivated ground. Regular cultivation for about four years generally alleviates the problem but, in the meantime, lift crops as promptly as possible so that the wireworms have as little time as possible to damage the crop.

Viruses

Many different viruses may affect the vegetable plot and between them may attack a wide range of crops but the most common is probably cucumber mosaic virus. Among its many hosts are cucumbers, marrows, courgettes, squashes and melons. Infected plants show a range of symptoms including stunted growth, yellowing (usually in distinct striped, ring-spotted or mosaic patterns), distortion and ultimately premature death. There are no cures for virus infections and most are readily spread, often by handling or sap-feeding pests. Infected plants should be removed and composted promptly. It is worth checking seed catalogues for varieties resistant to specific viruses.

Rust

Rust is common particularly in late summer in moist, warm conditions. Leaves develop numerous bright orange pustules. Leeks and garlic are frequently attacked but many vegetables may be infected. Remove affected leaves promptly and try to improve air circulation around plants. Avoid excessive use of high-nitrogen fertilizers as these may promote soft growth which is particularly prone to attack.

CARROT FLY DAMAGE

CLUBROOT ON A CABBAGE

TOMATO BLIGHT

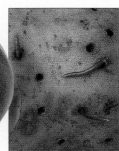
WIREWORM IN A POTATO

FLEA BEETLE DAMAGE

CHOOSING FERTILIZERS

THE RANGE OF FERTILIZERS available at garden centres seems to increase almost daily, and choosing the most appropriate product for your needs can be a confusing process. Just how do you decide what to buy and when, where and how to apply it? What do the main ingredients do? Which fertilizers are suitable for organic gardeners to use? And is it possible for garden compost and manure to supply plants with all the nutrients they need?

Q *Some fertilizers have three numbers on the packet, each separated by a colon. Presumably these indicate the proportion of ingredients, but of what?*

A The proportions of the major active ingredients of a fertilizer are often given in this way. The figures indicate the relative quantities of nitrogen, phosphorous (phosphate) and potassium (potash) in their available forms – forms in which they can be taken up by plants. These are the macro nutrients (often referred to by their chemical symbols, N, P and K respectively), the only ones needed by plants on a fairly regular basis in relatively large quantities. Other nutrients required in fairly large supply include magnesium, calcium and sulphur, but these are less likely to be applied regularly. In addition, plants need much smaller amounts of the trace elements. These include iron, manganese, copper, zinc, boron, molybdenum and chlorine.

Q *How do nitrogen, phosphorous and potassium affect a plant's growth?*

A Each has several functions but, in particular, nitrogen promotes lush, strong growth, phosphorous encourages a strong, well-developed root system, and potassium helps to ensure that wood ripens and matures well and that the plant produces plenty of flowers and fruit.

Q *How often should a general fertilizer be applied?*

A The only way to be sure is to check the instructions on the packet since quantity and frequency of application vary from product to product. Some are applied just once or twice during the growing season, whereas others, such as liquid feeds, can be used to good effect once or twice a week. Get rid of anything in an unlabelled container that has been lurking in the garden shed for a while. It will do plants no good if applied at the wrong concentration or frequency, and is likely to have deteriorated considerably since purchased.

Q *What are the options for organic gardeners?*

A Most organic gardeners rely heavily (and successfully) on improving the soil's health and fertility with manure and garden compost. In addition, pelleted chicken manure or a mixture of dried blood, fish meal and bone meal are often used as "general" fertilizers. Dried blood and bone meal may also be used separately to provide a high-nitrogen or high-phosphorous feed respectively. Both are easy to obtain and apply but bear in mind that blood, fish and bone meal is unlikely to come from an organic source whereas pelleted poultry manure from organic chicken farms is readily available. Foliar or root applications of comfrey may be used as a general liquid feed. This is easy to make yourself but may be rather smelly. Seaweed is becoming increasingly popular, particularly when used as a foliar feed.

Q *What are the advantages of using manure and garden compost, and do they supply all the necessary nutrients?*

A Bulky organic materials such as garden compost and manure not only feed the soil but also improve its structure and consequently its ability to retain moisture and nutrients. But weight for weight, these sorts of materials have a far lower ability to supply all the nutrients plants need than their inorganic or manufactured counterparts. However, they can have fairly high nitrogen levels and, if over-used, may produce an excessive amount of lush foliage at the expense of flowers. Remember that if used fresh, manure may scorch leaves, stems or roots if it touches them. After being left in a heap for about 18 months, it will still be extremely useful but should pose no threat to plants.

Q *Are there any drawbacks to using granular fertilizers?*

A These generally prove an easy, efficient way of feeding. However, if it does not rain for a day or two after applying the granules you

ESSENTIAL NUTRIENTS • OPTIONS FOR ORGANIC GARDENERS • USING MANURE will need to water the area thoroughly so that the granules dissolve and can be absorbed by the plants' roots. Remove any granules that land among plant foliage before they have time to scorch it.

Q What are foliar feeds and what are their main uses?

A Foliar feeds are usually sold as powder or liquid which is diluted to the required strength and applied directly onto a plant's foliage. It is generally easiest to use a watering can, but in some cases you can apply them using a dilutor on the end of a hose.

Precise ingredients and nutrient profiles vary from brand to brand, but on the whole these are a useful way to give a plant a "pick-me-up", although not the best method for long-term feeding. Foliar feeding is quick and easy and, provided you avoid wetting the plant in direct sunlight (which could cause bad scorching, especially of flowers), is generally problem free. The rapid uptake produces a rapid effect. It has been suggested, too, that feeding a plant through the leaves stimulates root growth. This can be very useful if a plant's roots have been damaged or are waterlogged and so cannot easily take up nutrients.

Q How do controlled-release fertilizers work?

A These are generally available as tiny, individual, resin-coated granules or as cylinder-shaped clusters of granules. Light brown in colour (occasionally blue-green), the granules are often mistaken for slug or other pest eggs. If the soil or compost is very cold or dry, the resin coating releases little, if any, fertilizer. It becomes more porous, however, when conditions are warmer and moister, so more fertilizer is released just when

the plants need it. These fertilizers usually have an active life of several months and are particularly useful in containers and hanging baskets.

Fertilizer sticks work in a similar way. These need to be pushed into the soil or compost and the fertilizer is released as the stick deteriorates.

Q Is a combined blood, fish and bone meal fertilizer suitable for most situations? And is it safe?

A This combination supplies many of the nutrients needed on a day-to-day basis and makes a good, widely used general fertilizer. As a safety precaution, wear gloves if handling any product containing bone meal.

Q Why is the use of bone meal often recommended when planting shrubs, trees and herbaceous perennials?

A Bone meal has a high level of phosphorous and so should help to promote root growth and hence establishment of the plant. Bear in mind, however, that it is likely to be alkaline in reaction and so is not the best choice when planting lime-hating plants such as rhododendrons.

Q How long do fertilizers generally last?

A It depends on the product. A few state the date by which they need to be used but unfortunately date-stamping is not yet common practice. Storage conditions also greatly influence shelf life. Most products need to be stored in a cool but frost-free, dry place, preferably out of direct sunlight. After opening, tightly reseal the packet and keep the fertilizer in its original packaging for future reference. Once a product has been

diluted or made up into any other form, use it straight away and do not attempt to store any that is left over.

Q What is the best time of year to apply fertilizers?

A Check for specific advice on the packaging but, as a rule, it is best to feed most garden plants only between mid-spring and early summer if using a high-nitrogen or general fertilizer. If you feed too early or too late in the season, you run the risk of promoting soft, lush growth that is liable to get frosted. Some fertilizers with a specific function may need applying outside this period: potash, for instance, is generally applied in early spring and autumn so that it can promote flowering and encourage wood to ripen. Similarly, lawn fertilizers may need to be used in spring or autumn. Manure can be applied at most times of the year, but mainly in spring around ornamentals and in winter to vegetable plots.

Q If storage space is limited, what is the best way of reducing the number of fertilizers needed? Will any one product be suitable for every job?

A It is probably best not to restrict yourself to just one product, but a combination of a general granular fertilizer plus a high-potash liquid feed will probably fulfil most of your needs. A high-potash liquid feed, such as a tomato feed, can be used to feed many other fruiting vegetable crops such as aubergines and courgettes, and also for flowering plants including annual bedding in borders, pots and windowboxes. If any plants show signs of specific mineral deficiences you will need to apply appropriate fertilizers (*see p.22*) to treat them successfully.

FOLIAR FEEDS • CONTROLLED-RELEASE GRANULES • WHEN TO APPLY • STORAGE

THE FRUIT GARDEN

HOME-GROWN FRUIT may seem to take up a lot of space and, like vegetables, look as though it requires expertise. Yet in reality, though it does attract a certain number of problems, it is no more troublesome than many strictly ornamental plants, and can often be fitted in among flower beds and borders or grown in containers. Growing your own fruit gives you the chance to enjoy it at its peak of freshness and flavour and to grow varieties that are difficult to find in the supermarket. And it is always possible to develop a philosophical attitude to frost and birds.

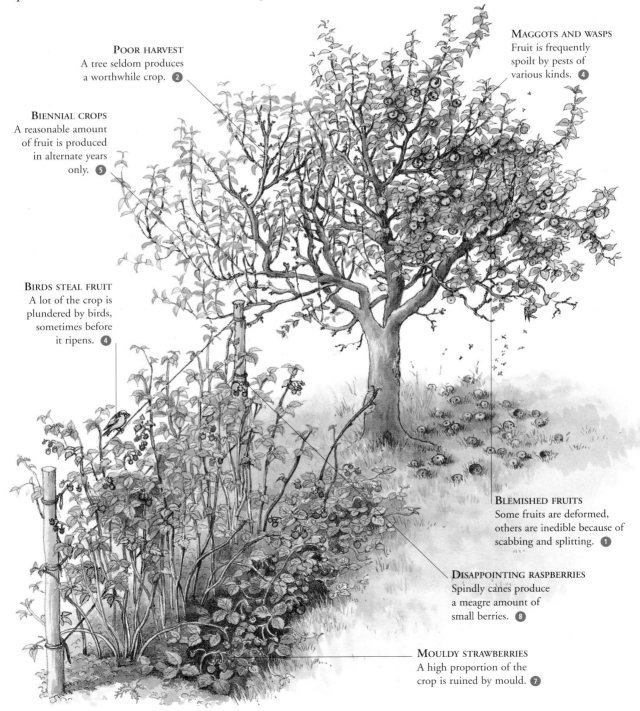

POOR HARVEST
A tree seldom produces a worthwhile crop. **2**

MAGGOTS AND WASPS
Fruit is frequently spoilt by pests of various kinds. **4**

BIENNIAL CROPS
A reasonable amount of fruit is produced in alternate years only. **5**

BIRDS STEAL FRUIT
A lot of the crop is plundered by birds, sometimes before it ripens. **4**

BLEMISHED FRUITS
Some fruits are deformed, others are inedible because of scabbing and splitting. **1**

DISAPPOINTING RASPBERRIES
Spindly canes produce a meagre amount of small berries. **8**

MOULDY STRAWBERRIES
A high proportion of the crop is ruined by mould. **7**

1 Split, blemished or deformed fruits

There are many different reasons for fruit having some sort of defect at harvest time.

APPLE MARRED BY SCAB

BITTER PIT DUE TO CALCIUM DEFICIENCY

Uneven watering

The most common cause of cracked or deformed fruit is an erratic moisture supply. If a period of dry weather is followed by heavy watering or rain, a fruit may put on a sudden spurt of growth then split. Keep trees adequately watered, especially while fruit is developing, and cover the root area with a good bulky organic mulch to help conserve moisture.

Frost and feeding

A late frost can injure the skin of fruitlets, resulting in surface russetting or scabbing of mature fruits. It may also cause cracking. If a tree has not been sufficiently well maintained, or if it is growing on thin or poor soil, inadequate nutrition may be responsible for the formation of rather pathetic fruits. Regular feeding with a general fertilizer and mulching with well-rotted manure or garden compost should get the tree back on track after a year or two.

Importance of thinning

Heavy crops are to some extent usually reduced naturally when the tree sheds a proportion of its fruit around midsummer. If this natural thinning is not sufficient, you will need to thin the fruits yourself. This is particularly important on young trees, where heavy crops in the early years can seriously weaken the tree and result in poor growth for many years to come.

Start by removing deformed fruits or any showing signs of pest attack. The extent of thinning needed depends partly on the tree's age and health and the size of the developing crop. Generally, dessert apples are thinned to one apple every 10–15cm (4–6in), pears to one or two fruits per cluster, and plums to leave one fruit every 5–8cm (2–3in).

Apple scab

When this fungal infection attacks almost-mature fruits, you may notice a greyish-khaki scabbing on the skin. This is usually only skin deep and the overall size and shape of the fruit is not affected. However, if the infection occurs at fruitlet stage or while the apple is still small, it can make it become very distorted and prone to cracking. Severely scabbed young fruits should be removed as soon as possible. When winter pruning, check young stems for signs of scabby growth and prune them out. Since apple scab will overwinter on fallen leaves as well as on shoots, rake up any leaves from beneath the tree and burn them or put them in the dustbin or on the compost heap. If the tree is small enough, you could spray with a suitable fungicide.

Bitter pit

If apples have faint brownish freckling or flecking within the flesh or just beneath the skin, this is due to a disorder known as bitter pit. It is the result of calcium deficiency within the fruit and may occur even on calcium-rich soils. In order to take up calcium, the plant needs an adequate supply of moisture. If this is not available and the tree does not get sufficient calcium, small areas of cells within the developing fruit collapse and turn brown. Nothing can be done once this has happened, but regular watering and the use of a good bulky mulch should help to prevent bitter pit occurring. If the problem recurs, you can spray with calcium nitrate at regular intervals throughout the season.

THIN OUT APPLES
To avoid small apples, reduce heavy crops (inset) after the tree has naturally shed some of its fruits in midsummer.

② Why does a tree produce such a poor harvest?

If you occasionally get a very poor crop, it could be due to weather or birds. But if it happens year after year, check there is not an inherent pollination problem.

In need of a pollinator

One of the most common reasons for fruit trees failing to crop well is that they have no pollinator. Most need another tree of a suitable type close by that is in flower at the same time to provide pollen for fruit set.

Tree fruits are divided into pollination groups, so check the group of any tree you buy and that you can provide it with a compatible partner. Pollination may occur if there is a tree of an adjacent pollination group in a nearby garden and flowering times overlap, but this is not reliable and will not provide the heaviest crop possible. If the neighbour removes their tree or prunes it severely, it may have a significant effect on your crop.

A few fruit varieties are self-fertile, notably among the plums and damsons. Triploid varieties of apple, however, need two companion trees because they make poor pollinators. There are not many, but one of the

'VICTORIA'

'MARJORIE'S SEEDLING'

SELF-FERTILE PLUMS
A few varieties are reasonably self-fertile and need no pollinator to produce fruit. These include the above plums and morello cherry.

most common is 'Bramley's Seedling'; others include 'Ribston Pippin', 'Belle de Boskoop' and 'Jonagold'.

Family trees

One way around the problem in a small garden is to choose a family tree. These consist of several different varieties (often three) that are able to pollinate each other, all grafted onto one tree. Although a useful idea, these trees can be difficult to maintain because the different varieties may grow at different rates, making pruning something of a nightmare.

Weather and insects

Frost, particularly a late frost, can damage the blossom or young fruitlets and cause partial or even complete

crop failure. This is quite common on relatively early-flowering trees such as plums. If your garden is prone to frost, try to choose later-flowering types of fruit which are less likely to be damaged. Providing temporary protection, perhaps by draping small trees with fleece or creating some form of windbreak, is also worthwhile in frost-prone sites.

If very cold or windy weather affects the number of insects reaching the trees, pollination may be poor. Pears may produce small, peculiarly elongated fruits lacking normal pips, and on cherries, fruits may start to develop but then drop from the tree. If the young fruit is cut open you will find that there is no seed developing inside the stone.

Fruit bud thieves

Birds sometimes eat or steal the fruit buds. The only way around this is to net trees early in the season. Bird scarers may have some effect, but it is generally short-lived. Birds and squirrels may also steal fruitlets or larger fruits before they are ripe, and again the only answer is to grow the fruit in a cage or net it.

③ An ancient tree bears only small, unappetizing apples

Renovation will encourage an old tree to crop better in almost all cases. However, an ancient apple tree is a beautiful thing to have in the garden, and if the apples are not needed, why not grow a clematis or rambling rose through it to add interest at other times of year?

Renovation

Start by removing the worst of the dead and diseased branches, and continue to remove deteriorating branches over the next few winters. Feed with a general fertilizer in early spring, then apply a mulch of well-rotted manure to a depth of about 5cm (2in) over the root area. If it

AN OLD APPLE TREE PLAYS HOST TO A CLEMATIS

does not rain within a few days of applying the fertilizer, water it in well, and wait until the ground is thoroughly moist before mulching.

In dry weather you may also need to give occasional thorough drenchings of water to alleviate stress on the tree.

Replacement

If you decide to replace the tree, remove the stump and as many roots as you can, or you may run into problems with soil-borne diseases. Do not plant an apple tree on the same site because it is likely to suffer from specific apple replant disorder. Any replacement tree should be planted as far away as possible so that its roots cannot tap into soil once occupied by the old tree's roots. Trees are rarely killed by this disorder, but are unlikely to thrive and crop well.

4 Much of the crop is spoilt by wasps, maggots and birds

Some creatures need to be kept at bay if you are to achieve a decent crop, but try to identify the culprit who started the damage.

Wasp damage

Wasps can do a lot of damage, particularly in late summer when fruits are ripe. Sometimes they actually initiate the damage on the fruit's surface or they may simply enlarge areas of damage created by other creatures. Try trapping them using the traditional method of a jam jar part-filled with a sugary solution or with a small amount of jam mixed into water. If the jars or, perhaps rather safer, plastic pots are suspended from branches of the tree, large numbers of wasps will be attracted to the sweet liquid and be drowned. Individual, particularly precious fruits may also be protected from wasps and birds if a small section of a pair of tights is placed over each fruit.

Maggots and caterpillars

The most common cause of maggoty apples are the caterpillars of the codling moth, which create a tunnel filled with brown frass (droppings). The female moth lays her eggs on the leaves in early to midsummer and the caterpillars then move into the developing fruits. By late summer they have finished feeding and leave the fruits in an attempt to find a safe place to overwinter. They often move out onto areas of loose bark or may hide away beneath tree ties. Spraying against codling moth on larger trees is almost impossible but if branches are accessible, a suitable insecticide can be used. This should kill a high proportion of the caterpillars before they get the chance to enter the fruits. You

EARWIGS
Although often blamed for damage, earwigs are seldom the initial culprit and invariably find their way into tasty fruit flesh that has already been exposed by another pest such as a bird or wasp.

can also lower the number of overwintering caterpillars by loosely wrapping hessian, old sacks or corrugated cardboard around the trunk and main branches of the tree in midsummer. The caterpillars will crawl underneath these tempting overwintering sites and spin silken cocoons around themselves. Then, you can remove the material and dispose of the caterpillars it contains.

The caterpillars of the apple sawfly may also tunnel into fruits, but because they attack much earlier in the season, infested fruits usually fall from the tree by early summer. It is essential to clear up fallen fruitlets as the caterpillars overwinter in the soil. In addition, you could spray with a suitable insecticide as soon as the petals have fallen.

Bird damage

Some birds may eat the buds on fruit trees early in the season and others may peck at ripe fruit. Although the damage done by the bird pecking may not be too great, it can cause problems because other pests may be attracted by the injured fruit. It may also become infected by brown rot, a disease that will very quickly reduce it to a brown, soggy mass. Netting fruit against birds is without doubt the most successful way of keeping the

crop for yourself. Temporary netting could be erected over plants just before the most susceptible period, for instance you could try this over a small cherry tree just as the fruits start to set and keep the netting in place until they are ready to be harvested. Netting is virtually impossible for larger trees, but it can work well on trained fans, espaliers and cordons. The netting needs to be held clear of the fruit so that birds cannot alight on it and feed through the holes. It must also be well anchored at the base to prevent entry at ground level. Erecting a fruit cage is obviously the best long-term solution, provided you have adequate space in the garden. Small fruit plants such as strawberries can be protected with netting mini-tunnels or a system of bamboo canes and netting. Flowerpots on top of the canes will help to stop the netting from sliding down the canes.

Scarecrows, glinting tinfoil pie cases, CDs, cat outlines and other bird-scaring devices can all be used with reasonable effect, but generally the birds soon become accustomed to them so it is essential to have a wide selection that can be used in rotation. Buzzing or humming line tied taut between posts or canes near to where the fruit is growing is also effective in some instances.

TEMPORARY NETTING
Protect low-growing fruit crops, such as strawberries, with netting draped over bamboo canes topped with plastic flowerpots.

❺ A fruit tree produces a crop in alternate years only

Biennial cropping is a characteristic of some apple varieties, or the problem may be due to an inappropriate pruning regime.

Biennial bearers

Some trees form a good or noticeable crop only every other year. Biennial bearing is particularly common on apples. The varieties 'Blenheim Orange' and 'Laxton's Superb' are biennial bearers; 'Bramley's Seedling' may also occasionally show a tendency to fruit biennially.

Spur- and tip-bearers

The majority of apple trees produce their fruit on two-year-old wood and spurs on older wood, but a few varieties bear the apples at the tips of shoots made during the previous summer. The latter require a different kind of pruning regime from the former. If one of the partial tip-bearing trees such as 'Discovery' 'Worcester Pearmain' or 'Bramley's Seedling' has been pruned as if it were a spur-bearer, this will have removed the tree's potential to fruit.

Pruning spur-bearers

The more an established spur-bearing tree is pruned during winter, the more growth is produced. If this growth is excessive, fruit bud production may actually be reduced. When you prune, always remove dead, diseased or dying wood, and with spur-bearers also shorten the previous summer's growth on main stems by 25–30 per cent, pruning back to a bud facing in the direction you want the new growth to go, that is to an upward-, outward-facing bud. Then tackle the laterals (the shoots from these main stems) that were produced the previous summer, cutting them back to between three and six buds.

Pruning tip-bearers

If you were to shorten all the laterals on tip-bearers, very little fruit would be produced, so instead prune any strongly growing laterals that are more than 22cm (9in) long, taking them back to leave five or six buds. You can also cut back a proportion of older fruited wood to a young shoot to give room for new growth to develop.

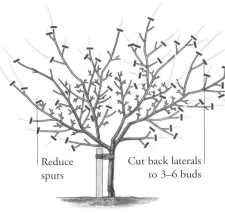

Reduce spurs

Cut back laterals to 3–6 buds

SPUR-BEARER

Remove large, older branches

Prune tips so they are not bent by weight of fruit

TIP-BEARER

❻ Which rootstock?

Choice of rootstock and variety are of prime importance when buying an apple, pear or plum. The variety, or scion, is grafted onto the rootstock giving a wide variety of combinations.

The best choice

The greatest choice of rootstocks is for apples. Among the most common and most useful are M26, a dwarfing

EFFECTS ON EVENTUAL HEIGHT
Rootstocks help to determine a tree's height, vigour and the amount of care it will need. Depending on the rootstock you choose, you can grow the same variety to make either a small or large tree.

rootstock which does well on most soils and produces a tree 2.5–4m (8–12ft) tall, and MM106, a semi-dwarfing rootstock which produces a tree 4–5.5m (12–18ft) tall. Both should produce fruit in three to four years from planting. If you need a much smaller tree, M9 is a very dwarfing rootstock which produces a tree only 1.8–3m (6–10ft) tall.

Although this can be useful, trees on M9 require a lot more care and attention than those on less dwarfing rootstocks and will need to be staked for longer and kept very well watered and fed.

The most commonly used rootstocks for plums are the fairly vigorous 'St. Julien A' and the more dwarfing 'Pixie'. Trees grafted onto 'Pixie' rootstocks will be about half to two-thirds the size of those on 'St. Julien A' but, as with dwarfing apple rootstocks, trees grown on this will require more attention.

Pears are often grafted onto quince rootstocks of which semi-vigorous Quince A is the most useful, producing trees 3.5–5m (11–16ft) tall. Quince C is used mainly for cordons.

❼ Soft fruit, particularly strawberries, often turns mouldy

The most common reason for soft fruit deteriorating and turning brown is infection by grey mould (Botrytis cinerea).

Methods of control

The typical greyish fuzzy fungal growth produced by grey mould quickly develops on fruit, making it inedible. It is particularly common on strawberries, but raspberries may also be affected. If fruits have been wounded in any way, perhaps by slugs or birds, grey mould is all the more likely to develop. Stagnant air or plant debris left around the plant also encourages the mould as does water or mud splash on the fruits.

Try to prevent damage and clear up plant debris regularly. Remove infected or damaged fruits promptly. Placing strawberry mats or straw beneath developing strawberry fruits will help to reduce the risk of mud splash. Removing runners so that the bed does not get overcrowded will help to improve air circulation and decrease the likelihood of mould.

Good hygiene and damage prevention are the most important tools in the fight against grey mould. However, you can also use a spray

STRAW HELPS TO PROTECT AGAINST MUD SPLASH

containing carbendazim if necessary, but it is important to spray early in the season because fruits can become infected at the flowering stage.

TRY ALPINES Alpine strawberries tend to be less susceptible to grey mould and less attractive to birds than larger-fruited strawberries. They also have a rather longer cropping season.

❽ Spindly raspberry canes produce a disappointing crop

If raspberries are not given a suitable site, cropping may be affected.

Site, soil and maintenance

Raspberries prefer a slightly acid soil with a pH of 6.5–6.7 that is well drained but not inclined to dry out in warm weather. In alkaline soil, plants are likely to show symptoms of lime-induced chlorosis (*see p.96*), where manganese and iron become deficient and new growth tends to be rather yellow, particularly between the leaf veins. Feed with a fertilizer formulated for acid-loving plants and, if necessary, apply chelated iron compounds.

Keep plants adequately watered while berries are swelling. Dry weather at the end of fruiting may result in the production of poor canes for the following season's crop, so it is often worth watering just after you have picked the last of the crop. Mulch to conserve moisture but avoid alkaline materials such as mushroom compost and do not let the mulch touch the canes, as this can encourage various diseases and may weaken the canes and reduce the crop.

Virus infection

Straggly canes and a poor crop may result from a virus infection. This is quite common in raspberries that have been on the same site for several years. Other symptoms include discolouration of foliage, usually in streaked, flecked or mosaic patterns, and small leaf size, sometimes with distortion. There are no control measures and infected plants should be removed promptly. Since some viruses are spread by nematodes in the soil, replacement plants should not be put on the same piece of ground.

CUT OUT SPINDLY CANES ON SUMMER VARIETIES

Old age

The speed at which plants decline depends on variety, growing conditions and cropping levels, but usually you can expect to see signs of deterioration after six to eight years. Even if there is no apparent disease, it is wise to plant replacement canes in a different position.

Too many canes

Some varieties tend to produce excessive new canes and the area becomes overcrowded with spindly canes that crop poorly. Thin canes out to about eight per plant, removing those that are weak, damaged or too far away from the support system.

With summer-fruiting varieties, cut the old canes to the ground as soon as they have finished fruiting to give space for the new canes to develop.

With autumn-fruiting raspberries, the fruit is produced on the top 30cm (12in) of the canes that were produced during that year. Cut down all canes to ground level in late winter. Once the new canes are produced, thin them out if necessary to about 5cm (2in) apart.

9 Blackcurrant crops get smaller year after year

Blackcurrants, and redcurrants too, need good cultivation for the best crops, but it is possible to revive neglected plants.

General care

Plants growing in too much shade or a frost pocket may produce poor crops. To keep plants cropping well, in early spring, spread a 5–8cm (2–3in) mulch of well-rotted manure, garden compost or other bulky organic material over the root area. Inadequate feeding also affects cropping. Apply sulphate of potash at a rate of 25g (1oz) per square metre (square yard) in midwinter.

Renovation

Neglected blackcurrant bushes can be restored to better cropping by pruning out all branches to within 2.5cm (1in) of the ground in early winter. This will encourage plenty of new shoots in spring. If necessary, these can be thinned out in autumn to leave only strong, well-placed stems.

Prune congested plants to improve cropping

Where growth is allowed to get too dense, poor air circulation may increase risk of disease and fruit may suffer because of the lack of light. Thinning congested plants should help to improve fruit quality.

THINNING A BLACKCURRANT BUSH
Up to 25–30 per cent of stems may be pruned out each year to produce a more open bush. Cut the stems at their base in early winter.

THINNING A REDCURRANT BUSH
Open up the centre of the bush (which is grown on a leg) and prune shoots growing from framework branches back to one bud.

Spread renovation of a redcurrant bush over two winters, cutting out unhealthy, old and badly-placed stems to leave 8–10 young, strong ones.

Reversion virus

On blackcurants, poor cropping is occasionally due to reversion virus, carried by the blackcurrant gall mite.

The mites feed and breed inside the buds, destroying them in the process. The problem is fairly easy to spot because the flower buds become noticeably plump. Leaf shape also becomes abnormal, but this is a harder symptom to identify. There are no control measures; burn plants or put them in the dustbin.

10 Grapes often rot or shrivel

Vines raised from seed or planted on an unsuitable site may never have the potential to produce a good crop in a northern temperate climate. If this is the case, remove or replace the plant with a more appropriate variety, or grow it simply for its attractive foliage.

Mildew on the fruit

If a plant forms a decent-sized crop but the fruits are covered with a whitish-grey coating, this suggests powdery mildew infection. Occasionally it is seen as a white fluffy growth on the surface of the berries, but more frequently it is a greyish growth which coats the young berries and prevents them from expanding normally. They are then prone to splitting with the result that the crop is wasted and then often

succumbs to further attack by wasps or rots off due to grey mould.

Powdery mildew is difficult to control, since there are no effective fungicides on the market. It is well worth checking the plant early in the year, as the infection often occurs first on the leaves. Any showing a white powdery growth should be removed promptly. Ensuring that the vine receives adequate moisture at the base and improving air circulation around the foliage will help to reduce susceptibility to the disease.

Shanking

Sometimes individual grapes within a bunch turn pale and shrivel. This is known as shanking and is generally due to a problem at the vine's roots and to general weakness. Remove individual damaged grapes or entire bunches, then make sure you keep the vine really well watered and fed with a general fertilizer plus applications of sulphate of potash around the root area. Poor drainage encourages shanking, so check that this is adequate and improve it if necessary.

MILDEWED GRAPES

SHANKING

11 What are the best fruits for containers on the patio

If space is limited or you want to make an area of hard standing particularly productive, several kinds of fruit grow well in containers.

Perfect for pots

Strawberries are without doubt the easiest fruit to grow in a container. Any variety is suitable although some, such as 'Pendulina', are specifically recommended. They can either be planted in large flowerpots or special strawberry pots; in either case they will look attractive and, provided they are kept well watered and fed, should be very productive. Life in a pot will help to provide figs with the root restriction they need and provided you choose apples on a very dwarfing rootstock these too can be grown in containers. It is also possible to keep nectarines or peaches in a pot.

Any fruit tree in a container will take a lot of looking after as regular watering and feeding is essential. Use a loam-based compost with some controlled-release fertilizer granules incorporated into it to reduce slightly the amount of feeding needed initially.

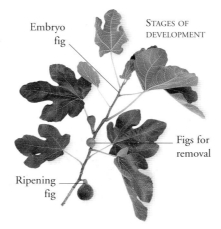

STRAWBERRIES ARE IDEAL FOR POTS

12 A large fig plant produces very few figs

Large, vigorous plants often produce small crops. Restricting root growth helps to reduce top-growth and increase the number of figs.

Contain the roots

If figs are wall-trained, it is quite easy to restrict the roots at planting time. Aim to create an open-bottomed "box", 45–60cm (18–24in) square, around the root area. One of the easiest ways to do this is to dig the planting hole, use the wall as one side of the box and line the three remaining sides of the hole with paving slabs. This should prevent the roots from growing out into the surrounding soil and, provided that the base of the box is left open to allow drainage, the fig should develop a good branch structure yet not become too vigorous.

Incorrect pruning

Poor cropping could also be the result of incorrect pruning. In northern temperate climates figs tend to produce two crops a year, but only one will actually ripen. Embryo fruits are produced in late summer, close to the tip of the young shoots. These fruits are only about 5mm (⅕in) in diameter and, provided you protect the fig adequately over winter or the winter itself is mild, they should develop to produce ripe fruits in late summer the following year. Fruits will also be produced on new growth in spring, but these rarely ripen because the summer is too cold. They are best picked off towards the end of autumn so that the tree's energy can be diverted to those figs which do have a chance of ripening.

It is essential to encourage the plant to produce plenty of short young shoots each year, as it is on these that the embryo figs develop. In early summer, prune off the growing tips of the shoots when they have made four or five leaves, so that more shoots develop from the leaf axils. Other pruning is best carried out while the fig is dormant, but to avoid risk of frost damage leave it as late as possible, usually mid- to late spring. Also thin out young shoots at the same time and remove any which are dead or diseased.

Embryo fig

STAGES OF DEVELOPMENT

Figs for removal

Ripening fig

13 Silvery plum leaves

Plum trees, and cherries too, can be infected by a disease which manifests itself by a silver sheen developing on the foliage.

Silver leaf disease

This disease is caused by the fungus *Chondrostereum purpureum*, which enters freshly created wounds, causes the leaves to develop a silvery sheen and then die back. Only certain parts of the tree are affected at first, but the number of silvered branches may increase year on year, possibly leading to the tree's death. If an infected branch is cut across and a central brownish stain is clearly visible in the wood, this confirms that the silvering is due to the fungal infection.

It may occasionally be possible to save a tree by removing the infected limbs, cutting back to a point at least 15cm (6in) past the point where the stain in the wood ends. Although using wound paints is no longer recommended, it is worthwhile on large wounds on trees that are susceptible to silver leaf. These include plums, cherries (edible and ornamental), almonds, peaches and nectarines. To a large extent, silver leaf can be avoided if major pruning is carried out in summer when the tree is better able to defend itself against the disease and there are fewer spores about to cause infection.

MAINTENANCE & STORAGE

THERE ARE INEVITABLY going to be a few utilitarian objects or features that don't fit in with your plans for a beautiful garden. Manhole covers, dustbins, washing lines and compost heaps can all seem like a blot on the landscape. What can you do to ensure that these ugly but necessary elements are disguised as well as they can be? In small spaces, finding a place to store the children's toys, the lawnmower and other tools can present a real problem, but if they are not to be the next items on a burglar's list, attention also needs to be paid to security.

NO STORAGE SPACE
There is nowhere to keep gardening tools safe and dry. ❷

DUSTBIN IS AN EYESORE
The dustbin needs to be hidden from view yet easily accessible. ❶

UNSIGHTLY COMPOST HEAP
The compost heap is essential but not very attractive. ❸

Washing line blues

Permanent washing-line posts that stick out of the lawn do nothing to enhance the garden. But for practical purposes, the washing line needs careful siting. Even in a big garden, don't put it too far from the house or you will regret it when you have to collect in the washing if it suddenly starts to rain. And wherever you site the line, the laundry must have sufficient space to blow without knocking the heads off flowers or itself being dirtied by fencing, stained by flowers or snagged by roses.

A collapsible rotary line that can be folded up and stored in a shed or garage when not needed is often the answer, especially in a small garden. If you have a permanent line strung between posts, you can camouflage the posts by fixing some chicken wire or vine eyes and wires and using them as supports for climbing plants so that you barely notice the line when it is not in use. Avoid climbers that are so vigorous they will tangle themselves around the line and make it unusable.

❶ Dustbins and other eyesores

Dustbins invariably lack aesthetic appeal but because easy access is essential they often occupy a prominent position. Fuel tanks, washing line posts and manhole covers, too, can mar the garden unless given camouflage.

Create a screen

A few sturdy pressure-treated posts driven securely into the ground will provide a framework for trellis or a system of galvanized wires and vine eyes to be used for supporting a climber or shrub. Such a screen should be capable of hiding a dustbin. Trellis has the advantage that it makes a reasonable screen even before planting up and allows you to use deciduous climbers. In addition to sweetly scented roses, jasmine, honeysuckle and sweet peas, you could use evergreen climbers such as *Clematis armandii* (which also has a delicate perfume) or an attractive ivy. Or plant a wall shrub, such as evergreen ceanothus or pyracantha. The latter may need its prickly stems cutting back regularly. Paint or stain the trellis to match colours in other parts of the garden. Alternatively, use willow or hazel hurdles which blend naturally into their surroundings.

Fuel tanks can be camouflaged in much the same way. Make sure you allow yourself easy access to the fuel gauge and filling point.

Diversionary tactics

It may be possible to make bins less obvious by drawing your gaze away from them to other, more eye-catching features such as containers of brightly coloured plants. A long-term planting could include small shrubs underplanted with bulbs or bedding.

Permanent quarters

In some gardens, a rather more robust structure may be the answer such as a brick-built enclosure. Make sure the base is easy to clean should there be any spillages and that you can remove

DISCREET DUSTBIN
Hidden from view behind ivy-clad trellis, a dustbin remains unobtrusive all year. A colourful hanging basket, carefully sited above, also helps to distract the gaze.

the bin or bins without having to lean too far inside. A door will conceal the dustbins completely and keep out animals such as foxes and dogs, which sometimes knock bins over while investigating the contents.

Hiding manhole covers

Manhole covers may be a necessity but have a nasty habit of being sited in prominent places, often in the terrace or patio. The best way of concealing them is to position one or two medium-sized planters on top. If the containers brim with plants that trail over the sides they should hide the manhole. Don't use excessively heavy containers, since they may need to be moved quickly to allow access in an emergency.

It is also possible to buy small platforms on wheels which can be positioned over the manhole cover. (These platforms are often sold for moving pots around the patio.) If you arrange a collection of pots on the platform, it is easy to wheel them away whenever necessary.

2 Storage in a small space

In a small space it may not be possible to find room for a shed, or you may feel that it would look too utilitarian and would dominate and spoil the whole garden. However, gardening equipment, and sometimes toys, still need a home.

Storage solutions

Many DIY stores and garden centres offer small wooden chests which can be used to store tools outside, and you can buy garden benches that include a storage area beneath the seat. Make sure that the space is sufficient to take long-handled tools such as rakes if you cannot store these elsewhere. If you need greater storage capacity, it may be possible to buy a small shed that has been designed to fit into a corner where it will take up less room and be less conspicuous. Inside the shed, make the best use of space by fixing plenty of sturdy hooks or brackets to the walls where tools can be hung in an orderly fashion within easy reach. Take care that the handles sit securely on the hooks or they could be a safety hazard.

ON THE BARBECUE
If building your own brick barbecue, incorporate a storage area into its walls for cooking utensils and charcoal. Doors will make the space as practicable as possible.

Shed appeal

Since sheds are rarely attractive, especially when brand new and an unpleasant shade of orange-yellow, it is worth considering painting or staining the wood, perhaps to make it blend in with existing garden features. A regular coat of wood preservative as necessary will help to prolong its life. You could also affix trellis or a system of posts and wires close by so that you can grow climbers around the shed. Similarly, a few hanging baskets or wall baskets will help to disguise it. Remember that hanging baskets or windowboxes can be planted up to create a display throughout the year, not only during the summer months. Check the roofing felt occasionally for cracks or holes. Once it starts to deteriorate, it is generally best to replace the entire surface, although small patches can be sealed using bitumen paint, which will act as a short-term solution.

A DESIRABLE SHED
A coat of paint and some tubs of flowers turn a standard shed into a model of charm and efficiency.

TOOL MAINTENANCE

• **GARDEN TOOLS WILL ALL** work more effectively and last longer if you find the time to maintain them regularly. At the end of each season, they should be cleaned thoroughly and any mud or other debris removed. Non-electrical tools can have their blades dipped into a bucket containing sand and oil to guard against rust. When tools have been used in wet conditions, dry them off thoroughly before bringing them inside and store in a well-ventilated place to decrease the likelihood of rust developing.

• **WOODEN-HANDLED TOOLS** are usually a joy to use, but if they become worn and develop splinters, try wrapping some insulating tape around the handle so that they can still be used with comfort.

Finding a home for the children's toys

A SHUTTERED SANDPIT MAKES A TOY REFUGE

Even toys that are designed for use outside will not stand up to too much sun and rain. Paint and plastic tend to fade, plastic is inclined to crack, wood may rot and metals start to rust. Providing some sort of storage area will not only help to avoid these problems, it should keep the garden tidier and improve your chances of encouraging children to put things away. Ready-bought sandpits sometimes incorporate a storage space for smaller toys, or you can add one in if designing your own. A big plastic box, tool-chest or bench with under-seat storage could also be designated for toys. If storage is required only during winter – for items such as paddling pools and sandpits – it may be possible to move these temporarily into a play-house that is no longer required once summer is over.

❸ Disguising the compost heap

A compost heap is an important element in the garden but in small spaces it may not be possible to hide it away in a corner, and even then, the smell may give it away.

Beehive lookalike
A well-made wooden compost bin will not be an eyesore provided it is kept well maintained. However, if you choose an ornamentally shaped bin, it can be a positive asset. It is possible to buy bins made to resemble beehives that look sufficiently like the real thing to fool visitors to the garden. Because they keep the compost well enclosed, there also tend to be fewer problems with odours.

Avoid odours
Compost that is well made and contains a good mixture of suitable ingredients should not produce too much odour. Avoid adding large quantities of grass clippings as these tend to produce a slimy, often very smelly mass instead of good friable compost. Similarly, do not add pieces of meat or any other animal products to the heap, since they are not only likely to produce unpleasant smells but will also attract vermin. Although compost needs to be kept warm, don't put the bin in too sunny a spot, as this may allow the contents to dry out and so slow down the composting process as well as increasing the chances of it smelling. A lid helps to retain heat, which speeds up the process and should help to kill any weed seeds. It will also ensure that the material inside stays neither too dry nor too soggy. Many of the plastic containers available are also good at not releasing unpleasant smells and, if you feel they spoil the garden, could be hidden by a screen of trellis or woven hurdles. Fragrant plants close to a compost bin can help to mask any unpleasant odours. Sweet peas, scented roses, honeysuckle or jasmine could all be allowed to clamber over a nearby fence or trellis.

COMPOST BIN CUNNINGLY BUILT LIKE A BEEHIVE

ADDED FRAGRANCE
Plant a scented climber such as honeysuckle to mask any smells from a compost heap.

SUCCESSFUL COMPOSTING
- **USE A LARGE BIN,** as the ingredients will get warmer quicker, making the process faster. Ideally, use a double-berth system so that you can be using well-rotted compost from one bin while filling the other.
- **ADD INGREDIENTS** in layers 15cm (6in) deep rather than in tiny handfuls.
- **ALTERNATE LAYERS** of soft, moist, high-nitrogen material such as lawn clippings with relatively dry ingredients such as small prunings.
- **TURN THE HEAP** regularly to mix and aerate it.
- **ADD SOME SPADEFULS** of garden soil every few layers to aid the process.

❹ Security fears

Gardens can make easy pickings for burglars so, although you may not want to turn your house into Fort Knox, it is worth taking some basic precautions.

Worthwhile deterrents
Particularly precious garden ornaments should not be displayed in a prominent place, certainly not where they can easily be seen from the road. It is sometimes possible to bolt ornaments to the ground if they stand on a hard surface. If necessary, you could also consider installing passive infrared detector-controlled lights at intervals around the garden which would illuminate any would-be thief. Other logical precautions include ensuring that potentially helpful items such as wheelbarrows are not left around the garden, since these could be used to transport items off the site with relative ease.

Take photographs of anything of value, including costly plants such as distinctive pieces of topiary, or discreetly mark containers and statues with your postcode or some other distinguishing feature. If the worst happens, this may help you to identify and recover stolen items.

Crime prevention
Make sure that doors to sheds and outbuildings are securely bolted and padlocked. Use a padlock designed for outdoor use. Windows can be fitted with mesh if necessary to prevent access that way. Where sheds or garages contain valuable, easy-to-steal ride-on mowers and power tools it may be wise to obscure them from view by covering glass in windows. Small burglar alarms can also be fitted to individual shed or garage doors. If placed in a prominent position, these may act as a deterrent and scare off any would-be thief.

WEEDS & WEEDING

IT IS OFTEN SAID that a weed is any plant which grows where it is not wanted, and it may feel as if your garden provides a better growing site for weeds than it does for anything else. Weeds are something we all have to battle against but, if you manage to recognize those that show a preference for your particular soil, start your attack early in the season, and continue to wage war whenever they regrow, weeds will prove less and less of a problem each year.

Q *What is it about weeds that makes them so difficult to eradicate?*

A As with herbaceous garden plants, weeds fall into two groups: annuals and perennials. Annuals seldom make root systems that are difficult to dig out, but many set copious amounts of seed which germinates readily, sometimes producing several generations from one year. Perennials persist from year to year, often dying back at the end of the growing season only to reappear the following spring. Some propagate themselves by seed, but many have extremely invasive root systems that are particularly difficult to remove.

Q *What is the best way of disposing of annual weeds once they have been removed from the soil?*

A If you hoe off annual weeds or use a hand fork to lift them from the soil, try to do this on a hot day. The weeds should then rapidly shrivel in the heat and can be safely left on the soil surface where they will act rather like a mulch. However, for this method to work, the weeds must have no chance of re-rooting, nor must they show any signs of setting seed.

Annual weeds can also be added to the compost heap but only if they are not starting to set seed, since many weed seeds seem able to survive the composting process.

Q *How should you best dispose of perennial weeds?*

A Perennial weeds pose more of a problem than annuals, as many of them have particularly pernicious root systems. They readily survive composting, and you certainly could not risk leaving them on the soil surface where they might easily regrow. The top-growth of most perennial weeds can be safely incorporated into the compost heap, provided it contains no seedheads, but be sure to put the roots in the dustbin or onto a bonfire.

Q *How effective is a motorized soil cultivator likely to be at clearing extensive areas of weeds in an overgrown garden?*

A If the weed growth consists entirely of annual weeds which have not set seed, using a motorized cultivator is a quick and efficient way of chopping them up and cultivating the soil at the same time. There would be a slight risk of some of the weeds re-rooting, but it is unlikely to be a severe problem.

However, if perennial weeds are present, a cultivator would almost certainly increase the weed population as the blades would chop them up, roots and rhizomes included, and spread them. In many cases you would end up with more weeds than you had originally. If the area contains couch grass, a cultivator will also make this problem worse as each segment is capable of growing into a new plant. You would be better off weeding the area thoroughly by hand or using a weedkiller. Then, once the ground is clear, use a cultivator if you feel it is necessary.

Q *What is the difference between a contact and a systemic weedkiller?*

A Contact weedkillers, for example those based on paraquat or diquat, are sprayed onto the foliage of the weed and then kill off those areas with which they have made direct contact. A systemic or translocated weedkiller, such as one based on glyphosate, is sprayed onto the foliage, but is then also carried around the plant in the sap stream. This means that a systemic weedkiller has the potential to kill off the root system of even a pernicious perennial weed such as ground elder or bindweed. In some instances it does take more than one application of a systemic weedkiller to do the job thoroughly.

Q *Is it all right to replant a border straight after using weedkiller on a large patch of weeds?*

A Some types of weedkiller are likely to remain active in the soil for a specified length of time. Since this may mean delaying replanting, it is essential to check the packet carefully when deciding what to use. Other weedkillers, such as those based on glyphosate, are inactivated on contact with the soil and so even if the weedkiller gets into the soil, it is perfectly safe to replant immediately.

Q Which is the best time of year for applying weedkillers?

A On the whole weedkillers are best applied when the weed is growing actively or when it is starting to die back towards the end of summer or into early autumn. The advantage of spraying when the weed is growing rapidly is simply that it has a large leaf area for receiving the weedkiller, which should then be taken into the plant quite speedily. Applying weedkiller towards the end of summer could, however, be said to have an advantage because the weedkiller will be pulled back into the storage organs of the plant in the same way that materials from the foliage are taken back. Certainly with weeds such as nettles, a late spraying is often found to be beneficial. In many cases it is worth spraying in late spring or early summer since this gives you an opportunity to apply a second spray later on in the year if regrowth occurs.

Q What is the best way to reduce the risk of a weedkiller contaminating nearby garden plants?

A Try to restrict the use of weedkillers to those times when it is absolutely necessary and make sure that you apply them only during suitable weather conditions. This means avoiding gusty or windy weather, in particular. Also bear in mind that in very hot weather miniature thermals can also carry weedkiller to unexpected places.

Although it is often suggested that a sprayer is the best way to apply weedkiller, in the majority of cases you would be better off using a watering can with a dribble bar attachment. This allows accurate application so that you should be able to avoid spraying nearby plants. In addition, the droplets which come out of a dribble bar are much larger than those produced by a sprayer and so are less inclined to drift. If you want to use a sprayer, fit a hood around the spray nozzle which will restrict the area over which the spray is projected. Hoods can usually be bought from garden centres.

Q What is the best way of coping with weeds growing up among herbaceous plants and shrubs?

A Annual weeds can often be gently pulled out from among garden plants, but perennial weeds are considerably harder to remove successfully, especially if growing up within the crowns of plants. You could try painting a gel formulation weedkiller directly onto the foliage of the offending weeds. If done carefully you should be able to avoid contaminating nearby plants.

Where the problem is severe or extensive, you may have to take a rather more drastic course of action. Wait until autumn or early spring, carefully lift all the plants which are infested with weeds and remove the weed roots from among those of the garden plants. (Avoid rinsing roots with water to make weed roots more visible as this is bad for the plants.)

If the weeds are growing among plants but not actually through them, it may be possible carefully to cover the garden plants and use a weedkiller. If you shield the plants with appropriate-sized pieces of card, cardboard boxes or plastic bin liners and apply the weedkiller accurately, perhaps using a dribble bar on a watering can, you should be able to treat the weeds without contaminating the garden plants.

Q Is it possible to kill off all the weeds on a new site by covering the area with black polythene?

A Covering soil and weeds with black polythene (which needs to be very dense and tough) will indeed gradually kill almost all weeds. However, it would be advisable to cut back much of the weed growth before laying the polythene. Weight it down with bricks or other heavy objects. Alternatively, bury the edges in the soil. The disadvantage of using polythene in this way is that it will not allow oxygen or rainwater through to the soil. If kept in position for long enough to ensure that all the weeds are killed off, the structure of the soil and important life forms in it may well suffer. As an alternative, you could cover the ground with old carpet. This will have the same light-restricting, weed-smothering qualities, but will allow a certain amount of oxygen to reach the soil and also a good degree of rain penetration.

Q What is the best way to deal with weeds such as nettles that keep creeping under the fence from the next-door garden?

A Provided the garden boundary is not so long that it makes this too tough a job, the best solution is to create an underground fence. This means digging a trench, preferably to a depth of about 30cm (12in), and then inserting a length of very heavy-duty polythene sheeting. Creating this kind of impenetrable barrier should prevent most of the weed colonization from next door. However, it will obviously not stop weed seeds being brought in on air currents or by birds and it will also not do anything about those weeds already growing in your garden. Provided you get these under control, you should see a dramatic improvement, although unfortunately, some weeds do grow very deeply and so a barrier at this depth will not provide total exclusion.

Q *What is the best way to deal with the long tap roots of docks and dandelions?*

A It is essential to do all you can to remove the entire root system of any tap-rooted weed. If you do not, or if you cut up the root, every section left in the soil has the potential to grow into a new plant. This means that you could end up with a worse problem than you started with. As long as they are not allowed to get too large, you can often remove tap-rooted weeds by hand. Carefully fork them out of the soil, gently easing out the root system so that it does not break, or insert a knife all around the root and lift it out together with a small surrounding plug of soil (*see p.57*). In paving, gravelled areas or lawns you can also use a spot-weeder (*see p.56 and p.85*).

Q *Weeds seem to appear from nowhere. Within a few weeks of clearing a large area ready for planting, the ground is covered in them again. How?*

A Many weed seeds are highly mobile and so can float in on air currents. Others may be brought into your garden by birds and animals. Do not forget also that many weeds produce huge quantities of seeds,

which can remain dormant in the soil for several years until conditions are suitable for germination.

It is highly likely, therefore, that there would already have been a number of weed seeds in your soil and the very act of removing the fully-grown weeds and cultivating the soil is likely to have stimulated these seeds to germinate. However, by carrying out thorough weeding early on, you will have broken the back of the problem. Now you could simply remove the perennial weeds by hand, then hoe off the annuals before they have the chance to set seed.

Q *What is the best way of coping with weeds growing in among bulbs?*

A It should be possible to hoe off or hand-weed annual weeds but if you decide that the problem is too extensive for this, or if perennial weeds are involved, you may decide to use a weedkiller. If so, it is essential to wait until the bulb foliage has died down, otherwise the weedkiller could easily contaminate the bulb foliage and be drawn down into the bulbs, damaging or even killing them.

Q *Weeds continually sprout in between paving slabs and on areas covered with gravel. What is the best way to keep such surfaces weed-free?*

A There are weedkillers available specifically for use on hard surfaces such as these and, provided there are no garden plants growing nearby, these can be used safely and effectively. If you do not want to use chemicals, it may be possible to remove the weeds by hand, but you are likely to have problems with regrowth. If you ever decide to lay a new area of paving or gravel, it is well

worth trying to kill off the weeds first. Consider covering the soil with some woven landscape fabric before laying gravel. This allows the soil to breathe and moisture to pass through but will help to prevent most weed growth. Some weed seeds, though, will inevitably manage to germinate and grow in the gravel.

Another alternative is to use a flame-weeder which burns off the top-growth of weeds. Obviously you need to be careful that you do not use this near any surface which could be damaged by the flame. Once you have killed or removed the weeds in paving, consider replenishing the mortar between the slabs to prevent more weeds growing through.

Q *What are the ideal weather conditions for applying a weedkiller, and will rain prevent it from working?*

A Try to choose a calm day that is also not excessively warm, since wind and extreme heat can both cause drift. Similarly, avoid wet weather since spraying during rain means that the weedkiller will have little if any effect and risk of contamination will also be increased. Also avoid spraying if rain is forecast. The amount of time without rain required after spraying does vary from product to product, but generally speaking you should try to spray during a period of fairly prolonged dry weather. Certainly if it rains within a few hours of spraying, the effectiveness of the weedkiller is likely be quite dramatically reduced.

Q *How can you tell if garden plants have been contaminated by weedkiller?*

A The symptoms vary from plant to plant and also with the type of weedkiller used, but the most common are scorching of the foliage (usually associated with contact weedkillers) or distinct distortion. On some plants, the leaves form extremely narrow blades, often in rosettes. This is particularly common on roses (*see p.185*) and raspberries. In some instances, the leaf blade becomes very distorted and thickened and leaves may become cupped. If tomato plants are contaminated by weedkiller, any fruits that form are usually peculiarly elongated and look more like plum tomatoes. When cut open, they do not contain any seeds.

Weedkiller contamination may affect the whole plant or, quite frequently, it is just seen on those parts that have been directly subjected to chemical drift.

Q Which is the best sort of weedkiller to use to treat lawn weeds?

A Remember that if there are only a few weeds in your lawn, or the lawn is reasonably small, it is quite easy to remove them by hand, perhaps using a daisy-grubber (a useful tool with a two-pronged fork which you insert under the leaves and lever out the roots). However, if you decide to opt for using chemical control, choose a weedkiller specially formulated for use on lawns. This will have no damaging effect whatsoever on the lawn grasses.

Most lawn weedkillers contain several chemicals or active ingredients which, between them, are capable of controlling a wide range of weeds. To choose the most suitable product, first try to identify precisely which weeds are present in the lawn and then compare your "hit list" with the weeds listed on the various proprietary packs.

You could also consider using a formulation which includes a fertilizer. This has the advantage that the fertilizer will encourage the rapid growth of the lawn grasses and these will quickly fill the gaps created after the weeds have been killed off. Alternatively, apply a lawn fertilizer a couple of weeks before applying the weedkiller. Although this method takes slightly longer, applying the fertilizer in advance ensures that the weeds are growing rapidly when the weedkiller is applied and so are likely to be killed more readily.

Q Is it safe to add lawn mowings to the compost heap if the lawn has just been sprayed with a weedkiller?

A Generally speaking it is always better to avoid incorporating any treated material into the compost heap, as there is a slight risk of contamination occurring with certain chemicals.

Q Are there any special ways of dealing with particularly resistant weeds, such as horsetail, where the weedkiller tends to run straight off the foliage?

A It is often worth crushing the weed's foliage slightly before applying weedkiller, especially if the leaves are shiny and quick to shed water. Abrading the surface of the weed will allow the weedkiller to be taken up more rapidly and effectively. When doing this, be careful not to sever any stems, or the weedkiller will be prevented from being taken down into the root system. With weeds such as horsetail, you can either jump up and down on it or press it sharply a few times with the back of a rake. Horsetail is particularly difficult to treat, because its foliage contains a lot of silica, making it extremely tough and particularly well adapted to shedding weedkiller.

Q A small shamrock-like plant has become something of a nightmare weed. The more it is dug out, the worse the problem seems to get.

A This is probably oxalis (*see overleaf*), a weed that is mainly spread by small bulbils clustered around the base of the plant. Early in the year these bulbils are fairly firmly attached to the plant and so when you dig it out you bring the bulbils with it. In summer, the bulbils become less firmly attached and are readily shed into the soil as you lift the plants. Each bulbil can grow into a new plant which means that you run the risk of increasing the numbers of this weed. Make sure that you do not risk exacerbating the problem by composting oxalis. This is a weed which should be put in the dustbin or on the bonfire. (There are also several ornamental species of oxalis.)

Q Is it possible to kill off weeds completely by covering them with a dense layer of mulch?

A It is indeed possible to drastically reduce or sometimes even completely stop the growth of certain weeds by covering the soil's surface with a 5–8cm (2–3in) layer of mulch. You may initially get some weeds growing up through this, but after a while they should be so weakened that they are no longer a serious problem. However, if you use organic material as a mulch, you may also find that some weed seeds are able to germinate in the mulch material itself. The finer the material, the greater the likelihood. If you cover the weeded soil with woven landscape fabric and then put a relatively thin layer of mulch or soil over the top and plant through the landscape material, you should find that you achieve good weed control.

COMMON WEEDS IN THE GARDEN

Bindweed

The elegant white trumpet flowers may be pretty, but this is an invasive perennial that is very difficult to control. It can strangle less vigorous plants and cause a lot of competition for light, water and nutrients. The underground stem segments root very easily.

It is difficult to dig out bindweed plants successfully, but regularly attempting to do so will gradually clear the problem. The process may, though, take several years. Bindweed often re-invades from neighbouring gardens by travelling underground. Once your garden has been cleared, it is worth sinking an underground barrier of very heavy-duty polythene along the fence-line in an attempt to prevent the bindweed encroaching again. A barrier like this will also help to keep out weeds such as horsetail and nettles.

Systemic weedkillers are effective but extremely difficult to apply to a weed entangled among garden plants. You can paint a glyphosate gel formulation onto bindweed foliage, as long as you can do it without contaminating the green stems and foliage of adjacent plants. It may be possible to wind a few stems of bindweed around a bamboo cane where, kept clear of neighbouring plants, they can be allowed to put on plenty of growth and will be much easier to treat safely.

Buttercups

If they were not so invasive, buttercups might be grown as garden plants. The silky yellow petals are held in a pretty cup shape and the divided leaves are often attractively marked. The most problematic type is the perennial creeping buttercup, which can become all too prevalent in beds, borders and lawns. In beds and borders,

regular hoeing to remove the top-growth or careful use of a hand fork to ease plants out of the soil will help to keep their numbers down. It is essential to get on top of these plants early in the season before they spread using their runnering habit, and before the seedheads ripen and the seeds are dispersed. Chemical control may be possible, too, but is not easy.

Chickweed

Delicate green leaves and starry white flowers are the hallmark of this annual weed. Although it may make beds and borders look rather messy, it is not as competitive as many weeds and is unlikely to become a problem if the soil surface is hoed regularly.

Creeping thistle

This perennial thistle can be particularly difficult to control as it has the ability to spread underground so effectively. Hand-weeding is often the most efficient means of getting rid of it, but you will need to wear stout gloves and try gently to lever the roots and runners out of the soil without leaving any pieces behind.

Dandelions

The bright yellow flowers followed by wispy "clocks" are rather attractive atop the rosette of leaves, but these are hungry plants and the leaves prevent other plants from reaching the soil surface or seeing the light. Dandelions spread easily and effectively, as each seed has its own parachute mechanism for good dispersal. Dandelions may prove a problem in beds and borders as well as in lawns. Their long and brittle tap roots are difficult to remove in their entirety and if a root breaks in to four or five pieces, say, each piece has the potential to form a new plant.

Most broadleaved lawn weedkillers will control dandelions and individual plants can be spot-treated with a systemic

weedkiller (*see p.56*). Alternatively, use a sturdy kitchen knife to carefully cut dandelions out of a lawn (*see p.57*), taking care to remove a plug of soil with the root so that no pieces of root remain. In some instances you can also use a knife to remove dandelions from clumps of herbaceous plants. On sandy soils, it may be possible to very carefully fork the infested area over in a border and remove the weeds, roots and all. Dandelion roots should not be composted since they are more than likely to regrow.

Docks

These perennial weeds with their fairly glossy, broad leaves may colonize lawns and borders. They are especially troublesome on areas which have only recently been converted into garden. Like dandelions, docks have long roots and again, if broken, each section can grow into a new plant.

On lawns regular mowing will gradually weaken docks sufficiently to cause them to die out, as will very regular hoeing in open ground. When possible, hand-weeding generally provides the most rapid method of removing them from in among garden plants. If you have a lot of docks, they can be sprayed with a suitable systemic weedkiller, but more than one application may be necessary to kill them off completely and great care must be taken not to contaminate nearby garden plants.

Ground elder

This rapid-growing perennial weed may have attractive heads of creamy white flowers but it is extremely invasive and can soon swamp less vigorous garden plants.

Careful forking out may work quite well but is a time-consuming and laborious process. Covering infested areas with old carpet for about two years may also be worthwhile, or the weed can be treated with a weedkiller such as glyphosate.

BINDWEED

COUCH GRASS

DANDELION

MIND-YOUR-OWN-BUSINESS

DOCK

CREEPING THISTLE

Hairy bittercress

This annual weed forms a small rosette of leaves from the centre of which develops a tiny flower spike of creamy-white flowers. In no time at all seedheads develop. The seeds are projected onto the surface of the soil around so that new ground is rapidly colonized by new plants. Bittercress is especially common on the surface of compost of plants growing in pots and is often introduced into gardens on newly purchased container-grown plants. It is essential to hand-weed or hoe regularly to remove bittercress before it has a chance to set seed.

Horsetail

The whorls of jointed, rough-textured, stems are very resilient, but digging out horsetail reveals that the underground structures are even more so. Occasionally horsetail occurs in lawns, in which case regular mowing will help to weaken the plants so much that they may die out. In most situations, however, chemical weedkiller is the method most likely to succeed.

Products based on glyphosate generally work best but to ensure that adequate weedkiller penetrates through the silica-reinforced stems you will need to crush them slightly before application (*see p.175*). Several applications of weedkiller are likely to be needed, each applied when the new growth appears.

Mind-your-own-business

This ground-hugging carpet-forming plant (*Soleirolia soleirolii*) may have tiny, tiny leaves, but it is intensely competitive and will swamp less vigorous plants. In winter, the foliage may sometimes die down but the plant invariably reshoots the following spring. Since it is sold as an ornamental, this is a weed you might unsuspectingly have planted yourself, or maybe inherited. In lawns, areas of mind-your-own-business can either be treated with a glyphosate-based weedkiller or the weed can be dug out, roots and all, and the area returfed or reseeded. In borders, it can be dug out or treated with a weedkiller, but great care must be taken not to contaminate nearby plants. Digging out is not simple, as the mat-like structure is difficult to remove completely and, because little pieces are easily left behind, the weed will soon recolonize.

Nettles

Perennial nettles are common in gardens that have not been well cared for or are close to neglected areas. They also appear in gardens created from rough ground. Well-known because they sting and can cause a nasty rash, nettles' only advantage is that they may act as a food source for the caterpillars of some butterflies. The tough, bright yellow roots and runners form an underground mat that is difficult to penetrate and which may swamp other less vigorous plants. Nettles' top-growth shades and causes stress to nearby plants.

On ground which has not been planted up, the whole area can be effectively sprayed off using a systemic weedkiller such as glyphosate, which should be carried to all below-ground parts of the plant, eventually killing it off. However, several applications may be needed before complete control is achieved. When nettles grow among and up through garden plants, control is much harder and can only really be achieved by repeated (and often rather painful) hand-weeding.

Oxalis

Although the pretty pinkish flowers and pale green leaves may, at first sight, seem appealing, this perennial weed is very invasive and will soon take over entire flower beds if left unchecked. It is spread mainly by tiny bulbils which form below ground.

Hand-weeding works quite well but must be carried out in spring or very early summer while the bulbils are still firmly attached to the plant. By midsummer, they very readily become dislodged and weeding after then may cause an infestation of oxalis to get worse. Systemic weedkillers will also have some effect on oxalis, as will the use of a thick mulch, at least 8cm (3in) deep.

Weed grasses

Grasses such as couch grass can be a real menace in beds and borders and in lawns. Couch grass, in particular, is extremely difficult to control as it is so easily spread – the underground stems are very brittle, readily fracturing and each piece then forming a new plant.

When present in a lawn, weed grasses are especially difficult to control because they will not be killed by the sort of broadleaved weedkiller used to treat other lawn weeds. (Any weedkiller that killed weed grass would also kill the lawn grasses.) Hand-weeding may be the answer in most cases but do not put any couch grass on the compost heap.

Weed grasses growing in lawns are unlikely to be cut when the lawn is mown because they tend to lie flat. Fluffing them up using a rake before mowing will help and, because they do not respond well to cutting, they will gradually start to die out if this is done regularly. Alternatively, try making parallel cuts across patches of weed grass using a sharp knife.

A weedkiller based on glyphosate will kill off couch grass and weed grasses but can only be used with the greatest care or in areas where you are aiming to kill off all types of grass and plant growth, perhaps when clearing a patch of rough meadow to create a flower bed, new lawn or even an entire garden.

HAIRY
BITTERCRESS

GROUND ELDER

HORSETAIL

PERENNIAL NETTLE

OXALIS

PESTS, DISEASES & DISORDERS

NOBODY IS PERFECT, and yet so many gardeners seem to expect their plants to be. Discovering evidence of a pest, disease or disorder can throw them into a state of alarm or panic. Disorders can usually be remedied by improved cultivation and, although it is true that some pests and diseases can do a lot of damage, provided you know which are the more important ones to be aware of and take suitable action promptly, most can be kept under control.

Q *Is there a simple way of avoiding pest and disease problems in the garden?*

A Unfortunately, however much care you take, you are likely to encounter a few pests and diseases but there are some things you can do to reduce the problems. Growing a wide variety of plants as opposed to concentrating on just one or two kinds "spreads the load" and makes your garden less attractive to any one particular pest. Giving plants a suitable site and looking after them well will make them better able to fight off infections or infestations and produce replacement growth should they get damaged. Plants growing in a position which makes them struggle will be much more open to problems in the first place. Keeping plants adequately but not excessively watered and fed and, if necessary, pruned will also be of benefit.

Check regularly for problems, since those which are caught and dealt with early are less likely to develop into something serious. They will also be easier to get under control relatively quickly, often without the use of chemicals. Prompt action also helps to prevent the spread of the pest or disease onto other parts of the plant or onto nearby susceptible plants.

It is possible to buy varieties of plants which are relatively resistant to some problems. When choosing what to grow from a seed catalogue, check to see if any varieties are described as being pest- or disease-resistant.

Q *How easy is it to garden organically?*

A Gardening organically is not particularly difficult and can certainly be extremely rewarding. However, it does take more thought than gardening using an armoury of chemical controls. Making sure that the plants are growing well in the first place is of prime importance, so more care and time probably need to be taken in looking after them. It is important to improve the soil (*see p.148*), keep it in good condition and prepare it well before planting. A compost heap will be a real help.

Because an organic gardener must do everything possible to avoid pests and diseases, you may need to give more thought to protecting plants against potential problems, perhaps by using fleece, netting or other devices to ward off pests and by trapping them, for instance using beer traps against slugs.

Growing resistant varieties is all the more important and so a little more time will need to be spent choosing plants. Remember, however, that if you garden organically you will not need to waste time or money applying large quantities of chemicals.

Q *Are all organic treatments perfectly safe?*

A Any chemicals that are sold as organic products and are acceptable according to official organic standards should have any restrictions and limitations of use noted on the packaging and you should observe these carefully.

It is worth bearing in mind that some organic chemicals such as derris, although acceptable in theory to organic gardeners, are actually quite broad spectrum in activity and will kill or damage a wide range of creatures, not just pests. For this reason, it may occasionally be more environmentally sensible to use a chemical which is specific in its action rather than using a much more wide-ranging "organic" chemical. For example, the very specific aphicide pirimicarb will kill only aphids, whereas a much broader spectrum organic product such as one based on soft soap is capable of also killing many innocent creatures.

Q *What is the best way to make sure chemicals are applied safely, and is it necessary to wear protective clothing?*

A Use chemicals only if it is really necessary to do so and make sure that you follow the instructions on the packet to the letter. If you cannot read these because the packaging has become damaged, buy a new pack.

Never apply chemicals at too great or too weak a strength or too frequently. Since many insecticides can damage harmless or beneficial insects as well as the target pests, always try to avoid them coming into

EASY AVOIDANCE MEASURES • ORGANIC TREATMENTS • SAFE USE OF CHEMICALS

contact with other creatures. Apply insecticides late in the day, preferably at dusk, as this will greatly reduce the risk of harming pollinating insects.

As far as your own safety is concerned, take care when mixing any chemical and never eat or drink anything until you have had a thorough wash afterwards. In theory there is no need to wear protective clothing when using the sort of chemicals available for amateur gardeners. Many people, however, prefer at least to wear gloves when mixing and some sort of protective clothing, even if it is just gloves and an old coat, while applying them.

Q *What are pheromones and how are they used to control insect pests?*

A Pheromones are occasionally used as a way of trapping or luring insects. The chemicals used in traps such as codling moth traps are, in fact, man-made versions of the insect's pheromones. They act as sexual attractants, luring the male codling moth into the trap in the belief that it contains females. The males are then caught on a sticky surface or drowned in liquid. The pheromones are normally impregnated into small rubber pellets which release them gradually. In most cases these pellets can be replaced and, provided this is done at the prescribed intervals, the trap can be used effectively for a considerable period of time.

Q *How and where can "biological controls" be used, and against which pests?*

A Biological control involves the introduction of a predatory or parasitic creature which will limit the numbers of the pest in question.

Unfortunately, only a few biological controls are available and because they are living organisms they cannot be purchased from garden centres. Instead you must rely on buying them from a specialist company by mail order. The mail order companies do, however, send them out promptly and in good condition.

The main pests against which biological control can be used are vine weevils, slugs, whitefly, greenfly, red spider mite, mealy bugs, certain leaf miners and scale insects.

Many of the predators and parasites used in this kind of control come from much warmer climates and as such they can only be relied upon to perform effectively in the relatively protected environment of a greenhouse or conservatory. The exceptions to this are the controls for vine weevils and slugs which can be used outdoors. The one available for vine weevil is, though, only really effective if used in relatively light garden soil or preferably in proprietary compost.

Q *Once biological controls have been introduced into a greenhouse, what stops them from escaping through the vents and windows? Should these be sealed in some way?*

A The vast majority of biological controls are very "well-behaved"! With the exception of the adult stage of the control used for mealy bugs and the *Delphastus* beetle which is used to control extensive whitefly infestations, the biological control agents invariably stay very close to their source of food or the creature that they wish to parasitize. This means that you can quite safely open vents, windows and doors in the normal way. Indeed, if you did not, the plants would undoubtedly suffer. When introducing biological controls,

ensure that you do it exactly according to the instructions that arrive with them. If placed in the most suitable position, creatures are less likely to attempt to move and will provide more reliable control. If you are dealing with one of the beetle predators, which may have a tendency to attempt to fly off, you should find that covering the plants with horticultural fleece for a day or two after introducing the predator helps to keep them in place. Once they have spent about 48 hours on the intended plant, they will be more inclined to stay there.

Q *How successful are biological controls in the greenhouse?*

A Provided you use these controls according to the instructions supplied with them they should work well. The fact that they are used by commercial growers of glasshouse crops indicates that they are efficient and economic.

Precise instructions for applying them vary from creature to creature, but usually you should introduce your predators or parasites while the pest level is still fairly low. Waiting until numbers have increased could present the predator or parasite with too much of a struggle. Similarly, there needs to be a reasonable number of the pest present or the biological control may die out too rapidly. Many biological controls also need a minimum temperature to function properly. This is generally around 21°C (70°F).

It is important not to use chemicals in a greenhouse or conservatory while attempting to use biological controls. Many insecticides and some fungicides could kill the predators and parasites as well as the pests. Since some chemicals have a lasting residual effect, even if it is several weeks since they were used, they could still kill the predators. If you have recently applied chemicals, list those that you have used and when and discuss this with your biological control supplier.

Q Can diseased or pest-infested plants be composted safely?

A It is best to follow the rule "if in doubt leave it out". Although many diseases will safely compost down, there is always a risk they will not and with some problems, such as honey fungus and clubroot, the organisms involved are extremely resilient and should definitely not be composted. Similarly, if you are making chippings from woody stems by passing them through a shredder, be careful not to include any diseased material. Some problems such as apple canker are likely to persist and, when you use the shredded bark around the garden, you may well spread the problem. Put this sort of material either into the dustbin or onto a bonfire.

Q It looks as if the powdery mildew which has attacked some roses is now spreading to some nearby phloxes. How can it be stopped from spreading to yet more plants?

A Although it may appear that the same disease is attacking all these plants, the chances are that several different types of powdery mildew are involved. They may all look similar, and they are all caused by closely related fungi, but each fungus usually attacks only a specific type of plant or closely related group of plants. Certain weather conditions (generally moist air and dry soil) encourage powdery mildews of all sorts and so it looks as if exactly the same problem is spreading around the garden. Do all you can to discourage the disease

by keeping plants adequately moist at the base, improving air circulation around stems and leaves (by thinning out growth, spacing plants well and controlling weeds) and also by removing severely infected parts of a plant. You could also use one of the many chemicals for controlling powdery mildew (*see p.185*).

Q The greenhouse is plagued by problems. Why do things get out of hand so much more quickly there than in the garden?

A Greenhouses provide a warm, protective environment for plants. Unfortunately, these conditions are also perfect for many pests and diseases, which tend to build up and spread far more rapidly and efficiently in a greenhouse or conservatory than they do outside. In addition, there tend to be fewer natural predators in a greenhouse.

As far as diseases are concerned, the relatively warm conditions and often fairly poor air circulation also provide ideal conditions for these to build up and spread. Anything you can do to improve air circulation will help, and be vigilant at spotting pests and diseases and taking prompt action.

Q You often hear that natural predators are important in keeping pests at bay. How can these be protected or encouraged?

A There are lots of creatures which are actively beneficial in the garden. Some of the larger ones include frogs, toads, hedgehogs and birds, while the smaller ones include spiders, ground beetles, devil's coach-horse beetles, ladybirds and their larvae and the larvae of lacewings and hover flies. It is worth trying to find good pictures of some of the larval forms of these beneficial insects since

many bear absolutely no resemblance to the adults. Avoiding the use of garden chemicals will help to protect beneficial insects and other creatures. Excessive tidiness, on the other hand, tends to remove places where they can hide and breed.

Q If you want to grow as many pest- and disease-resistant plants as possible, how can you find out which these are?

A A good reference book should give some indication of varieties resistant to the pests and diseases you want to avoid. It is also well worth combing through as many seed catalogues as possible every year. The majority now note this kind of information. Sometimes they state which specific pests or diseases are involved or they may simply describe varieties as disease- or pest-resistant. Some catalogues also note varieties as being "particularly suitable for organic gardening" and basically this means that they, too, are relatively pest- or disease-resistant.

Q How do viruses spread from one plant to another?

A The ways in which viruses spread vary from virus type to virus type, but some methods are quite common. These include spread by sap-feeding insects, in particular aphids. As the aphids feed on the infected plant they take up the sap containing the tiny virus particles. These can then be passed on to another susceptible plant when, in turn, the insect feeds on it.

Some viruses are also spread by organisms that live in the soil, in particular nematodes or eelworms. Again, the spread is likely to occur when the nematodes feed on the infected plant's roots.

Handling is another cause of virus spread. When you handle an infected plant, even if you do so gently, you slightly crush the surface and in the process a minute quantity of sap gets onto your fingers. If you then handle another susceptible plant, it is possible for the sap containing the virus particles to be transmitted into the sap stream of this second plant. The sap can also be passed on via secateurs or a garden knife.

Some viruses can be transmitted when seed is collected from an infected plant, although this is fairly rare. You should also bear in mind that, generally speaking, viruses are within the entire plant so you should never propagate from a plant which may be infected, as cuttings are an obvious source of trouble.

Q Are millipedes and centipedes goodies or baddies?

A Millipedes are generally regarded as being potentially damaging to a few plants since they sometimes damage soft plant tissues or young seedlings. But they are not a significant pest because most of their feeding matter consists of rotting organic material. They do, however, have a tendency to extend damage that has been started by other pests, for instance they may enlarge slug holes in potatoes.

Centipedes (*see overleaf*), on the other hand, are predatory and attack a variety of small soil-living animals including some soil pests. If you have difficulty distinguishing between these two creatures, remember that centipedes are generally yellowish-brown and each of their many body segments bears a single pair of legs. Millipedes have two pairs of legs on each segment. Centipedes also have quite long antennae and, because they are predatory animals, they move much faster than millipedes.

Q Could some plants be damaged by chemicals?

A When you decide to use a chemical to control a pest or disease, it is important to check that the chemical could not have any damaging effect on the plant itself. Generally speaking, this should be clear from the product label. Some carry a list of plants on which the chemical cannot be used because what is known as a phytotoxic reaction is produced. On the whole, plants such as ferns and fuchsias or fairly exotic plants are more likely to react badly. If you are in any doubt about the safety of a chemical on a particular plant, test it on a small area before spraying the whole thing.

Q What sort of barriers can be used to prevent pests attacking plants in the garden and which would be the most useful to start with?

A Horticultural fleece is extremely useful stuff and whether you buy it by the metre or attached to metal hoops so that it forms a mini-tunnel, it will help to protect plants against most winged pests and their larvae, especially carrot fly, cabbage root fly on brassicas, aphids and caterpillars. Make sure it is in position at all times and that there are no pests on the plants when you put it in place. This means covering plants very early in the season, preferably as soon as they appear above soil level or are planted out. Check regularly that the fleece is firmly in contact with the soil, with no gaps.

Barriers can also be used to keep slugs and snails away from plants. Those commonly recommended include cocoa shells, grit, crushed eggshells, pine needles and soot. In addition, you can buy self-adhesive copper strips and small copper-coated

"fences" which, because the copper contains a small electric charge, act as a useful barrier.

Sticky barriers around the trunks of fruit trees susceptible to the winter moth work well. The female moth cannot fly and relies on climbing up the trunk to lay her eggs. You can buy either fruit tree grease or grease bands to apply to the tree trunk.

Similarly, the vine weevil cannot fly, so anything which prevents her from gaining access to the surface of the compost or soil where she lays her eggs will help to reduce or even eliminate problems with the larvae. You could apply non-setting glue all around the rim of a container to stop her climbing up, making sure that no foliage can act as a bridge, or place a deep, fairly impenetrable mulch of pebbles or gravel on the surface of the compost. In the greenhouse, stand the legs of the staging in small bowls of water, since adults cannot swim.

Q Can you advise on the safe storage of chemicals?

A Chemicals must be stored in a cool, frost-free place where they can be kept dry and at a relatively constant temperature. This should ensure they remain effective. It is also essential to bear safety in mind so, ideally, store them in a lockable cupboard that is not accessible to children or pets. Chemicals should always be stored in their original containers and care needs to be taken to keep the labels legible. If the containers become damaged in any way, discard them.

If you need to dispose of chemicals, contact your local council or refuse collection centre to find out where they should be taken. Never pour chemicals down the lavatory or into any area of the garden where they could possibly contaminate an underground water supply.

COMMON PESTS IN THE GARDEN

Aphids

Commonly called greenfly and blackfly, aphids actually come in a range of colours. By sucking sap they may cause leaves to yellow, pucker and distort and, while feeding, sometimes spread viruses.

In some instances, aphids can be hosed off using a strong jet of water, or you may use a systemic insecticide. Ideally, use an insecticide based on pirimicarb; it is aphid specific and so poses little, if any, threat to beneficial insects. Biological controls are available for aphids in greenhouses, conservatories or other protected environments.

Caterpillars

There are numerous different caterpillars – the larvae of moths or butterflies – some of which you may want to preserve, but many of which can cause serious damage. Some chew holes in leaves, sometimes also spinning fine tent-like shelters or fibres that stick the sides of a leaf together to create a pocket in which the caterpillar can live. It may be possible to collect up large numbers by hand but, since many feed at night, a torch-lit expedition may be necessary.

Covering edible crops such as brassicas with fine mesh or netting from early in the season should prevent butterflies and moths from laying eggs. You could spray with a suitable insecticide or use a bacterial spray which controls caterpillars but does not affect other creatures.

Deer

In rural and semi-rural areas deer can be an extreme problem, wrecking whole gardens and eating back a lot of growth on almost any garden plant.

The only real solution is to erect high-tensile deer fencing around the entire garden, a job best done by a specialist fencing contractor. In addition, you can try to deter deer by placing muslin bags full of unwashed human hair around the garden or dangling CDs from string – the reflected light is said to scare them off.

Glasshouse red spider mite

This minute mite feeds by sucking sap and can devastate plants or kill them in a short time. Affected leaves are spoiled by numerous tiny cream or white flecks and soon curl and die, rapidly becoming crisp and brown. Very fine webs are sometimes seen. The mite enjoys hot, dry conditions and dislikes wet, so regularly misting plants with water and damping down the greenhouse path will help to keep it at bay. You could also try introducing the predatory mite *Phytoseilus persimilis*, which will kill red spider mite at all its life stages. Chemical controls are available, but there have been problems with build-up of resistant strains of this pest.

At the end of the growing season, have a thorough clean-up, removing all infested plants and scrubbing down the greenhouse structure and staging to prevent mites from overwintering.

Glasshouse whitefly

All stages suck plant sap and also produce a sticky excreta known as honeydew which then attracts black sooty mould. Eliminate this pest without using chemicals by introducing a parasitic wasp, *Encarsia formosa*, which lays its eggs in the young stage of the whitefly, killing off the developing larva within. New generations of wasps continue to control the whitefly. A certain number of whitefly can also be trapped on yellow sticky traps, pieces of card covered in a non-setting glue, hung from the roof. However, the traps are often more useful for indicating what creatures are in the greenhouse and if any are at damaging levels. Although the cards trap some whitefly, they also catch other flying insects, including parasitic wasps. If high numbers of whitefly have built up, try using a vacuum cleaner fitted with a hose to suck them up, but take care not to damage the plants.

Various chemical controls are available, but many whitefly have now become resistant to them and, because of the nature of their life cycle, it is extremely difficult

to spray successfully against this pest. Insecticides based on bifenthrin and soap-like substances are generally still effective.

Leaf miners

The larvae of some moths, sawflies, flies and beetles may cause leaf-mining symptoms, usually seen as white or brown meandering or straight lines on affected leaves. Occasionally circular or irregular blotches may be seen and, if an infested leaf is held up to the light, it is often possible to see the larva feeding on the inner part of the leaf. Later in the season, you may be able to see the stationary, rather plumper, pupa. The best way to control leaf miners is to remove affected leaves regularly or spray with malathion or pirimiphos-methyl as soon as the first signs of mining are seen. Leaf miners are unlikely to cause significant damage and although a plant's appearance may be spoilt, it is unlikely that this pest will cause extensive damage on a regular basis.

Pollen beetles

Numerous tiny black or metallic beetles can be a real nuisance when clustered on garden flowers, particularly when you want to pick them to take indoors. Pollen beetles are most troublesome when large quantities of oil-seed rape plants in nearby fields are sprayed off or removed. Once the beetles' normal source of pollen is removed, they tend to move into gardens in search of alternative food.

Although irritating, these beetles do no significant harm to plants and it is sometimes thought they may help in the pollination process. There is, therefore, no need to control them. The best way to remove the beetles from flowers destined for the house is to sharply tap the flowers to shake out as many beetles as possible. Then place the flowers in a vase in a darkened room or shed which has a single light source such as a window or table lamp. The vast majority of beetles will soon fly out towards the light where they can be collected up.

APHIDS

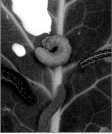

CATERPILLARS

GLASSHOUSE WHITEFLY

LEAF MINER DAMAGE

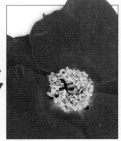

POLLEN BEETLES

Rabbits

In country gardens, rabbits can cause severe damage, ringing trees by eating bark and devastating the top-growth of herbaceous plants and even shrubs. The best way to avoid problems is to fence off individual plants or, preferably, the whole garden. Protect individual plants using galvanized chicken wire held in place by canes. If the whole garden needs protecting, make a chicken-wire fence 90–120cm (3–4ft) high and bury it in the soil to a depth of at least 15cm (6in) with this lowermost section of "underground fence" angled outwards.

Sawfly larvae

These pests are the young stages of various types of fly and though they may look like caterpillars, they are quite different. They feed by eating young foliage and are particularly common and troublesome on gooseberries and Solomon's seal. Large quantities of eggs are laid towards the centre of the plant, with the result that the sawflies rapidly eat their way outwards but may only be noticed once they are near the edges of the plant. By this stage, they will have done a significant amount of damage. Inspect plants in mid- to late spring and pick off young sawflies promptly. Affected plants can be sprayed with a suitable insecticide such as one based on derris, bifenthrin or pirimiphos-methyl.

Scale insects

Raised, rounded, waxy, hood-like structures appear, most commonly, on the lower surfaces of leaves and plant stems. Beneath them are scale insects which feed by sucking sap; they produce a lot of sticky honeydew in the process. Scale insects can be very difficult to control. The insects are most vulnerable to insecticides such as malathion at the newly hatched, nymphal, stage of their life cycle. On outdoor plants, nymphs are most likely to be present in midsummer; on glasshouse and indoor plants, scale insects can breed throughout the year in the protected environment.

Slugs and snails

These pests eat holes in leaves and occasionally stems and even flowers, leaving a silvery, slimy trail behind them as they move around the plant. Some slugs also tunnel into the underground parts of plants such as potatoes and carrots. (Potato varieties that show some slug resistance include 'Kestrel', 'Estima', 'Charlotte' and 'Wilja', among others.) Many slugs spend a high percentage of their lives underground and are most likely to be seen on the soil surface after rainfall or watering. Since slug pellets are generally regarded as environmentally unacceptable, most gardeners prefer to use milk or beer traps, half grapefruit skins or large cabbage leaves, positioned in areas that slugs and snails are known to visit. They then crawl under these and can be collected up and disposed of. A biological control, using a soil-dwelling nematode, will kill slugs but is, unfortunately, not effective against snails which live all their lives above ground. It is often worth conducting early evening slug hunts, particularly after rain or watering when you can often quickly collect large numbers. Creating barriers around slug- or snail-prone plants can be effective. Numerous materials can be used including cocoa shells, pine needles, crushed eggshells, sharp grit, copper strips and petroleum jelly (*see p.181 and Containers, p.98*).

Vine weevils

Adult vine weevils are about 1cm (½in) long, matt black with tan-brown flecks, and have elbowed antennae. The adults eat holes around leaf edges, particularly towards the base of the plant. Their soil-dwelling grubs (*see p.98*) cause much more significant damage, however, because they eat plant roots and can kill them in a relatively short space of time. The grubs can be extremely damaging to plants in containers. Do all you can to prevent any adults (which are all females) from reaching the soil or compost surface where they tend to lay their eggs. Covering with a

BENEFICIAL CREATURES

Many creatures which live in the garden feed on pests such as aphids and slugs and will help to control them. Since adults and larvae often look quite unlike one another, take care to protect all life stages.

LADYBIRD LARVA

CENTIPEDE

GROUND BEETLE

HOVER FLY

LARVA AND ADULT LACEWING

dry mulch such as grit will help to some extent. Trapping vine weevils may also be possible using loosely rolled-up sections of corrugated cardboard. The weevils tend to hide in these during the day and can be collected up and disposed of regularly. Chemical controls are available which can be used as a drench around the roots of affected plants and are said to keep the pests away for about six months. You can also buy chemically impregnated compost said to prevent vine weevil attack for up to a year. For those who prefer not to use chemicals, there is a biological control using a nematode. This is diluted according to the manufacturer's instructions and drenched onto roots of infested plants.

SIGNS OF RED SPIDER MITE

SAWFLY LARVAE

SCALE INSECTS

SLUG

SNAIL

VINE WEEVIL ADULT

COMMON DISEASES AND DISORDERS

Apple scab

This is a fungal disease that is especially prevalent in wet or damp years, particularly when there has been a wet spring. Apple scab causes greyish-khaki-coloured patches to develop on the foliage, young woody shoots and the surface of fruits. A similar disease may also be seen on pears and pyracantha. The infected leaves fall prematurely and in extreme cases the tree may be bare by summer. Infected fruits may become distorted because they are unable to expand normally and, if the infection occurred early in the season, fruits may split or crack.

It is essential that all infected leaves are raked up and disposed of on a regular basis. During the winter you should try to prune out any infected stems. Keeping the crown of the tree relatively open will help to reduce the build-up of humid air but, if necessary and if feasible, the tree can be sprayed with a suitable fungicide early in the year.

Downy mildew

These fungi are less commonly seen in gardens than those of powdery mildew (*see opposite*). They have a much fluffier appearance, usually being an off-white colour, sometimes with a hint of very pale lilac. Downy mildews need a good deal of moisture to survive and spread and so are almost exclusively found on the lower surfaces of leaves. The upper surface is often discoloured and the entire leaf is likely to shrivel and die off relatively rapidly.

Improving air circulation around infected plants and those which are prone to getting this disease (for instance brassicas, lettuces and hardy geraniums) will help to reduce the amount of damage, but it is also essential to remove all infected parts of plants promptly. Spraying with a fungicide containing mancozeb should help to control the spread of the infection.

Fasciation

This disorder causes strangely distorted stems or flower stems, which often appear as if formed from several stems fused together. Growth of the rest of the plant is generally perfectly normal, but the affected stem itself may be curled.

Fasciation occurs when the growing point of a stem is damaged in some way – late frosts and insect attack are common culprits. There is no need to do anything about this deformity, since it is not infectious. If the stems are deemed unsightly, they can simply be pruned out as soon as they appear.

Grey mould

This fungus is present in pretty well every corner of the garden and although it may often live on already dead plant material it can infect living tissue and cause a great deal of damage. Most plants may be attacked on any part that is above ground. Patches of deteriorating tissue turn brown and become covered with a fuzzy grey fungal growth. Large numbers of spores are readily dislodged from these areas by air currents and rain or splash from watering. In some cases, they enter perfectly healthy areas of the plant but, more often, they start by colonizing a dead or damaged area and then spread into the healthy areas. On some plants, extensive rotting may occur and the whole plant may then die. Even woody stems can be killed by grey mould, and death of soft stems and leaves is a common occurrence, especially in damp weather and in greenhouses.

Good garden hygiene helps to prevent grey-mould infections and to minimize the spread of the fungus. Removing dead, damaged or infected areas of plants promptly is especially important. Improving ventilation and air circulation will also help to reduce the problem, particularly in greenhouses and conservatories where grey mould is often rife. If necessary, spray with a suitable fungicide such as carbendazim.

Leaf spots

Most leaf spots are a grey or brown colour, often with concentric zones of discolouration within each spot and sometimes with clearly visible tiny fungal fruiting bodies in their centres. Leaf spots are common on a wide range of plants but in most cases do little significant damage and generally only attack plants which are weakened in some way. Exceptions to this include diseases such as rose black spot and apple scab, which cause severe premature leaf fall.

To minimize spread of the problem pick off affected leaves and, in extreme cases, spray with a suitable fungicide.

Magnesium deficiency

This deficiency is generally seen as a distinct yellowing between the veins on the leaves. The outer edge of the leaf may also be affected, and in some cases the yellowed areas become red, purple or brown once the green pigments have been withdrawn. The oldest leaves are always affected before the newest ones because, once magnesium is in short supply, the plant transports it out of the older leaves and into the younger ones.

Plants which are fed using a high-potash fertilizer are likely to show the symptoms of magnesium deficiency particularly rapidly because the high levels of potassium in the soil or compost may make the magnesium unavailable to the plant. If the plant is watered very regularly, or rainfall is high, the deficiency is also more common, this time because magnesium is very readily leached or washed from the soil.

During dull weather, water the foliage with a solution of Epsom salts mixed at a rate of 150–200g (5–8oz) salts to 10 litres (2½ gallons) of water. Adding a couple of drops of washing-up liquid will help to ensure that the solution adheres to the foliage for long enough for it to penetrate. Any excess will then be absorbed through the roots.

APPLE SCAB

DOWNY MILDEW

FASCIATION

GREY MOULD (*BOTRYTIS*)

LEAF SPOT

Oedema

If numerous small, raised outgrowths, each about the size of a pinhead, develop on the lower surface of plant leaves, it may be caused by oedema. At first the outgrowths are the same colour as the leaves. Then they turn brown and dry. Oedema occurs when the plant takes up more moisture than it can use and as a result small groups of cells swell up. As the problem worsens, the cells swell so much that they burst, becoming dry and brown as they do so. Overwatering and excessively wet soil are generally the cause of this disorder. It may be further aggravated by poor air circulation or high humidity, both of which will decrease the rate at which moisture is drawn up through the plant and lost to the atmosphere.

Decreasing the amount of water given – even withholding it entirely for a while – is important. Every effort should also be made to improve air circulation around the plant, perhaps by opening greenhouse vents and windows or removing nearby plants. It is essential that the affected leaves are left on the plant – they are not infectious and indeed removing them will actually worsen the problem as it will further decrease the plant's ability to lose moisture. Oedema can affect any plant, but pelargoniums, camellias, eucalyptus and succulents are the most susceptible.

Powdery mildew

The fungi of this type of mildew can, among them, attack a wide range of plants. In most cases the symptoms are a characteristic white, powdery fungal growth, coating the upper (and occasionally lower) surfaces of the leaves. This may cause distortion and, in some instances, flowers, buds, stems and even prickles may be infected. On some hosts, such as rhododendron and gooseberry, the fungal growth is a buff colour and rather more felty. Infected leaves often fall early. Plants that are dry at the roots are most susceptible, and so regular and adequate watering combined with the use of a good bulky mulch will help to reduce the severity of the symptoms.

Stagnant air, resulting in high humidity around the plant, will also encourage powdery mildew. Pruning or thinning top-growth may therefore help in some cases. Once the disease has appeared, try to remove as much of the infected growth as possible and, if necessary, spray with a suitable fungicide such as one based on supercarb or bupirimate with triforine.

Rust

Rust fungi are most likely to attack foliage but may occasionally develop on other above-ground parts of plants. Infected leaves may be distorted and fall early. The spores are usually bright orange or dark brown and in some cases, on roses for instance, there are different stages of the fungus present at different times of year. In early summer, bright orange spores appear beneath rose leaves and then, towards the end of the summer, the dark brown over-wintering stages develop. Spores may be grouped into random "spots" or arranged into patterns, such as the concentric rings seen with pelargonium rust.

Improving air circulation may be sufficient to prevent rust infections from becoming too troublesome, but prompt removal of infected leaves is definitely worthwhile. Excessive use of high-nitrogen fertilizers, manure or garden compost will produce soft plant growth which is more prone to rust attack, so this should be avoided wherever possible. If necessary, spray with a suitable fungicide such as one based on mancozeb, triforine with bupirimate or penconazole.

Viruses

Viruses cause a range of symptoms including general stunting, distortion, poor flowering, streaks of unexpected colour on the flower petals and leaf-yellowing in the form of distinct patterns, usually ring spots, flecks, streaks or mosaics. There are no cures available for this type of disease and prompt removal of the infected plant is usually advisable.

In many cases, the virus particles are readily spread, often by handling or by sap-feeding creatures including aphids, thrips and soil-living nematodes. Some viruses may also be seed-borne. Once a plant is infected, the virus particles are likely to be within the whole plant even if the symptoms are not apparent in all areas. No part should therefore be used for propagation.

Many viruses have a large host range, often comprising a wide range of very different and unrelated plants. After handling an infected or suspect plant, wash your hands thoroughly before handling any other plants.

Weedkiller damage

Damage resulting from drift from hormone- or growth-regulator-type weedkillers is common in gardens and usually occurs soon after a weedkiller has been applied to the lawn. Leaves become very distorted, often losing any resemblance to their normal shape, and strangely thickened. Growth may also be stunted and, if caught at precisely the right moment, a tomato plant may produce plum-shaped fruits which have a thin flesh and contain no seeds. Once contaminated, there is little chance of doing anything to prevent the symptoms occurring, so it is important to try to prevent contamination in the first place.

Always use weedkillers with great care and never apply them when the weather is windy, gusty or very hot. Ideally, apply weedkillers using a special watering can, reserved for this purpose, which you have fitted with a dribble bar. The droplets produced from a dribble bar are larger than those from a sprayer and so less likely to drift. It also makes sense to cover any garden plants with large polythene bags or cardboard boxes before you start applying weedkiller.

MAGNESIUM DEFICIENCY

POWDERY MILDEW

RUST (FUCHSIA)

VIRUS (CUCUMBER MOSAIC)

WEEDKILLER DAMAGE

INDEX

Page numbers in *italics* refer to illustrated material.

ACKNOWLEDGMENTS

Author's acknowledgments
With thanks to Pamela Brown, the best editor I have ever
worked with (and who put up with all the problems I
presented and she was left to solve!), to Murdo Culver, for
his artistic inspiration, Lee Griffiths, David Lamb and
everyone else at DK who, once again, made producing a
book with them a pleasure. Also to Justina Buswell, who
helped with so much of the word processing, and Alasdair,
who helped to keep me smiling throughout.

Index Hilary Bird
Editorial assistance Candida Frith-Macdonald

Picture Credits
(Key: t = top; b = bottom; l = left; r = right; c = centre)
Commissioned photography by Peter Anderson: 2, 26tc,
    56cr, 85br, 95tc, 95cl, 99tc, 100bc, 101bl, 108t, 124bc,
    134t, 134c, 135bc, 145t, 163t.
Eric Crichton Photos: 109tc, 154tc, 169tr.
DK Picture Library: Andrew Butler 15tr, 15br; C. Andrew-

Henley 41cr; Jerry Young 55cl; Juliette Wade 139br.
Garden Picture Library: 12tr, 42tc, 45bl, 89cr, 102tc,
    170tc, 170bl.
The Garden Magazine: Tim Sandall 1c and 36bl.
John Glover: 79tr, 89bc, 125bl, 146bl; designer John
    Baillie 125tc.
Holt Studios International: 22tcb, 96tl, 157bcl, 182bc,
    183tr, 183bc, 183tcr, 185bcr.
Andrew Lawson: 60tc, 125tr; designed by Diana Riddell
    88tc.
Clive Nichols: 87cr, 108br, 139tc inset.
Photos Horticultural: N.J. Landscapes 127br.
Harry Smith Collection: 11br, 14br, 54tr, 72bc, 88bl,
    103tr, 155bc, 162bc, 183bl, 185br.
Jo Whitworth: 129bl.

All other photographs are from the DK Picture Library

Main problem illustrations by Gill Tomblin.
Additional illustrations by Karen Gavin: 77cr, 81tc, 81tr,
    86tc, 90b, 91l, 94b, 107br, 127t, 138tc, 146t.